Praise for Angels and Archetypes

"A remarkable achievement with strong visual appeal. *Angels and Archetypes* is somehow scholarly and lively at the same time."

Marilyn Ferguson
Author, **The Aquarian Conspiracy**

"Impressive and scholarly! *Angels and Archetypes* is an excellent work— profound, readable, enlightening and useful. It is written for both men and women who are interested in accessing the feminine resources within themselves to become healed and whole. This work follows the lineage of Carl Jung whose pioneer work on archetypes opened new directions in psychology and contributed to the human potential movement. Like Carol Pearson (*Awakening the Hero Within*) and Clarissa Pinkola Estes (*Women Who Run With the Wolves*), Boulter enriches our understanding of ourselves by enlivening feminine archetypes."

Doreen G. Nystrom
Book Review Editor, **Synchronicity Magazine**

"So much of Spirituality as it is expressed and experienced in today's world still—surprisingly—comes through a male perspective. What a joy to find a work that expresses itself through the female. *Angels and Archetypes* adds a valuable dimension to a large body of study—one that opens up new ways of thinking and learning. It takes feminism and the feminine into the full flower of a new age. To recognize feminist consciousness and to celebrate it is not to replace or repudiate that which is male and masculine, but to add to our world its often neglected femaleness."

Catherine Ford
National Columnist, **Southam Newspapers**

*Winter Solstice
and
Christmas
1997*

*Susan Dear – I met Carmen
in Egypt in March – She has
become one of my main
teachers.*

Angels
And
Archetypes

An Evolutionary Map
of Feminine Consciousness

*If she were to autograph this book
for you she would say something like this*

*May you ride the galactic spiral
of the Dreamer ☺ with the
Angel of Karmic Destiny*

Love always

Flower

Angels
And
Archetypes

An Evolutionary Map
of Feminine Consciousness

by
CARMEN BOULTER

Library of Congress Cataloging-in-Publication Data

Boulter, Carmen, 1954–
Angels and Archetypes: An Evolutionary Map of Feminine Consciousness
p. cm.
Includes bibliographical references and index.

I. Title.

BL325.F4B68   1997
291.2'114—dc20

96-36167 CIP

ISBN 0-926524-38-0 : $22.00
1. Goddesses.
2. Angels.
3. Women and religion.
4. Women–Religion.
5. Feminist theory.

COVER ART: Robert H. Foster
COVER PHOTO CREDITS: Geordie Facey, Suze Baumann, Josef Szujker
COVER DESIGN: Maynard Demmon
DESIGN IMPLEMENTATION: Cliff Kadatz

Printed in the United States of America
Address all inquiries

Swan•Raven Co.,
P.O. Box 2875
Rapid City, SD 57709
U.S.A.

1-800-366-0264
1-605-341-9060

⊙ Printed on recycled alkaline paper.

Table of Contents

Preface xi

Introduction xvii

I   **ARCHETYPES**
The Gateway to the Empowered Feminine 1

II   **ANGELS**
The Link to Our Higher Consciousness 11

III **THE EVOLUTIONARY MAP**
The Road to Multidimensional Initiation 15

IV **0** — *The Dreamer*
The Archetypal Seeker 25
The Angel of Karmic Destiny 30

V   **1** — *Persephone*
The Archetypal Victim 35
The Angel of Surrender 41

VI **2** — *Isis*
The Archetypal Initiate 45
The Angel of Cosmic Intelligence 51

VII **3** — *Hera*
The Archetypal Wife 55
The Angel of Prosperity 61

VIII **4** — *Pele*
The Archetypal Gate of Power 65
The Angel of Empowerment 69

IX **5** — *Inanna*
The Archetypal Queen 73
The Angel of Descent 81

X   **6** — *Aphrodite*
The Archetypal Beauty 85
The Angel of Love 90

XI 7 **Medusa**
The Archetypal Amazon 95
The Angel of Focus 97

XII 8 **Kuan Yin**
The Archetypal Meditator 101
The Angel of Peace 103

XIII 9 **Hestia**
The Archetypal Vestal Virgin 107
The Angel of Discernment 110

XIV 10 **Athena**
The Archetypal Animus-Driven Woman ... 115
The Angel of Magnetic Resonance..............120

XV 11 **Lillith**
The Archetypal Unshackled Woman 125
The Angel of Courage and Conviction 129

XVI 12 **Baba Yaga**
The Archetypal Hag 133
The Angel of Reversal 137

XVII 13 **Kali**
The Archetypal Destroyer 143
The Angel of Ultimate Release 147

XVIII 14 **Uma**
The Archetypal Ecstatic Dancer 151
The Angel of Temperance 154

XIX 15 **Hecate**
The Archetypal Crone 159
The Angel of the Illumined Shadow 162

XX 16 **Demeter**
The Archetypal Great Mother 167
The Angel of Strength and Nurturing 174

XXI 17 **Nuit**
The Archetypal Cosmic Gate 177
The Angel of the Galactic Beam 180

XXII   **18**   **Artemis**
The Archetypal Wild Woman 185
The Angel of the Lunation Cycle 190

XXIII   **19**   **Hathor**
The Archetypal Shapeshifter 195
The Angel of Multidimensionality 202

XXIV   **20**   **Maat**
The Archetypal Seeker of Truth 207
The Angel of Cosmic Consciousness 210

XXV   **21**   **Gaia**
The Archetypal Humanitarian 215
The Angel of the One Heart 218

XXVI   **APPLICATIONS**
Activating the Angels and the Archetypes
Making Angels and Archetypes Runes 221
How to do a Reading 223
Divinatory Meaning of Angels and Archetypes
in a Reading 224
Personalized Goddess Charts 229

APPENDICES
SUMMARY CHARTS 233
The 22 Archetypes 234
The 22 Angels 237

CHAPTER NOTES 241

PHOTO CREDITS 247

BIBLIOGRAPHY 253

INDEX 273

To
Jenara
whose name means *joy to the wind*
my precious spirit daughter
who I have loved in realms beyond space and time
and in the here and now
forever more
I honor you.

The Great Pyramid as seen across the gardens of Mena House.

Preface

A hunger has been unearthed for material that provides a framework for understanding ourselves, our spirituality, and our ancient roots. Our personal evolution, and our collective evolution as a species, relies on bringing the entire inventory of our selves into consciousness. But how do we go about such a monumental task?

When exploring unknown territory, we find it helpful to have a map. With such a tool, we can assess where we have been and chart a course for where we are going. We can also ascertain which parts of the territory are foreign and which are familiar.

As founder and director of the Women's Therapy and Research Center in Calgary, Canada, I have worked with thousands of women throughout North America. Most had read a variety of material on personal growth, had taken numerous workshops, and were committed to developing their spirituality. They were searching for something to help them understand themselves, and their daughters, as women. They were craving the wisdom of feminine consciousness.

In 1979, I began sifting through massive quantities of information. I knew that archaeological sites of peaceable matriarchal cultures were being unearthed, but no one seemed to have a grasp of how those cultures functioned. They were inevitably viewed through the eyes of modern researchers who deemed them primitive and quirky, not productive and technological. My burning question was: "*What happened in matriarchal civilizations before the patriarchy took over?*"

This original work is a synthesis of information gathered in the academic archives during twelve years of college, university, and graduate school, and extensive travel in 27 countries to archeological sites, world museums and libraries such as the National Archaeological Museum in Athens, the British Museum in London, the National Museum in Cairo, and the Simone de Beauvoir Institute Library at Concordia University in Montreal.

My research focused on gender differences, the effect of the socio-cultural context on sex-roles, archetypal psychology, all aspects of Jungian psychology, dream analysis, and mysticism throughout the world. As I studied pictures of frescos and artifacts of pre-historic Greece and pre-dynastic Egypt in the archives, I began to notice more and more images of the empowered feminine. I found that ancients all over the planet shared a reverence for the mysteries of the Universe. Evidence of star maps, space ships, sacred geometry, energy patterns, numerology, and archetypes were explicit on ancient art.

I began to weave archetypal stories about various goddesses, disclosing a complexity of symbolism and mythology. An underlying framework that could comfortably contain this extensive information revealed itself. I embarked upon the task of creating an original work, a multidimensional evolutionary map of feminine consciousness. The system that emerged is rooted in the ancient arts of numerology, astrology, and the Tarot. It is multidimensional in that it maps out social roles, patterns of behavior, and stages of spiritual evolution that are relevant to feminine consciousness. It is evolutionary in that it charts levels of consciousness and spiritual initiations.

In the first three chapters, *Angels and Archetypes* presents a theoretical context for the mastery of feminine consciousness. The chapters that follow present 22 archetypes, or goddesses. Each archetype possesses an original glyph and a number, and is rooted in an astrological sign with its complementary characteristics. Each has an Angel who guides her, who manifests her Higher Self, and who is a tone in the harmonic journey toward higher consciousness. The individual chapters describe the mythology of each goddess, her place in the Tarot, and how she touches the psyche of a modern-day woman. Finally, a chapter entitled "Applications" offers practical information on creating runes and doing readings using the *Angels and Archetypes* system.

This book is written for an audience that is well-versed in new age material. It is not designed to be an introductory text: there are many valuable reference to enhance your basic knowledge in specific fields. You will notice an extensive bibliography of some 370 references is included in this book. For more information about astrology, see Arroyo, Burt, Davidson, George, Goldsmith, Green, Hand, Hodgson, Long, Luxton, Oken, Pelletier, Rudhyar, or Thierens. For discussions on Tarot see Crowley, Gray, Kaplan, Konraad, LeMieux, Morgan, Nichols, Pollack, Roberts, Thierens, Walker, Wanless, or Woudhuysen. For basic information on numerology, consult Cheiro, Konraad, or Walker.

Angels and Archetypes is written in an academic style: numbered endnotes throughout the chapters reference the sources of information. Unless you are using the document for research purposes, the endnotes are meant not to interrupt your reading but only to substantiate statements.

When I proposed an evolutionary map of feminine consciousness, both men and women immediately voiced concern regarding the relevance of such a map to men and to masculine consciousness. Was a corresponding map of a parallel structure for masculine consciousness forthcoming?

Men, in fact, have not been left out. The scholarly work of Robert Moore, Sam Keen, Robert Bly, and Joseph Campbell have designated numerous masculine archetypes of warrior, king, magician, and lover. The simple fact is that the past 5,000 years of culture has supported the archetypal masculine.

Making a safe place for the archetypal feminine was the task at hand. As men come to value their own internal feminine, they may indeed welcome the opportunity to occupy a chair at the table designated for the archetypal feminine.

I invite you to join me in the journey toward consciousness and to reacquaint yourselves with profound truths. I offer you an evolutionary map of feminine consciousness, a treasure that has been lost for a brief time in the relative scheme of things.

Carmen Boulter
May, 1996

Acknowledgments

To Priscilla, for setting my career path, for restoring my academic zeal, and for helping me find the *Simone deBeauvoir Institute* Library.

To Gail, for handing me pertinent books, and for all the enlivening conversations and for taking me to *The Recoletta* in Buenos Aires, Argentina.

To Galen, my son, for your immense patience and for your technological help.

To Jackie, for understanding Jung and for recognizing who I am.

To Trace, for grasping my vision, for containing my process, and for being just like me.

To Michael Freeman, Robert H. Foster, and Dwayne Edward Rourke for your invaluable artistic interpretations.

To Boyd Holloway, Ron Rathburn, Suze Baumann, Geordie Facey, Josef Szujker, Denis Murphy and Brian McCutcheon for permission to publish your photographs.

To Rita, for loving me and believing in me no matter what, and for your example as a spiritual warrior.

You have given me strength.

The following authors made an enormous contribution to my thinking. I hope to thank you in person:

Jean Shinoda Bolen	James Redfield	Barbara Hand Clow
Marilyn Ferguesson	Marion Woodman	Erich Neumann
Marion Zimmer-Bradley	Dr. David Ash	Barbara G. Walker
Susie Orbach	Merlin Stone	John Randolph Price
Clarissa Pinkola Estes	Charles Berlitz	John Michel
Judy Chicago	Sally Nichols	Fritz Perls
Gabrielle Roth	Elinor Gadon	Carlos Castenada
Marija Gimbutas	Cris Grisom	Jean Houston
Zacharia Sitchin	Thomas Moore	Sam Keen
Sylvia Briton Perrera	Demetra George	Barbara Mor
Monica Sjoo	Ken Carey	Barbara Marciniak

Two magnificent pillars guarding the entrance to the Holy of Holies, the sacred sanctuary at the temple of Karnak, Egypt. One pillar has a papyrus flower and the other has a blue lotus flower.

Introduction

The seeds for the development of the *Angels and Archetypes* system were planted when I was a young child. Standing under my favorite maple tree when I was six, I realized that I had light energy radiating from my hands. I knew there were worlds beyond the physical, but I simultaneously knew I would not be met with understanding if I told anyone. When I was 11, I found two books on my father's bookshelf. One was an Edgar Cayce channeled piece on prophesies of the future and the ultimate purpose of life on earth; the other had pictures of the Great Pyramid. Seeing my first photograph of the interior of the Pyramid, I was thunderstruck. In that moment in Montreal in 1965, I pledged to go to Egypt and to learn all I could about the pyramids and their *raison d'être*. Little did I realize that this experience would set the course of my career.

In 1977, I traveled to Porto Santo (a tiny Portuguese island off the coast of Africa where Christopher Columbus launched many of his expeditions before sailing to the Americas) where for several glorious months, I studied astrology and cast hand-calculated charts. I then traveled alone in search of ancient mysteries. I already had memories of past lives, but I had no idea that direct exposure to sacred sites would trigger more of these memories with such intensity. I journeyed to Mediterranean islands, to Turkey, Iran, Afghanistan, Pakistan, India, and Nepal. My quest drew me to spiritual communities, palaces, monasteries, and archeological power points. I was profoundly stirred by auspicious experiences at Stonehenge, the Glastonbury Tor, Findhorn, Knossos, Mycenae, the Parthenon, Delphi, and the lands that were Persia, Tibet, and ancient Egypt.

On Crete, at Knossos (which means "knowing from within"), there is a remarkable archeological site. When I read the plaque stating the "historical" explanation for the site, my stomach turned. A voice within exclaimed: *"That's not what happened here!"* I wandered around the temple complex, which felt strangely familiar. While contemplating an artifact from 3000 BC, an ornate pin that was reputed to have changed the nature of fashion worn at the time, I fell into a deep state. Transfixed, I gazed into the marble sanctuary, envisioning maidens luxuriously draped in white gowns, leisurely reposing in the sacred waters of the shallow pools.

Struck with an impulse, I was pulled outdoors, and inexplicably propelled across the grounds of the complex. As suddenly as I had been led across the courtyard and up a hill, I was stopped. Perplexed, I looked around and saw an empty grassed area. I looked toward the site with its immensely precious view of the Mediterranean Sea. I questioned: "Why am I here? What relevance did this location have to those who lived here in times past? What force propelled me to witness this?"

Released from the grip of the experience, I anchored the resolve to seek an explanation for this fascinating episode. I committed myself to carrying out serious research on the origins of ancient cultures. I soon found that although academic articles on matriarchal cultures had been written and published, the publications were not stocked in the University or public libraries in my province. My search continued and my zeal to find the answers grew.

Ten years after my experience on Crete, I traveled to Montreal because I had heard that the Simone de Beauvoir Institute Library at Concordia University had the most complete collection of feminist journals in the country. There, after weeks of digging through archives, I discovered a map of the ancient site of Knossos: the site to which I had been propelled was none other than the sacred grove where temple priestesses had performed rituals.

Angels and Archetypes is a result of intuitive hunches, profound experiences, and channeled information followed up by research. Academic investigation has revealed enormous confusion, misinterpretation, and contradiction within the literature about the nature of gods and goddesses. For example, two identical photographs of a figurine were claimed in one document to be a particular goddess and in a second to be another. Some references took two distinct goddesses and proudly amalgamated them into one. Frescos of barebreasted women were described as men. Frescos depicting Egyptian women transmitting energy were labeled "men hunting birds." The energy of Astarte, Ishtar, and Inanna, which all seemed to have the same roots, were claimed by subsequent cultures and unabashedly renamed in the various civilizations of Egypt, Sumer, Babylon, Mesopotamia, Greece, and Rome.

At first I was disconcerted, but what came clear was that definitive truths about our ancestral past were largely unknown. I began doing pictorial research, meaning that I began viewing photographs of ancient sites and artifacts while consciously refusing to read the interpretations. This released me to follow my own hunches and to piece a new version of the story together.

This system is the ultimate result of that undertaking. During the process, the goddesses began revealing themselves to me. They unveiled definitive characteristics of their own and exposed a staggering depth. My fascination grew. With new eyes, I began to see how the goddess energy was not a mass of confusing and contradictory data, but rather had the potential of becoming an organized, cohesive system with an inherent intelligence of its own.

This work is a multidimensional evolutionary map of feminine consciousness, retrieving the ancient mysteries that have been veiled through the ages and offering a template for the actualization of the feminine in balance with the masculine.

A Transformation of Consciousness for Mankind

A global shift in consciousness is occurring. In this time of great upheaval and collective reevaluation, accurate knowledge of the grand jigsaw puzzle of the Universe is becoming available in quantum leaps. Many great thinkers have gone against the grain of culture and showed the courage to expose material that explored seemingly uncharted realms. In the synthesis of this information, and in its accessibility, truths can resonate and meaningful transformation within individuals can occur. These transformations occur on many internal levels: physical, emotional, mental, and spiritual. They occur simultaneously in individuals and in communities, and they coincide with global and galactic shifts reverberating throughout existence.

Retrieving Our Heritage

Examination of the origins and influences of these changes is a vast prospect, but the ancients left sculptures and temples encoded with powerful matrices that can shed light on the unexplainable. They are miraculous gifts left for our discovery and evaluation.

Clear, intelligent, and definitive information about the past is sketchy and distorted. History has been repeatedly rewritten, from the perspective of the victors. In the twentieth century, there has been much speculation about prehistoric cultures, notably from a limited patriarchal vantage point. As a consequence, data now available about prehistory are often scrambled, largely unsynthesized, and grossly misinterpreted. Much of the sacred information from our ancestral past remains shrouded in mystery, and our predecessors have been dismissed as infantile and misguided. Not understanding multidimensionality, scholarly texts will promote absurd notions that the Egyptians were obsessed with death, that hunter-gatherers were preoccupied with possession by spirits, and that pagans worshipped the devil. Seen as a direct threat to the new order, whole libraries were burned, along with the people who compiled the books and those who maintained the self-empowering beliefs.

Evidence about peaceable cultures that honored the feminine is scattered, and fragments often appear in texts written for all kinds of other purposes.[1] But they are not entirely lost, and as we expand our capacity to comprehend the spiritual character of the ancients, we are able to retrieve important pieces and re-weave the tapestry of our heritage.

Ancient traditions and oracles left their mark through legend, artifact, ancient fresco, or psychological remnant. With enough digging, synthesizing, intuiting, and determination, a larger story can be told. Be it myth, magic, visioning, or pure fantasy, let our wings take flight, let the brush stroke the palette of our collective imagination. May we connect with ourselves so that we can once again know the truth. May our souls be nourished and released as we sort through illusions, shed veils, illuminate our shadows, dance within the polarities, and embrace a higher consciousness. In this state we can commune with the divine and alleviate the malaise of our times. Here, we can see that humanity is standing at a gateway. Here, we hear the Angels sing. Consciously or unconsciously, we know this. We are ready, on a planetary level, to bring it into consciousness. After all:

The unconscious is ready to witness a miracle.[2]

The Gate of Power, also known as the Gate of the Sun, Tihuanaco, Bolivia.

Chapter I

Archetypes
The Gateway to the
Empowered Feminine

As we explore the realm of the unexplained in our search for meaning, we stir ancient memories. It is truly an auspicious phenomenon, for a wave of inspiration links the vast network of megalithic structures to terrestrial patterns that measure both the earth and the heavens and reveal a universal civilization.[1] As we consider that the devisors of these sacred monuments *are* our progenitors, we help ourselves to consciously understand the values and symbolism that constitute our ancestry.

But what comprises the molecules of our ancestral past? Carl Jung believed that there are universal and impersonal motifs in folklore, mythology, and dreams that are transmitted by tradition and heredity. These mystical, spiritual images can exist in conscious reality or be largely unconscious. Jung referred to this body of symbolic data as the *collective unconscious,*[2] or cultural psyche common to us all.

The patterns of the human mind cluster into universal, primordial images that are called *archetypes*. Archetypes are eternal and compelling. They constitute the very structure of the collective unconscious.

> The archetypes are formal factors responsible for the organization of unconscious psychic processes: they are "patterns of behavior" At the same time they have a "specific charge" and develop numinous effects which express themselves as affects.*[3]

Archetypes are, by their very nature, alive. They emerge without conscious effort. They are connected to our instincts and trigger us emotionally. They provide a psychological map that can help us identify our stage of growth and our place in the world. These roles can be categorized, dramatized, and explored. The maiden, the warrior, the mother, the hag, and the lover are transformative, re-generative, and transcendent archetypal personifications. When an archetype constellates, a psychosocial field radiates from the deep unconscious.

---

*Affect: feeling or emotion; an expressed or observed emotional response.

Our task is to develop the capacity to comprehend archetypes and to learn to differentiate between them. It is an enormous developmental achievement to bring archetypal images into consciousness and to flow freely between them without getting caught in the seductive grip of a single archetype. At various stages in our life, we dance with different archetypes. When we emulate one archetype to the exclusion of others, we run the risk of being caught in an archetypal complex, meaning that we lose perspective and flexibility.

Primordial archetypes contain paradoxes. They can simultaneously represent the light and the shadow, the good and the bad, the beautiful and the ugly, the male and the female. They exist for us to identify with and to project into. As we embrace the continua they represent, we begin to reckon with the parts of ourselves that have been unconscious.

Femininity and Masculinity as Archetypal Forces

The repression of femininity and of feminine consciousness is at the root of many global and personal issues. As we balance these forces within ourselves and within culture, we will experience a collective healing. Not surprisingly:

> Maleness and femaleness are archetypal forces. They constitute different ways of relating to life, to the world, and to the opposite sex. *The repression of femininity, therefore, affects mankind's relation to the cosmos no less than the relation of individual men and women to each other.* Sociological solutions serve some purpose, but lack a basic understanding of feminine psychology.[4] [emphasis mine]

Masculine and feminine energies are clearly in dichotomy on earth at this time. The communication gap has widened, as reflected in the divorce rate and in instability in male-female relationships. We are all born male and female, not masculine and feminine. We have characteristic differences and are birthed into a cultural context that has emphasized sex-roles stereotypes. Yet, qualities of feminine nature play an important role in the psyche of a man and vice versa. Masculine and feminine traits themselves can be comfortably contained within both sexes. Contrary to our socialization process, the balancing of these polarities is essential for the full functioning of either gender. Carl Jung introduced the concept of *anima,* the feminine side of a man, and *animus,* the masculine side of a woman The empowerment of the feminine in both genders and a return to our inherent wholeness is essential to the healing of individuals and the healing of the planet.

Even so, hierarchical culture has had an investment in maintaining the gender gap. Over the past several millennia, psychic, intuitive, and emotional functioning have systematically been denigrated in both genders. Repression of the feminine ways of processing has created a deep wound and had a crippling effect on relationships between men and women. In healing of this dichotomy and retrieving the conscious feminine, we can all engender balance.

> Dialogue between masculine and feminine aspects of the Great Spirit has been going on in this universe for twenty billion years. The creation that has appeared as a result of this dialogue has appeared on each vibrational frequency of manifestation in turn, with degrees of specificity and precision on each frequency directly related to the quality and clarity of the exchange among the embodied representatives of male god and female god who there come into being.[5]

In the beginning there was oneness. The "Pearl of Beginning" divided into the two great rhythms, *yin* and *yang*, the interaction of which gives rise to all phenomena in the Universe.[6] The essence of creation is a deeply meaningful and wise connection between the sacred and the bio-sexual. Magnetism is created between the polarities spiraling around the two fundamental principles at the atomic core of our beings that do not compete but complement each other as harmonious parts of a whole.

The two great rhythms are represented in the difference in dominant brain functions in males and females. Given the socio-cultural context and the longstanding divisiveness between traditional roles for males and females, it is not surprising that these contrasts manifest at cerebral levels as well. Females, then, predominantly manifest *yin* functions, and tend to be right-brain dominant. On the other hand, males represent *yang* functions that are dominant in the left hemisphere of the brain. It is known scientifically that full functioning of individuals and the ultimate creative thinking occurs when there is lucid interaction between both hemispheres of the brain through the corpus callosum, or mid-brain.[7] (The brain stem, or reptilian brain, also has an invaluable function as it contains the ancient memories at the cellular level.) The following list designates the attributes of the two hemispheres as adapted from Robert Ornstein's *Psychology of Consciousness*.[8]

Psychology of Consciousness:

YIN	YANG
Right Hemisphere	Left Hemisphere
Left Side of the Body	Right Side of the Body

Feminine	*Masculine*
Night	*Day*
Eternity, timelessness	*Time, history*
Sensuality, Intuition	*Intelligence*
Tacit	*Explicit*
The whole	*The parts*
Cyclical	*Linear*
Simultaneous	*Sequential*
Diffusion	*Focal*
Synchronicity	*Causality*
Experience	*Argument*
Ritual	*Dogma*
Expansion	*Contraction*
Softness	*Hardness*
Process	*Analysis*
Flexibility	*Rigidity*
Symbolism	*Concrete*
Altered States	*Waking Reality*
Associative	*Dissociative*
Magic	*Rationality*
Receptivity	*Action*
Lunar	*Solar*
Internal	*External*
Perceptual Leaps	*Systematic Thinking*
Art	*Science*
Creative	*Analytical*
Divergent Production	*Convergent Production*
Irrational	*Rational*

Culture has glamorized and popularized the concrete functions of the left brain, leaving the more symbolic realms largely uncharted and forbidden. This book will map out the rich landscape of feminine consciousness that validates intuitive, mystical, and timeless dimensions in balance with the active and the concrete. The successful blending of the energies and the graceful dance between them brings us home to our essential selves. North American native culture inherently respects the energy within the polarity:

> When male and female meet on the Medicine Wheel, they each carry a distinct, creative charge. Though their roots weave together and spring from the same source in the same Great Spirit, they incarnate on earth to face one another with distinct sexual charges, profoundly attracted, with immense capacity to create through the universal power of the love that can flow between them.[9]

In our culture, seekers of both sexes are engaged in the disciplinary work of bringing into consciousness that which has been repressed. We are thus re-empowering ourselves, resonating with our own truth, regaining our voices, and once again becoming whole. Both sexes are learning that denial is central to repression and that external control is the antithesis of functional expression. In validating our essential natures, we are freed to live soulfully and to illuminate that which has been lurking in the shadows of our unconscious.

There are fundamental differences in the experiences of femininity and masculinity. Women are contextual and relational. They are holistic in their approach to reality.[10] A woman's attachments provide the foundation for her sense of self. They are the soil from which her emotions and behavior originate.[11]

> A woman does not draw a clear distinction between herself and her children, herself and her mate, herself and her religious community. Rather the relationship is the primary organism within which the 'self' is only somewhat under her personal control. This diffusive quality of women makes them particularly vulnerable to loss of self and voice in relationship and community.[12]

On the other hand, the male psyche is attuned to repressive discipline and often compartmentalizes emotions. The female psyche is hurt by such denial and sees it as evasion, therein demonstrating an essential difference in orientation between the sexes.[13]

In order for a woman to become balanced in every aspect of herself, she must retrieve and honor her own way of processing feelings. Instead of projecting outwards and seeking an external mirror for self-reflection, it is essential for a woman to consult internally.

Self-affirmation for women means, first and foremost, acceptance of their differentness from men, rather than identification, imitation, and competitiveness with them by androlatric standards. Only by first finding this basic feminine stance can they also claim their Yang element and give expression to their masculine drives and capacities, in their own ways, as women. The raw impulses—to hurt, to possess, to make something or someone conform to one's expectation—can be destructive when vented as they occur. This is true for men no less than women.[14]

Understandably, many of the interpretations of our reality have reflected linear thinking and dualistic, patriarchal values. Contrary to prevalent opinion, "patriarchal" does not mean sovereign authority of men over women. It is the prominence of an archetypal masculine consciousness that has dominated culture for the last 5,000 years. This imperative reflects a phase of human development. It is characterized by the urge of the ego to free itself from the unconscious and to exist independently from it.

Similarly, "matriarchal" does not refer to the dominance of women over men. When ideologies predict the end of patriarchy, fantasies are conjured of women getting even with men for the past centuries of violent suppression. Alternatively, references to pre-historic Amazons invite abstractions of barbaric androgynes devouring men and turning them to stone. Neither of these misguided images contain the notion of the Matriarchate. The supremacy of the archetype of the Great Mother was a pervasively psychic situation, in which the unconscious prevailed and the fertile womb of the feminine was intimately connected to the periodicity of the moon and revered. At the dawn of time, the mystery of procreation was the magical activity of the woman, and the masculine ego-consciousness was still in the childhood of its development, not yet attaining autonomy and independence.

The phase of matriarchal feminine consciousness was nocturnal, reflective, and enchanting. By gazing into the night sky, the ancients observed the dramatic phases of the lunation cycle to which woman is eternally bound. Humankind's earliest cultural developments were the work of women. Counting and calendars were precipitated by basic recordings of menstruation cycles. Planting and harvesting, spinning and weaving, preparation of food and intoxicating beverages were all birthed by the feminine. These were not the technological achievements of the masculine, but were the primitive, symbolic rituals of the feminine.

We are immersed in a phase of global psychic renewal[15] that has brought us full circle and has us reconsidering our position in the grand scheme of things. The technological patriarchal solar consciousness has brought us to a pinnacle of modern culture, yet if it remains separate from its shadow, humankind could most certainly destroy life on the planet.

Patriarchal consciousness threatens our understanding of the whole by promoting dualistic thinking. Subscribers to this mindset in fact may refer to themselves as "realists." The central tenet of this position is that if something cannot be seen, it does not exist. Yet, much of our experience of our very existence, our internalized view of our daily reality, our conscious and unconscious processes are mental, emotional, and spiritual and thus wholly unseen. To purport that unconscious processes do not exist is simply to limit one's experience of that which is. People who cling to this perspective often do so by rote, tenaciously manifesting self-righteousness.

There is a link between authoritarianism, self-righteousness, and religiousness. In this time when many people feel an urge to connect with their spirituality, many inadvertently equate spirituality with religiousness and become easily confused when they are not drawn to go to church. They are instinctually suspicious of organized religions that have gone to great lengths to monopolize and control spirituality. Dogma and rigid dualism rages through authoritarian religions insisting that God is male, vengeful, and punitive. Church fathers re-interpreted the miraculous, invented hell, and trained us to feel unworthy and fearful of an external spiritual authority. This is a departure from the original essence of matriarchal spirituality that connects our souls directly to the mysteries of our divinity, where Father-God and Mother-God are deeply in love.

It is common knowledge that although the bible has been the object of massive interpretation and revision, it still consistently reflects the divisiveness of patriarchal consciousness and overtly denigrates the feminine. It is widely known that the New Testament was composed centuries after Jesus' death. When Church and State were linked, the Inquisition violently tyrannized and terrorized, and the oppression of matriarchal consciousness was institutionalized. Those who attempted to reverse the flow of ignorance and superstition were systematically defeated. Though the original scriptures still hold kernels of the evolutionary template that Christ was sent to exemplify, the fear and pain of the persecutions have been locked into our cellular memories and into the collective unconscious. The huge effort spent in eradicating the truth about the past has been effective and, for the most part, the old tradition has been lying dormant. Even if the reasons for the suppression have been forgotten, the attitudes remain, and we as a culture have been unconsciously committed to maintaining the veil of illusion that puts the sexes in opposition to each other. As Whitmont so aptly states:

> ...extroverted religiousness taught us social consciousness. But in our time, it has reached its saturation point. It has degenerated into moralistic preaching and into a world view that can see only material and economic dynamics, devoid of any relevance to the mystery

of existence. The resurgence of the feminine, however, reopens the possibility of access to this mystery by revalidating the *inward subjective dimension*.[16] [emphasis mine]

Integrating Material from the Subconscious

It is inevitable that we will get wounded in our process of growth. Modern culture is so addicted to denial and so phobic of pain that it systematically avoids opportunities for real growth. The ancients had a reverence for and a deep understanding of the value of emotional lessons on the earth plane. One of the mottoes of the Delphic Oracle was *that which is wounded shall heal.*[17] The rituals offered comfort, solace, and guidance for dealing with the cycles of life. The stages of life were honored. Learning to let go and grieve losses and loved ones was part of the sacred rites. The populace faced the issue of death and dying head on, understanding them to be spiritual initiations. The burden of self-knowledge was placed on the student whose struggle to understand led to real intellectual power. It was widely known that a teacher's explanations were not as durable and useful as personal insights achieved through internal effort. Deciphering the truth within and the truths recognized by all peoples was a practiced art.[18] As we attune to our own tides and instinctual directives, we too can decipher our own internal codes and end the cycle of self-betrayal. We learn who we are and what we need and are thus released from the anchor of meeting artificially imposed agendas and demands.

In this process of self-reflection, we see our relative position on our journey of personal and spiritual evolution. We thus illuminate our *shadow*s, or the aspects of ourselves we have not been able to witness and have relegated to the unconscious. Likely, they were pushed asunder because they did not fit with the notions that culture purported acceptable. The material was quite simply denied. As already noted, many of our issues as women are relational, or occur in the context of a relationship. Culture has been in denial about the repression of the feminine, about physical, emotional, and sexual abuse. We have all had ample opportunity to participate in the conspiracy of silence. In order to release the trauma, we require containment, validation, and support. In the absence of an adequate container, we are left with shame and guilt. Healing hinges on facing our secret weaknesses and our formerly rejected shadow. Thus we achieve a balance within our psyches.

In this state of grace, duality evaporates. All is seen as integral in the continuum of wholeness. The only way a shadow can be cast is in the presence of light. The light of the moon is a pearly emanation of the projected light of the sun. Each contrariety contains the seed of its opposite within which we can confront ourselves and thus discover our indivisibility. *Duality* is about separation, but *polarity* creates a force field of opposites, gracefully interacting with one another. In Whitmont's words:

> Strictness requires looseness. Courage must discover where it is afraid and needs to fear. Honesty needs to find out where it cheats and is untruthful to the needs of life. Love has to see where it hates and rejects or is indifferent to the realities of the other. Hate has to discover where it is attached, and loves. We must endure the full reality of ourselves, not only the part that we wish to be. The full reality of the living being requires a down for every up just as it leads to an up for every down. That is the pulse beat of existence.[19]

Our ultimate goal is to be able to contain all archetypes and to chart our interaction with these elements of the collective unconsciousness. If we fear or resist any particular archetype, our unconscious will be haunted. If we are overly enamored of a particular archetype, we will be driven by an archetypal complex and could become rigid, imperialistic, and narrow. The graceful flow between various archetypal energies allows us full expression of all aspects of self and allows for the wisdom of the Higher Self to interact successfully with us. It is here that we meet the Angels, the link to our higher consciousness.

Chapter II

Angels
The Link to Our Higher Consciousness

Angels live in perpetual ecstasy in the celestial realms of harmony and light. They offer us a glimpse of a larger universe and of the evolutionary impetus that is our destiny. Angels and humans function like a powerful set of magnets. Angels exist to spiritualize the material world, while humans exist to materialize the spiritual world. Humans and Angels draw toward each other to fulfill a divine purpose and to perform major celestial work. By descending into the material world, Angels benevolently create a bridge across the dimensions. By purifying ourselves, we attune to more subtle energies, and begin to ascend into that finer frequency range where the Angels dwell.

Angels are cooperative companions to our souls that resonate with the true concepts of the absolute.[1] They infiltrate the environments of our lives, offering guidance, support, and perspective. They are beings of connection, not of control.[2] Universal law provides an atmosphere of the greatest respect, for Angels have the cosmic mandate to respond only when we ask for help. Angels function like the social workers of the Universe: if we are a danger to ourselves, they can reach out their wings and protect us.[3]

Culture has offered massive visual stimulation and has trained us to experience reality through the five physical senses. Though this has been sensationally rich, it has kept us focused on our *outer* vision, and disconnected us from the intuitive and imaginative frequencies in the realms of the unseen. These inner communication devices are designed to keep the Angels in frequent communication with humans.[4] It is our receptivity that allows the Angels to bond to our souls. We may be *under their wing*, but if we are not conscious of their presence, their wisdom inevitably escapes us.

Angelic entities are highly evolved beings that vibrate at a more refined, or faster, frequency than is perceptible in our ordinary waking reality. Society, materiality, and duality exist in the third dimension, a dense or slow vibrational level, while Angels exist in the fourth dimension and beyond. We can easily miss seeing an Angel when we are focused on the constant visual stimulation of the third-dimensional world. Yet, our lack of awareness does not prevent the Angels from seeing us. Technically, an entity vibrating at a faster frequency can perceive and see entities vibrating at slower frequencies. Meanwhile, entities vibrating at slower or denser frequencies can be completely oblivious to the more refined, or more evolved, beings.[5]

Being in an open, loving-hearted state with ourselves paves the way for spiritual energies to move through us with grace and ease. When we are not living in our hearts, the spiritual forces are scattered. The open heart is the holy meeting place, the sacred flame of the internal temple that allows for spiritual evolution to take place.[6] Through focused intent and purification of our bodies, our minds, and our emotions, we can foster our connection with the divine. In so doing, we increase our capacity to channel cosmic energies and thus raise our vibrational level. We become connected to the luminous web that encircles the planet. We then open to direct transmission with our Higher Selves. As duality and separation evaporate, we can learn to consciously access the Angelic realms. This process is in itself an initiation. We become part of a tremendous revolution in consciousness that is grounding spiritual energy in the world.

Angels are the vehicles for the distribution of creative influences. When we are infused with genius,[7] creative energy rises to the brain, and we are elevated to the Angelic state. Angels function as our spiritual perceptive faculties that dwell in the higher consciousness. In their own words:

> We bring you an Angelic awareness that historically has not often been incarnate in human form. We bring an eternal continuity of consciousness that henceforth you might know yourselves as we know ourselves. Together in loving cooperation, we join to provide spirit and matter with the optimal balance.[8]

Angels have always existed. Angelic messengers have had powerful impacts and the stories are kept alive in mystical texts. They appeared in auspicious moments and have inspired biblical stories and religious prophecies throughout history. One of the most famous visitations was when Archangel Gabriel appeared to Mary to announce her pregnancy and the precious significance her son would have on the world.

Contact with Angels may be far more prevalent than is surmised. In a 1993 poll, 69% of Americans stated they believe in the existence of Angels, 55% believing them to be spiritual beings with special powers to act as agents of God on earth. Almost one-third of them (32%) had consciously experienced an Angelic presence.[9] As the earth and its people evolve, consciousness of other realms is becoming increasingly relevant and believable. Incredibly, 71% of Americans believe in life after death[10] while a 1987 poll revealed that 50% believe in the existence of extra-terrestrial visitations.[11]

Many of us are aware that we have been blessed by Angels in moments of radical transformation. Some secretly hope to one day know an Angel, while others are actively preparing themselves for contact. It may be worth looking through our memory banks for such an experience. For, when we consciously open to the reality of angelic friends and guardian Angels, we may realize that, in retrospect, we have already met with Angels, even as our conscious minds ruled out the possibility. Many of us are able to retrieve and integrate past experiences that have been lying dormant in our subconscious minds. When we do not understand that Angels move between frequency ranges, or dimensions, we may not grasp that they are influencing us. When serendipity has blessed us, we may have assumed the miracle was luck or fate. Recognizing our affiliation with Angels can be immensely comforting and is a gateway to a profound and soulful world.

To Angels, all is vibration. Having no material density, they consciously move from one world to another, re-forming their light bodies in an appropriate pattern when they arrive in a different dimension. Changes in the electromagnetic field around the planet has made it easier for Angels to lower their vibrational frequencies and to approach us. When they descend into our reality, the third dimension, they creatively clothe themselves in the "beautiful, feminine, crystalline latticework of the material plane."[12] They function as vortices, transmitting the pure essence of their beings. The human body is designed to function as an electromagnetic, biochemical receptor for these transmissions.

We are living in an age of synthesis and of recollection. It is clear that the pure of heart, prophets from every age, and the spiritually awakened were touched by Angelic encounters. It is possible now for us all to remember.

The divine evolutionary plan is unfolding. In preparation for the evolutionary leap, there was a *cosmic dispensation* of thousands of Angels, sent to assist in materializing the Age of Light. As galactic beams move into alignment, the Aquarian Age is being birthed into physical reality on earth. As we come to the crest of our own evolution, we are only beginning to fathom the expanse of knowledge our progenitors possessed and the depth of union with the divine that motivated them.

The Angels are our midwives as we make this great transition. It is now possible to perceive Angels when they are in our presence. If we listen very carefully, we can also hear their words.

> We are the Pattern Beings, the Winged Ones, the Light Bearers. We are the reality of your perfect spirits, coming now to consciously incarnate in your human fields.[13]

Angels themselves are immortal. They represent the future of our own evolution.[14] They exist in a unified field, and function on many levels at once. Our genetic code engenders this form of evolutionary programming. In this age of ecological consciousness, we recycle material objects. From this point of view, it is plausible that we would also recycle our souls. Having so many lessons to integrate, it makes sense that we would cycle through many incarnations to achieve the mastery necessary to evolve, synthesize, and bring to consciousness the totality of our existence. By understanding where we come from, we can return home to *Source*.

> The original spark is a very sacred, holy thing, because upon its development depends [humanity's] immortality. It is represented as occupying the most holy place in the temple and as being protected and cared for with great devotion. All that [humanity] is has been brought forth from this central spark, yet the sense-conscious man often neglects it and ignores its very existence. The attention is taken up with the things of sense to the exclusion of Spirit.[15]

Bonding with Angels increases our capacity for trust in the perfection of our evolving universe. In this ascended state, our innocence is restored. We inspire a state of consciousness in which the cosmic reality of the Universe, and beyond, is revealed. This is sometimes referred to as *Christ consciousness*, or "the higher self of [wo]man."[16] As we transcend the limitations of space and time, we loosen the hold of third-dimensional existence and experience ourselves as multidimensional beings. The body loses its limitations and takes on the vital substance of Father-Mother God. Here, duality knows no place. Moving beyond fear, we reclaim our radiance and we become one with the Angel within us. By bringing consciousness into our etheric fields we illumine our *light bodies* and spread our wings. By touching the divinity of the unified field, we are in full communion with the omnipresent source and the essence of the Universe. This is the process of *ascension*, an evolutionary step for humankind, "the final step in the attainment of Christ consciousness."[17]

Prior to meeting our Angels we are typically outer-directed, immersed in materiality and the sensationalism of culture. When we nourish our souls, honor our visions, and resonate with inherent truth, we transform from within. By constantly communing with Spirit, the "union is made with the indwelling substance and the soul is fed and satisfied with the abundance of good."[18] From an inner-directed stance, we transcend culture, embrace our higher selves, and consciously participate in the evolution of the species and the simultaneous evolution of Mother Earth.

14

Chapter III

The Evolutionary Map
The Journey of the Soul

The Evolutionary Map

Each chapter begins by showing the position of the Archetypes on the Evolutionary Map. The Evolutionary Journey takes us to one of twenty-two stations along the Red Road. We meet an Archetype at each station and hear her story. Next, her companion Angel offers us a spiritual lesson. The journey takes us through four Realms: the Realm of the Underworld, the Realm of Roles, the Realm of Renunciation, and the Realm of Cosmic Consciousness.

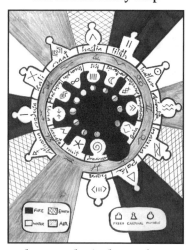

The Astrological Template

The Astrological Template arranges the Archetypes on the astrological wheel. Eleven archetypes are arranged on the outer rim and are Solar, or extroverted, representing roles that are culturally visible. Eleven archetypes are arranged on the inner circle and are Lunar, or introverted, illuminating the internal, intuitive nature of the feminine. Each are represented by an element and are either earth, air, fire, or water. Each is either cardinal (initiating), fixed (maintaining), or mutable (changeable).

The following anecdotal story sets the stage for the Evolutionary Journey. It takes into consideration that we are spiritual beings having experiences on the Earth Plane. The story introduces each Angel and each Archetype by name. To really know them in depth, delve into their individual stories in the chapters that follow.

Join The Dreamer, the one who takes the journey of the Soul. Walk the Red Road, meet the individual archetypes, and be initiated by their Angelic companions.

In the beginning, after the physical earth was formed, it was decided, as part of the Master Plan, that the Earth would be the location of a cosmic experiment. Earth was designated a *free will* zone. Fascinated by the concept, civilizations within the Universe and beyond it were to monitor the experiment as well as participate in it.

A galactic clarion call was emitted, inviting souls from various star systems to consider voluntary participation. In addition to free will, souls would have the advantage of *emotional bodies* and the immense freedom to access the *karmic wheel* of cause and effect. With purity and intent, there was vast opportunity for spiritual evolution.

The challenge was that the Earth was to vibrate in the density of the third dimension where duality reigned. The polarities of light and dark, good and evil, would co-exist and interpenetrate each other with infinite subtlety. Where *chaos* would represent disorder and dissolution, *cosmos* would represent the harmonic order of creation and time. The ultimate intent was for participating souls to return to the light and to be free of karma by the end of the experiment when

Earth entered the Age of Light.

It was understood that the Earth existed in a solar system where planets rotated in an electromagnetic field around a single star. Because most souls in the universal family applying to participate in the experiment on Earth originated in binary star systems, their electromagnetic field was necessarily of a higher vibrational frequency. This follows the idea that when a planetary star system is formed, the electromagnetic energy available at creation dictates the vibrational frequency of the entire system. In other words, more stars create more energy, which necessitates vibration in a higher dimensional field. The Earth, then, vibrated in the third dimension, while the planets of origin vibrated in the fourth, fifth, and the higher dimensions beyond.

The Descent to the Earth Plane

As a consequence, the souls' individual vibrations had to be adjusted so they could tolerate the limitations of a denser field. Pathways of descent were established. Souls coming from the dimensions beyond would typically descend to the fifth dimension of Sirius, then to the fourth dimension of Venus, and eventually to the third dimension of Earth. After entering the frequency of the Earth plane, the densification continued and the other dimensions were veiled. The further they descended, the more they forgot the cosmic sophistication of their origins.

All volunteers participated in training sessions that necessitated a complete understanding of the relevance of the experiment. All participants were performing a cosmic duty, and would be called *light workers.* Their eventual task would be to become conscious and to remember who they were before they descended to Earth. They were to understand that all beings are part of a universal family. They were to cycle through multiple incarnations on the Earth plane, to be exposed to all polarities of rich and poor, healthy and sick, dominator and dominated, immersed in the linear reality and limited by time and space, yet steadily evolving breaking the karmic chains and embracing an evolving consciousness.

There was to come a time when the veils would be lifted, when the Earth herself, personified as Gaia, would be ready to make an evolutionary dimensional shift. This would be when the light workers would consciously remember their mission. Miraculously, they would unite with one another and be midwives to Gaia herself as she passed through the cosmic gateway and was birthed into the harmonics of the multidimensional Universe.

In the beginning, it is as though there was pure consciousness in the beings who came to Earth. They understood the laws of the universe,and of cause and effect, that thought is creative, and that they were here on a spiritual mission. They flew with the Angels and understood the movements of the planets and the influence the stars had on us. Furthermore, creation and pro-creation were valued as precious gifts from the universe. The Sky Goddess birthed the Mother Goddess who gave birth to a divine human prototype.

The Angel of the One Heart guided the Angel of Cosmic Consciousness. The Angel of Multidimensionality brought along the Angel of the Lunation Cycle. Looking ahead along the path, the Angel of the Galactic Beam saw a gateway. It was guarded by the Mother Archetype who spans between the Realm of Cosmic Consciousness and the Realm of Renunciation.

Another vibrational densification was required to travel the pathway descending into the earth plane. In the Realm of Renunciation, light became shadowed. Lessons were issued by the Angel of Strength and Nurturing, the Angel of Temperance, and the Angel of Ultimate Release. It was seen that multiple incarnations would be required to fulfill the mission to earth. The Angel of Reversal was the gatekeeper to the Realm of Roles, which followed as the path wound its way down.

The Angel of Courage and Conviction stood at the gateway, not wanting to be trapped in the Realm of Roles. The Angel of Magnetic Resonance had become quite proficient in the Realm, characteristic of her portfolio as an Angel. The Angel of Discernment was busy ascertaining which lessons would best contribute to the overall spiritual goals of those they guided. It was the Angel of Peace who revitalized the mission when the Angel of Focus declared the Realm of Roles an acceptable domain for exercising the emotional body. With that in mind, the Angel of Love played cupid, stirring rapture and passion and stimulating multiple essential lessons.

Meanwhile, in the Realm of the Underworld, the Angel of Descent worked diligently to have Inanna discharged and returned to the Realm of Roles. The Angel of Empowerment stormed through the Underworld, also seeking release to the Upperworld. The Angel of Prosperity knew that no matter what the strife on the earth plane, the spiritual law of abundance would ensure bounty. Nonetheless, it was the Angel of Cosmic Intelligence who set the record straight, declaring that the Underworld bore precious fruit, that shadows were only cast when there was light, and that ultimately all souls had an equal chance for growth. It was then that the Angel of Surrender understood that the earth plane was sometimes perplexing and ironic. The Angel of Karmic Destiny was overjoyed, for the Dreamer began her journey, the pathway was opened, and the trailblazers could embark upon the ascension process required for the *light workers* to return home.

The Ascent of the Dreamer

The Dreamer had spiraled to the depths of the Realm of the Underworld. There she encountered Persephone, who was carrying the oppression and victimization of all women in modern culture. Although Persephone spent half the year in the Upperworld, she was tied to the depths of the Underworld with all its shadow and illusion.

The temple of Isis was veiled and submerged in the Underworld, but the high priestess understood and lived the secrets of the ancients. After experiencing an initiation, the Dreamer had a vision of the refinement of consciousness that Isis personified. Continuing along her path, she came upon an arrangement of large ceramic vessels, abundant in women-centered cultures, that represented Hera's ability to contain. Filled by Hera, the Dreamer gazed out across the horizon and witnessed the volcanic eruption of Pele's mountain. Pele had been repressing molten emotional matter for quite some time, exploding into the Upperworld as the sun shone red.

Turning, the Dreamer saw a woman emerging from the Underworld, and she knew her to be Inanna. Why had the Queen of Heaven and Earth descended to the Underworld? How would she re-establish herself upon her return? Perplexed, she saw a gateway and was guided blindly into the Realm of Roles. There she first saw Aphrodite in a passionate embrace on the shore of the restless sea. Love was in the air.

Next, the Dreamer saw Medusa, the Amazon Queen, standing guard outside a temple. She quietly strolled past Kuan Yin, who was meditating outside the marble temple, and said a prayer for world peace. As she passed, the Dreamer saw a woman at the hearth, stoking the fire. She dreamed of times past, when the sacred flame was passed from mother to daughter, and wondered why this woman, Hestia, was alone.

Now, her journey brought her alongside the Parthenon, a temple to Athena, the goddess of war. Why would a goddess support a war? It did not make any sense. This Realm of Roles was a bizarre, disconnected place. Why were these women not relating to one another?

The Dreamer came upon a vast, unsettled sea. She trudged along, forlorn, and after a time she met Lillith who was fleeing the Realm of Roles. Wondering what came next, the Dreamer followed Lillith to the portal of the Realm of Renunciation. Not knowing what the rules were on the other side, the Dreamer hesitatingly peered through to see a Hag, none other than Baba Yaga, the old wild crone. Baba Yaga scowled. She welcomed them, yet warned them of what was to come. They were about to meet the Destroyer, Kali, who wore a necklace of skulls and who understood that rebirth followed death in every Realm.

After confronting her fears, the Dreamer wandered along and found a cave. She crawled in. The night fell and, feeling safe enough, she fell into a deep sleep. She dreamed of a time when women were strong, self-assured, and divinely connected to Spirit and the powerful energy from distant stars and planets.

As day dawned, there was a crack of thunder, and a bolt of lightning struck the mouth of the cave. Suddenly, the Dreamer noticed that there was another being in the recessed cavern in the earth. As the light shone in, she could see that the woman had dark skin and was scantily clad in a leather tunic torn away at the bottom edge. She was laden with beads and amulets and had a tremendous energy field around her. Curious, they starred deeply into each other's eyes. Then the exotic woman spoke pointing to herself, "Uma." They stood transfixed. Intuitively, the Dreamer discerned that Uma had within her an almighty spiritual force. The Realm of Renunciation was becoming more interesting.

Uma and the Dreamer spent a long morning gathering herbs and playing by the water's edge. The journey urged the Dreamer onward, and it was not long before she saw a mysterious cloaked figure standing by a stone arch with two heavy doors, one dark and one light. Perplexed, she inched forward.

"It is the gateway to duality," she heard a croaking voice referring to the stone doorway. "I stand at the crossroads."

"What is that tower?" the Dreamer inquired, looking beyond the crossroads.

"It is the temple of the Great Mother, Demeter's house, and it is filled with people, for everyone has a mother. The Great Mother spans between the Realm of Renunciation and the Realm of Cosmic Consciousness. She knows the ways of both worlds."

"How does one get through the gateway?" the Dreamer pressed.

"One has to have to pure intention and has to balance the body, the mind, and the emotions," Hecate answered. "Come with me," she motioned up the steps. From there, the Dreamer could see into the Realm of Cosmic Consciousness.

First she saw a tree. Hecate explained that the sky goddess Nuit connected heaven and earth through the electromagnetism of the branches and the roots. "See the village beyond the great tree? Artemis, the virgin wild woman, lives there. She belongs to herself and is the protectress of the initiate animals in the Realm."

"Initiate animals!" exclaimed the Dreamer.

"Yes, the initiate priestesses in the temples on the horizon control them telepathically. There is much magic and mystery beyond the gate of duality. I have been wanting to go back there for five millennia. There was a time when priestesses on the shores beyond this very Sea were free and strong. I am the keeper of that memory."

"What would it take to get into the Realm of Cosmic Consciousness?" the Dreamer insisted.

"The Angel of Strength and Nurturing has been waiting for you to complete your lessons. She came to me in the violet hour and whispered that you would be along before the crescent moon. The moon is dark and we are in our lunar power. Come, it is time to sit and to turn inward. The journey home is imminent. You must be prepared for the ascent," encouraged Hecate.

"Won't you come along?" the Dreamer pleaded.

"Well, come to think of it, prophesy stated that at the end of the Great Round, there would be an opportunity for all incarnate earthlings to move through the cosmic portal. Perhaps it is time," the wise sister contemplated. "You go on ahead, I will go tell the others it is time."

With that, Hecate and the Angel of the Illumined Shadow disappeared into the dark night. The Dreamer boldly climbed over the stone wall, spread her wings, and leaped onto the desert sand. She was instantaneously aware of energy in this Realm that was distinct from the other three Realms she had journeyed through. She felt light, at ease, and bursting with anticipation. Finding a trail, she headed onto the plateau toward the village. She caught a glimpse now and again in the corner of her eye and felt sure there were Angels were guiding her, finally revealing themselves to her in the physical.

Dogs barked as she passed the sleepy hamlet. A gentle radiance illumined the horizon as night gave way to day. Off in the distance, silhouettes of pyramids glowed mystically. The Dreamer wandered amidst the gentle bluffs until she came upon a majestic stone lioness goddess. She was thunderstruck beyond her wildest imaginings.

After a laborious walk she arrived at the Sphinx and made her way down over sacred stone blocks toward the paws. Looking up, she was brought to her knees by the majesty and grandeur. Trembling, she wept with release, stationed herself against a sandstone block, hummed lightly, and fell asleep.

In her dream, she was met by Hathor, who appeared as a gentle giant radiating loving splendor. Hathor cradled the Dreamer, and together they traveled through the astral plane to Saqqara, site of the step pyramid and home of Maat. Hathor revealed how initiates learned to levitate at Saqqara many, many millennia ago, before the great descent and the ultimate densification of the Earth. The training was arduous, yet it allowed priestesses and priests to teleport in corridors and chambers in the pyramids.

It was clear that the Realm of Cosmic Consciousness was beyond space and time. In no more than a thought, Hathor escorted the Dreamer to *the Pit,* an ancient subterranean chamber deep below the Great Pyramid. They slid down the descending passage. Was this the Underworld? Or was this the very womb of Mother Earth, of Gaia herself?

Hathor explained that this sacred chamber existed in another dimension and the laws of the universe were magnified therein. Hathor cautioned that any residual fears would be augmented in this chamber as well as any hopes and dreams. The Dreamer dreamed of going home and knew at once that there were Realms beyond the Realm of Cosmic Consciousness. She set her sight on returning to the planet where she had lived before she agreed to participate in the experiment on the earth plane.

Hathor's image evaporated and the Dreamer was left alone in the Pyramid. She moved toward the portal and felt herself magnetically charged and lifted up the long corridor. She emerged fully realized, never to be the same again, understanding her soul's destiny, ascended and at peace.

The Dreamer

The Spiraling Galaxy

The Dreamer

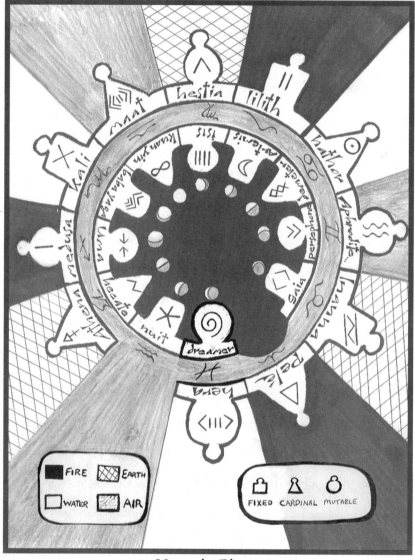

Moon in Pisces
Mutable – Water

Chapter IV

The Dreamer

$\mathcal{T}$he Dreamer is the archetypal Seeker, the one whose journey toward consciousness is represented in the twenty-one stages, or lessons, in the *Angels and Archetypes* evolutionary journey. The Dreamer rides on the galactic spiral and carries spiritual debts from past lives. The Dreamer has no number, and, in her quest for psychic wholeness, she is free to wander at will through the archetypes.

The Dreamer harnesses the power of zero that is intrinsic in the circle. The circle represents the unconscious nature that achieves a state of wholeness through the development of the psyche. The Dreamer shows us that the end of the journey is also an invitation to begin again on the archetypal spiral. The circle is both the beginning and the end. This is symbolized by the *Uroboros*, the mythic snake that swallows its tail.[1]

In traditional Tarot, the Dreamer is symbolized by the Fool. In Italian, "To be like the Fool in *Tarocchi* (Tarot)"[2] means to be welcome everywhere. Like the court Jester, the Fool mingles with any group, popping up here and there, and then disappearing. Related to the Joker in modern playing cards, the Fool is full of games and can fill in for a lost card. Like the Trickster, the Fool blends serious truths and lighthearted jest, reminding us that the journey toward consciousness is about light and lightness. In many Tarot decks, the Fool card depicts a carefree wanderer moving from right to left. This symbolizes the move from concrete, measurable reality to the symbolic and the unconscious. The Fool's task, like the Dreamer's, is to begin to journey into the internal world, resplendent with the richness and depth of self-realization.

The Dreamer is anchored in the astrological energy of the Moon in Pisces. A mutable water sign, this archetypal energy is responsive to the depths of human experience. There is an optimism that sometimes borders on romanticism. There is an emotional naiveté, a silent magnetism, and an emotional sensitivity. The energy is dreamy and gentle, and adapts well to change.

MYTHOLOGY

In past times, the Feast of Fools, later known as April Fool's Day, was an occasion for underdogs to unleash repressed hostility, lust, rebellion, or just plain silliness. There was a formalized attempt to ward off unexpected uprisings by offering periods of "universal permissiveness."[3] The Fool's energy is uncontained by social structure and protocol and reminds us that order and anarchy are close cousins lurking in the rafters of our consciousness. In Nichols' words:

> The maintenance of jesters at court and in titled families began in ancient times and continued until the seventeenth century. This practice dramatizes the idea that we must make room for the renegade factor in ourselves and admit [her] to our inner court, which means psychologically we must admit to [her]. It is usually a good idea to place our Fool out front where we can keep an eye on her.[4]

The Dreamer also conjures the Navajo trickster *Coyote*. In native Indian teachings, the appearance of Coyote is a warning to loosen up and not take ourselves so seriously. It may be an invitation to see who is deceiving us or how we are deceiving ourselves. It can be a foreshadowing of unpredictable energies that push us to take a chance or to own another aspect of ourselves that has been "projected" out. Once we open our eyes and take the risk, growth is assured.

One of the most common psychological "tricks" we play on ourselves is contained within the largely misunderstood idea of *projection*. The obvious is often elusive. When we point a finger at someone, three fingers point back at ourselves. The factor that prevents us from fully understanding projection is simple: it appears easier for us to blame another and to see fault as existing outside ourselves rather than within.

Carl Jung, one of the most brilliant thinkers of our century, introduced the concept of projection. Consciousness involves taking full responsibility for our perceptions. Each of us, regardless of our gender, has an internalized, receptive feminine aspect or "anima," as well as an activating, masculine aspect or "animus." Culture has sanctioned sex roles, and most of us have been socialized to dichotomize the masculine to men and the feminine to women. Before we begin the journey toward consciousness, we function in the domain assigned to our gender and seek to fulfill the opposite polarity with another human in the form of an intimate relationship. Inadvertently and unconsciously, women project their idealized masculine outward onto an unsuspecting man. When a man participates in this unconscious arrangement, he will in turn project his idealized feminine onto women.

Whether something is perceived as outside ourselves or is owned and seen as an integral part of ourselves, it is connected to the greater universal whole. Gnostic doctrines taught that before each rebirth, the soul drank from the waters of forgetfulness, blanking out the memories of previous lives and bringing us back to "zero" consciousness.[5]

Yet the Dreamer is an inner sage full of irrational knowing that fires impulses, triggering the psyche. We are programmed to become conscious, and the Universe constantly provides gifts to awaken us to greater truths. Typically, the aperture of our awareness is limited and we experience our lives in a linear sequence. Yet uncanny, synchronistic events penetrate third-dimensional reality, and we find ourselves pondering and searching for an explanation.

Jung described synchronicity as *meaningful coincidence*. It is the portal to other dimensions that expands our consciousness and leads us to question the nature of reality. As electromagnetic energies change and frequencies increase on Earth, most of us are experiencing more surprising coincidences. The phone rings and we know who it is. We resist going to a meeting and find out it was unexpectedly canceled. We think of friends we have not seen in years and run into them shortly after. It is as though there is a crack between the worlds, a connection between dimensions, and we are being made privy to it.

> Jung's research confirmed the existence of a secret storehouse in our minds from which dreams, never before seen, and facts yet unknown can rise to the surface and become part of our conscious equipment.[6]

The Dreamer wanders in the Underworld and answers the shamanic call to enter the darkness, the birth canal that awaits the soul and allows entry into one's own astral territory.[7] Consciousness comes at a high price through the arduous task of learning the lessons offered in each stage of the journey. Each circle through the stages offers new insight and a deepening of perception and experience. The Dreamer throws up mysterious symbols from our unconscious for us to ponder. She is often led by the Riddle Mother, who is sure to trick us with psychological puns and acquaints us with the language of illusion. We soon begin to see that dream language is meant to tantalize our psyches as it gently awakens us to the profound lessons on our archetypal journey. The winds of dissolution blow and we are invited to transcend opposites, surrendering to the bliss of union where we find the still center.

The unfolding of spiritual consciousness is related to the expansion of emotional capacity. As we expand our emotional body, the power of universal love can enter the being, and the force of freedom can connect us to our free will. Before the emotional opening, we stumble upon our lessons and our understanding is limited.

The Dreamer, then, contains the extremes and bridges the dichotomies. We have all been raised in a culture that thrives on measurement, competition, and being on top. We have been taught about good and bad, right and wrong, and we have been exposed to morals that are black and white. The Dreamer focuses on the gray areas, the depth, the unseen, the not-so-obvious. She knows all about shadow and is well aware that it is only in the presence of light that a shadow can be cast.

The Dreamer makes blunt observations that are beyond space and time, and, as in our dreams, she throws up bizarre interpretations from the material we encounter in our waking reality. If we are trying hard to be "good," we will dream of Madwomen and Demon Lovers. We are being asked to reckon with our shadows, to embrace and acquaint ourselves with our unconscious selves. Culture encourages us to focus on Upperworld activities, and offers us little understanding into the realm of the unseen, or the unconscious. It has only been in the last hundred years that Western culture and Freud acknowledged the existence of and defined the unconscious mind.

If we do not pay tribute to the unconscious processes operating within us, we disadvantage ourselves greatly. Our complexes, intense emotional reactions, relationship patterns, functioning in groups, and life choices are largely governed by our unconscious. The clearest access to our unconscious is through our dreams. Dream images, when harvested over time, begin to form a personalized "dream language." Dream images play a major role in our understanding of self. They lend meaning and significance to the ordinary, and they dramatize aspects of self. In Nichols' words:

> Dream characters, like friends and relatives, need to be taken seriously. They like to feel that we are interested in them and their doings—that we are involved with them.[8]

By thinking we cannot remember our dreams, we may push our dream symbols deeper into the unconscious. Powerful dream images may forcefully percolate to the surface in the form of nightmares. The denied shadow rears its ugly head. If the dream images are unattended to, they will recur. Even in the face of denial, the Dreamer has important information for us.

Carl Jung offered us much in the way of insight into dreams on both the collective and the personal levels. He introduced the idea of *active imagination* as a way of finishing a dream, or as a way of recreating portions in waking reality to heal an aspect of self. He was certain that if a dream was "unlived," the vital symbolism remained undigested and thus was locked in the unconscious. The dream had allowed hidden parts of the psyche to percolate to consciousness, and the task of his analysands was to attend to its significance. In Jungian analysis, a new dream will not be considered until the last dream has been *lived*. This could mean painting an abstract version of the emotion of the dream, anger being represented in red and grief in black. It could mean the conversation between the dream characters would be extended through journal writing. If we dreamed of being a figure skater, it could mean getting our skates from the attic and literally getting on the ice.

> Jungian psychology today reflects the idea that modern people experience initiation rites and symbolic ventures into the ancient mystery realms through the unconscious — mainly our dreams and our artistic expression. Through these avenues, a person is able to integrate experiences and the parts of the being until reaching wholeness.[9]

Fritz Perls, the founder of Gestalt therapy, made a significant contribution to dream analysis. He emphasized that each aspect of the dream was a reflection of the self. Too often, if we dream of a madman or a madwoman, we objectify the dark deeds as outside ourselves. In reality, there is a connection to an aspect of our own psyche that is represented by that individual in our waking reality. Dream interpretation for Perls involved owning these fragments as our own. By "becoming" each aspect of the dream, speaking in the present tense, giving a voice to each fragment, we empower ourselves to hear the hidden messages embedded in the dream. For example, "I am an abandoned house. I am dingy and cold inside. The joy and warmth have gone from me."

The work of the Dreamer connects us to these seemingly miraculous encounters. It is also the way of the future that the veils between the dimensions will be lifted. Our task is to search for the meaning embedded in the synchronistic events. Whether we are conscious or not, the Dreamer teaches us to understand these events as the workings of spirit that lead us to a collective initiation.

THE DREAMER WOMAN

The Dreamer manifests in the modern woman whose subconscious mind is active. She is oriented to change and adapts readily to a variety of situations. This woman reflects feelings of compassion for herself and for others. The Dreamer woman has affection for all people. She can easily be fooled and led on, and can fall prey to disillusion as a consequence.

The Dreamer will be sympathetic to the underdog. She is dreamy and gentle and is prone to change her mind often. She has the tendency to live in a world of imagination. Because she vacillates and is unsure of her direction, she can easily become discouraged or depressed.

Still, she has potential for identifying with a true vision. The Dreamer woman ultimately seeks the Truth that puts her on the path of spiritual discovery. She is perpetually renewing herself and preparing for rebirth.

Unresolved issues incubate in her subconscious mind and manifest in elaborate dreams. This is a woman who keeps a dream journal. She watches how symbols transform over a series of dreams and interprets them within the development of her psyche. She knows that the thousands of symbols she is exposed to each day sort themselves psychically to produce a dream that assists her in deciphering her process.

THE ANGEL OF KARMIC DESTINY

The Angel of Karmic Destiny nudges us along our journey offering circumstances that promote growth. She introduces us to the Realm of the Underworld where our journey toward consciousness begins. She stands at the doorway to the Earth plane and births us into third-dimensional reality. Once we pass through the doorway, we promptly forget our divinity and become unconscious. It is the Angel of Karmic Destiny that blesses us with lessons that assist us in clearing our karma.

It is the non-physical intelligences that work with our karmic destiny. Our *karma* is the sum of all our unprocessed actions, emotions, desires, and patterns that hold energy. They are repeated in an incarnation and spill into subsequent incarnations until they are clarified and released.

It is not human love but divine, unconditional love that is said to have created the cosmos. The Angels were discovered thousands of years ago by the mystics who understood the concept of karma. Part of the journey of the Dreamer is to first fathom and then grasp the idea that love is not connected to action or reward. We have all been raised in a culture that rewards behavior in keeping with stringent rules and values. This breeds fear, guilt, feelings of repression, and restriction in consciousness. We try to please and to achieve, and we learn to compete for the rewards of the culture.

Spiritual mystery schools taught that the entire world is but a dream. Dreams are projected fragments of consciousness parading in our mind's eye offering information from our psyche. We can begin to think of our perceptions as a divine movie being projected. We are the projector, and our consciousness is the movie. We can easily become convinced that events are "happening" to us. What we think about, we begin to perceive. We magnify the power of whatever we focus on. Thus we create our own reality.

The Angel of Karmic Destiny reminds us that the Earth is a Free Will Zone. She invites us to remember that we are divine beings having an earth experience. At the gateway to our incarnation, we are granted physical, emotional, and mental bodies that are mutable and impermanent. Our ultimate spiritual goal is to comprehend this and to transcend to a place of higher consciousness about our purpose for being here.

Persephone

Entry to Underworld

Persephone

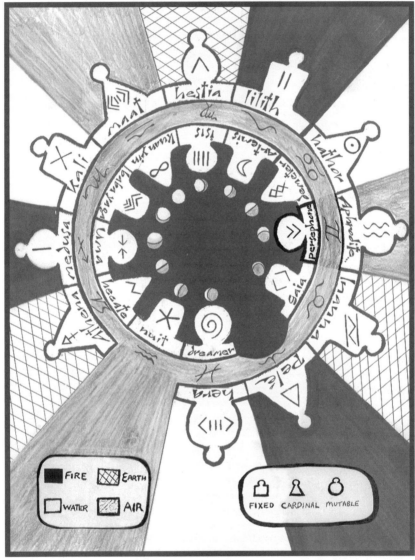

Moon in Gemini
Mutable–Air

Chapter V

Persephone

Persephone is the archetypal Victim who was abducted by her uncle and taken to the Underworld. She is the virgin goddess whose story is interwoven with those of Demeter, the mother, and Hecate, the crone. Persephone is a loner, and with her powerful will, she shows us the way to triumph over our own oppression and victimization. Surmounting victimization is the quintessential developmental task for the conscious feminine. Persephone archetypally leads us through this collective initiation.

Persephone holds the seat of the prime number, one. It is as though we have only one mission, one great overcoming to accomplish, that sets us on the Red Road of the Evolutionary Map. It is of primary importance that feminine consciousness collectively releases the burden of victimization, breaking the conspiracy of silence and uncovering the truth about molestation, sexual abuse, and incest. The monumental task is to overcome denial and to process that which has been relegated to the unconscious.

Persephone's energy is fueled by Tarot Magician's power. The Magician mediates between two worlds and becomes the conductor of souls through sacrifice, the death of the self, and the descent into the Underworld. Thus begins the process of individuation, which involves the transcendence of the ego. The ability to transcend the restrictions of ordinary time and space is central to all magic, rites of passage, shamanic experiences, and multidimensional learning.

> It is understandable that the Magician who lives in the depths, at the psychoid level of the unconscious where there exist no divisions of time, space, body and soul, matter and spirit (and where the four elements themselves have not been separated out of the great void), should have the power to put us in touch with the great Oneness of perfection, health, and harmony.[1]

Persephone's energy is anchored in the Moon in Gemini. A mutable air sign, the Persephone archetype is emotionally versatile. Represented by the twins, Persephone can adapt well to two situations. She is dramatic, retrospective, superficial, and easily swayed. She likes the variety and novelty, though her mind can be changeable and chaotic. She is able to sustain impressions through thought rather than feeling. It is hard for her to trust her instincts so she can appear cold and reserved. Her senses serve her intellect rather than her emotions. She lacks concentration and can be a worrier.

MYTHOLOGY

Persephone was a spring maiden living in Olympian Greece who was abducted and raped by her uncle Hades. Her mother, Demeter, had been abandoned by Zeus, Persephone's father. Persephone was raised as a priestess and a healer. One day, Persephone wandered off to roam the countryside. She stopped to admire a narcissus flower when suddenly, out of nowhere, she was confronted by Hades who kidnapped her, thrusting her through a crack in the earth holding her captive in the Underworld.

When Persephone disappeared, Demeter became frantic. The violent, forcible abduction precipitated gut-wrenching grief in Demeter, and she could not rest until Persephone was found. Her maternal attachment and the cellular connection from having carried Persephone in her womb created a deep and permanent bond. Demeter abandoned her duties in the Upperworld as the Goddess of Grain and searched incessantly for her beloved daughter. She remembered her own "deflowering" and the comfort and joy it had brought her. Now that the patriarchal imperatives were taking over, the horror of rape and of masculine domination was becoming commonplace.

> In prepatriarchal cultures like Minoan Crete, a girl's sexual initiation would have been joyful and free. Persephone would have lain down with her lover in the fertile fields, like her mother Demeter did before her with Iason. But all these sources are the product of patriarchy when the puberty initiations of a woman-centered Goddess culture had already been transformed in alignment with the new ethos of male domination.[2]

Meanwhile, in the Underworld, Hades had trapped Persephone in his domain, both psychologically and physically. Hades was intermittently charming and domineering. He created a psychological circumstance that both seduced Persephone and controlled her.

Hades was Persephone's only contact. He created an atmosphere of isolation and then began to offer Persephone the attention she craved. Her fear abated and she cautiously began to relate to him.

As time passed, Persephone began to participate in Hades world, serving him and spending her days in leisure. Still emotionally impoverished, Persephone refused to eat.

Meanwhile the growth of grain had ceased in the Upperworld and the populace was stirring. Demeter was preoccupied, frustrated, and angry. She sought out Zeus, who reported that Hades had approached him about mating with his daughter Persephone, and he had approved the abduction. Demeter was incensed and deeply wounded. She begged Zeus to tell her of Persephone's whereabouts to no avail.

Time passed and the populace was faced with a famine. No one was able to be nourished while the Great Goddess Demeter was absorbed in Persephone's trauma.

It became apparent that a rescue mission was in order. Zeus was informed that Hecate, the Crone of the Underworld, had seen Persephone and Hades in the Underworld. Zeus found Hades and told him Persephone was to be rescued in the coming days.

Hades had been continually concerned that Persephone had refused any food while in the Underworld. The law of the Underworld states that if one is nourished there, one must remain forever. Knowing she was about to leave, he offered Persephone a pomegranate. Persephone refused. Hades turned on his charm and finally persuaded Persephone to eat. She ate six pomegranate seeds. Because she willingly partook by ingesting Underworld nourishment, Persephone was made a participant in her own demise.

Hades was victorious and Persephone was trapped. When Hecate and Demeter found Persephone, Hades smugly informed them that Persephone was required to remain with him. Besides, they were to be married.

Disheartened, Demeter made a deal. Because Persephone had eaten six seeds, she was to be released from the Underworld for six months of the year. The other six moons, she would be Queen of the Underworld and Hades' wife.

Persephone was released and reappeared in the Upperworld at Eleusis. A procession of priestesses brought power objects from the temples in Athens. A major celebration occurred, and the populace rejoiced. Crops once again produced grain. All was restored to harmony and peace.

> Thus the always physically beautiful maiden acquires the psychic beauty whereby she truly becomes herself: Psyche. Perhaps Psyche is that aspect of Persephone that cannot stay in the Underworld, the human soul that knows it is not the goddess.[3]

In the centuries that followed, the populace re-enacted the story of Persephone, Demeter, and Hecate in the Eleusinian Mysteries at Eleusis. Initiates would confront their fears, delve into their unconscious selves, face their mortality, and emerge with a deeper understanding of the mysteries of life and death.

The Persephone archetype teaches us to free the spirit that has been imprisoned in matter. This lesson is crucial in identifying underlying soul patterns of victimization that have been governing our experiences on the earth plane.

THE PERSEPHONE DAUGHTER

The Persephone daughter never really grows up. When she matures, she will identify with another archetype. The Persephone daughter is immersed in her subjective experience. She can be curiously insightful, yet her innocence makes everyone wonder whether she is aware of the seriousness of her circumstance. Persephone manifests as the molested one, the one who is vulnerable to victimization and to scapegoating.

It is a paradox that the oppressed begin to participate in their own oppression. This, in fact, is a coping strategy. When we have been repeatedly subjected to invasion, our sense of what is acceptable and what is not becomes damaged. When our perpetrators operate with no remorse and justify their actions, we are lured into self-doubt. We can only imagine how these distortions affect the sensitive, psychic maiden now trapped in the delusions.

The Persephone daughter's move toward consciousness makes her quite expert at recognizing shadow and bringing the material forth into the light. The energies devoted to resisting shadow become available for creative use. In a developing psyche, archetypal vocabulary develops. Just as we learn to walk and to talk, using building blocks of knowledge and integrating them in steps, we learn to understand archetypal energies one by one as we mature. In this way, the inner spiritual and the outer physical processes connect in a meaningful way, linking the deep self with the ego. When the hidden languages of the unconscious are deciphered and brought to light, there is a surging gift of energy and release.

Persephone is inevitably psychic. Her sensitivity to other's emotions has her carry the family shadow and attempt to process the denied material. This is done in service to the family, and it becomes the imperative for the functioning of the family. For this reason, when she is moody or unresponsive because she is overburdened with emotional material, the family judges her as the least able to cope. Little do they know she is processing for each member who cannot and will not feel and integrate their own shadow. The Persephone daughter does not want to add to the problems of the family. As a consequence, she will become perfectionistic and "too good."

Nevertheless, she is often scapegoated, perhaps out of her willingness to carry the familiar burdens. As long as family members do not have to face their own pain, they often do not. Because she dwells in the Realm of the Underworld, where illusion and reality dance, she accepts the projection defenselessly. She then wanders around her psyche aimlessly searching for meaning, depth, contact, or understanding as a means of consoling the woes of her clan.

This puts her at risk. Seeking solace, easily swayed by others' wishes, starved for contact and acceptance, being sensitive to others' needs, Persephone is vulnerable to molestation. In a hierarchical society, there is always someone in a dysfunctional family ready to control a sweet, young, open, unassuming maiden.

The Persephone maiden willingly accepts the projections of the males in her clan and of the women who wish her to be a patriarchal daughter. Secretly they may think she is adorable and desirable. To honestly acknowledge this image of desirability conjures up the threat of incest that is clearly taboo in the Upperworld. Mix dysfunctionality, unmet needs, and lust in the clan cauldron, add a heaping measure of culturally sanctioned denial, and the recipe for molestation is complete.

As the years go by, the baggage becomes excessive, and the Persephone daughter will often develop coping strategies to deal with unprocessed emotions. The disorder of choice for the maiden who is locked into this archetype is often bulimia. The dilemma of the bulimic personality is a profound reflection of the collective that offers beautiful and disempowered role models to women.

The Persephone daughter often develops a bulimic personality. The bulimic wants to please, so much so that she will attempt to emulate the cultural ideal for beauty that emphasizes thinness. Advertisers choose 13-year-old models with narrow hips and innocent faces to pose as women. Culture has dictated for decades that the full figure of the average woman is unacceptable, while the childlike waif is considered appealing. Similarly, the full strength and self-assuredness of a whole woman have until the recent past been considered threatening.

Bulimic daughters are masters of illusion. Because they have been controlled and manipulated and have seen reality twisted so thoroughly, denial becomes their best friend. After all, denial rules the roost they were raised in.

Locked in the complex, the Persephone daughter grows up. She can play the societal game, and she often marries. The Persephone bride will live out the roles assigned to her of charming hostess and demure wife, and her children will have every culturally approved opportunity. She will accept her lot. Yet, there will come a time when she will wonder if any part of her life is real. She has been smiling when she is not happy, and she has been giving from an empty vessel for so long, while no one seems to have noticed. If no one validates her feeling of being utterly lost in her own world, she gives up hope that there is anything she can do to make her inner self visible.

When the psyche cannot resolve a complex, it seeks distraction or a door of compensation. Anything that supports the illusion will seemingly support the woman caught in the Persephone complex. Alcoholism, over-exercise, compulsive eating, excessive television, gambling, sexual addiction, or any compulsive behavior begin to rule the life of the escapist.

While the Upperworld activities of dinner parties, concerts, and family dinners continue, the Persephone woman is roaming the Underworld. Right there in front of her family, she is disconnected, lost, and alone. Her suffering is excruciating, yet if no one can validate it, she wonders if she is making it up. Because no one else can see her, she loses her ability to see herself. Such is the curse that springs from the original trauma of abduction.

Healing for the Persephone archetype begins as soon as there is the psychological strength and support to unravel a fragment of the complex. Then, buried memories are activated and come into consciousness. The Persephone daughter may distract herself. She may drift and become consumed by Upperworld activities. She may go on a bulimic binge or drown herself with a bottle of liquor. Nevertheless, on some level, the Persephone daughter is always aware of her pain. After all, "pain is the custodian of our undiscovered treasures."[4]

In an atmosphere of denial, a multiplicity of behaviors develop to maintain denial. Family members have characteristics they prefer not to own because it would tarnish their perception of themselves. Thus, these seemingly negative traits are projected out onto the Persephone daughter. The family becomes convinced that she is the undesirable one, while the darkness of their own unconscious selves lies dormant and unowned. The dark figures will often haunt the dreams of those who project. Those committed to remaining unconscious will also believe the madman stalking their dreams is outside themselves.

The Persephone daughter is undoubtedly the most emotionally sensitive child in the family. Conflicts between mother and father, whether they live under the same roof or not, are vectors of tension that flow like conduits through the Persephone daughter's belly. She will know who is upset and how much tension exists even if the family member is in utter denial. She may not know the reason or the whole story because many families function with denial as the paramount "protector" of the secrets.

In families, these projections then become roles that members act out. Inevitably, the unprocessed projected judgments cluster and stick to the most sensitive child in the family. It is she who becomes scapegoated. It is she who carries the shadow of the family.

This inescapably engenders isolation within the psyche* of the one carrying the projection. This can be seen as a form of psychic slavery. It serves the family well to blame Persephone for being absent-minded, or too sensitive, or an illusionist.

The ultimate demise of this archetype is the fear of being judged. The Persephone daughter will go to great lengths not to rock the boat. Thus she enables the family to continue to make decisions about her without her consent, involvement, or agreement. In other words, she will be labeled, everyone in the family will agree, and they will live it out as a truth. Persephone will know she is being abandoned in the moment she is judged. Left to her own devices, she could like herself. In this psychological environment, Persephone begins to lose her confidence. She may conclude that these people simply do not like her. In any case, the psychological isolation is agonizing. All she wants to do is join and be intimate and safe. She is deeply saddened when she realizes that she is psychologically orphaned.

In any case, the opening from the original molestation and the years of psychological weightlifting assist the Persephone woman to grow up quickly. It is true she may collapse and drown in the overwhelming burden of psychic slime. Usually, however, the spiritual path of the Persephone woman is one of personal power and strength. These women are survivors. And survive they do.

THE ANGEL OF SURRENDER

Persephone lives with the Angels. Her beauty and innocence are a direct transmission from Spirit. Her willingness to receive and to surrender is an ultimate engager for a hungry heart. The masculine polarity that seeks to connect its diametric opposite is enchanted. Persephone is alluring in her innocence, yet she is already wounded. Because she is the emotional conduit and container of her clan's subconscious, she is burdened with projected psychological content. She is accustomed to being projected upon, to carrying the shadow, to descending to the Underworld until she can emerge from the illusion.

The Angel of Surrender is the guardian of the Realm of the Underworld. To reach a more conscious state of being, we need to allow this Angel to help us see more clearly what is real. We often suffer from mental illusions caused by misperceptions and misunderstandings. Because the psyche develops reaction patterns to circumstances, it tends to repeat the patterns until the consciousness can grasp the message embedded in the drama. Certainly, we act out these false perceptions to retrieve a truth that was denied.

*"Psyche": The structure of the mind; ego projections, themselves attached to the psyche; the part of the brain mind that self-reflects; inside the mind's eye.

Thus the Persephone maiden, fueled with the Magician's power, becomes the conductor of souls through sacrifice, death of self, and descent into the Underworld. As she mediates between two worlds, she is initiated into the elemental mysteries of the conscious and the unconscious.

> On the microscopic level, the ego alone cannot effect this magic. Only our inner Magician can master the intricate choreography of revelation. Only [she] can demonstrate the correspondence between the central core and its outer wrappings; only [she] can reveal that they are made of the same stuff.[5]

Healing will always involve sorting through what is illusory and what is real. The Angel of Surrender is well equipped to assist in the lifting of veils and the perception to see through them. She helps us be enthralled by the inner work that leads us into the Light. She roams in the Underworld, illuminating truths, revealing falsehoods, and encouraging us to decipher the differences. Thus, our journey toward consciousness gains momentum and prepares us for the next initiation along the Red Road.

Isis

Ornate Pillars

Isis

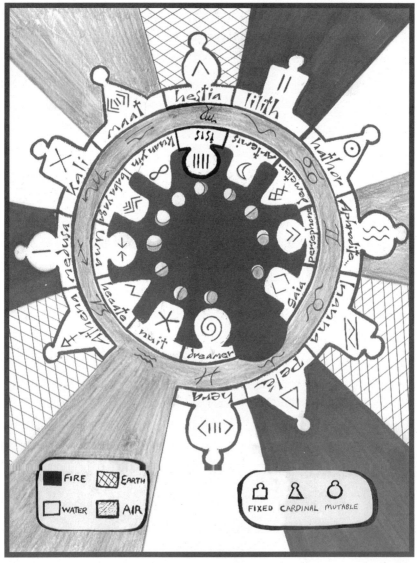

Moon in Virgo
Mutable–Earth

Chapter VI

Isis

2

Isis is the archetypal Initiate, the High Priestess. She is the embodiment of the feminine as a vessel for holiness and for divine expression. She is an open channel and receives energy from the Cosmos. She sits patiently between temple pillars, providing equilibrium and guidance on our journey. Isis is the guardian of ancient wisdom. To the modern seeker she holds the keys to the mysteries of the Great Unknown. Yet she is veiled. She lives in the Realm of the Underworld, and only those who unveil her will be able to solve the mysteries of life, death, generation, and regeneration.[1]

In numerology, Isis manifests the number two. With one, there is the self. With two, there is the consciousness of the self, reflected in the mirror of the other. Polarity is contained and balanced in two: masculine and feminine, spirit and matter, heaven and earth, external material and inner spiritual.

In Tarot images, she is the High Priestess, seated, rooted in place as though she had always been there and will remain on her throne until the end of time. She rules by slow persistence, love, and feminine patience. She governs the world of internal knowledge and is, by nature, introverted and reflective. She is the essence of Spirit descended into matter. She is merged with the creative essence of the Holy Spirit,[2] the Moon, and the emotional body. She does not raise the veil before the sacred shrine but allows the seeker to mature and to seek the Truth for herself. She keeps her lips sealed, yet she also lets us know there is a world inside the temple. The gateway between the pillars invites us to enter.

Isis is anchored in the energy of Moon in Virgo. A mutable earth sign, the energy is grounded and has a great capacity for change. The archetype is quiet, shy, unpretentious, and adaptable. She possesses great intuition and is an excellent teacher. She has a deep hunger for knowledge and for mysticism that she wishes to synthesize and to apply.

MYTHOLOGY

Isis herself was a triple goddess integrating the roles of the virgin, the mother, and the crone. Her mother was the goddess Nuit, who contained the energy of the galaxy. The story of Isis is a cosmic myth with its origins beyond the Earth. Isis has always been connected to the Sirius star system, while her consort Osiris came from Orion.

> Mistress of the gods, thou bearer of wings
> Praise be to thee, O Lady, who art mightier
> than the gods...[3]

The Name of Ra

The Sun God Ra contained the mysteries of his secret power within his name. As he grew old, his mouth trembled and his spittle fell to the ground. Isis observed this and mixed his spittle with earth and fashioned a snake that she lay in Ra's path. As he approached, the snake bit him and he cried out in pain. Isis pitied him and offered to cure him with her magic in exchange for his real name. He listed a series of impressive names, yet held his real name and power back from her. Isis was not deceived and insisted on the revelation of his true secret name. Forced to comply with her demand to be relieved of pain, Ra whispered the magic name into her ear. This myth accentuates the truth that the creator god is unknowable. Isis alone, the initiate goddess of wisdom, has insight into him.[4]

Isis and Osiris

When Isis enters history, she is already the renowned wife of her half brother Osiris. A mythical drama unfolds in the tale of Osiris' jealous brother, Set. Set, competing for the throne that was promised to Osiris through the royal bloodline, invites Osiris to lie in a beautiful sarcophagus. Set's helpers rush in, lock the coffin, and lower it into the Nile.

Isis is frantic at losing her lover and consort and, with her sister Nephthys, seeks him without rest. Her sorrow is evident and is left like a trail throughout the land. Isis' tears swelled the river. The yearly flooding of the Nile, which provided the essential moisture for the crops, was seen by the ancient Egyptians as connected to the grief of Isis.

Finally, Isis and Nephthys find the coffin by the bank of the Nile. When Isis is alone with the coffin, she opens it, kisses the face of her dead husband, and wails in lamentation. Brokenhearted, she expresses her gut-wrenching grief.

Ancient records show much evidence of the connection of lamentation and grieving to funerary practice. Depicted with wings, Isis provides a shadow for the body. Isis then "raises the slackness of the weary."[5] She rises above Osiris, lays her winged self on his phallus, receives his seed, and impregnates herself with an heir so his soul can live on.

Thus the ritualizing of grieving, as mirrored in the legend of Persephone and Demeter, was seen as an important part of the emotional training of the populace. This is in sharp contrast to modern culture, which insists that we hold back our tears especially in public, even at funerals. Today we are expected to grieve without crying and resolve the trauma of loss within a scheduled time. The depth of our relationship to the one who made the passage to the other world, the expansion of our emotional capacity, and the fueling of the mystery of the afterlife are all submerged. The ancient Egyptians ritualized within the collective. Our cultural commitment to denial submerges grieving to the domain of the Underworld. However we descend to the Underworld, unprocessed grief lurks in its recesses, patiently awaiting our attention.

Isis Waves Her Wings

As the story of Isis continues, she revives Osiris from the Netherworld by waving her wings, providing revitalizing air to him. Osiris is thus resurrected. He returns with knowledge of immortality and knew that "only the unconfined light of pure spirit is immortal."[6]

In time, Set plots again to attain the throne. Well aware of the powers of Isis to raise Osiris from the dead, Set murders Osiris again. He mutilates the corpse into fourteen pieces and scatters them throughout the land.

Isis, weary with grief, is determined to find her man and to bring him back to her side. She searches and finds him, piece by piece. In 14-day cycles, the moon waxes and builds in scope, then wanes and diminishes in size. Metaphorically, she *re-members* Osiris. We symbolically go through the same process when we are grieving a relationship. Piece by piece, we reconstruct and *remember* the object of our affections. Left to our own devices, we will either slant the memories favorably or negatively. Re-membering is a restorative and creative act.

Isis and the Manhood of Osiris

Osiris was thus entirely restored to life by the magic powers of Isis, who found all of him except his manhood. A mythological rumor suggests that the phallus of Osiris was devoured by a Nile crab.[7] Isis then fashioned Osiris a new phallus out of clay.

Horus is the son born of this magical act. He symbolizes balance between the male and the female. Although Set was a constant threat, Horus was raised in secret and eventually became a legitimate heir to the throne. All subsequent pharaohs in Egypt carried the name of Horus to symbolically legitimize their right to rule.

Isis' acts of courage and wisdom were integrated into teachings for the populace to touch and experience universal Truths. She represents a doctrine of piety and consolation in the face of loss. The story of Isis and Osiris is an expression of archetypal sibling rivalry.

The Temples of Isis

By emphasizing the eternal nature of the soul and the importance of making a passage through a dimensional doorway, initiates understood their origins as starry beings. Isis, from Sirius, was birthed by Nuit, symbolized by azure sky studded with yellow stars.

In *The Lost Years of Jesus*,[8] the Christ is said to have traveled to Egypt and to have studied in the temples. It is clearly stated that these ancient practices, initiations and purifications are the tools that contributed to Jesus Christ's ability to perform miracles in later years. According to Samuel Woer, all clairvoyants need initiation. He states:

> The Divine Savior of the world chanted the powerful sacred Mantram of fire, *Inri*, with the priestess when he practiced with her in the Pyramid of Kefren. The Lord of all Adoration practiced in Egypt with *his Isis*. He combined the five vowels IEOUA: ... for the connection to the divine, ... for the magic ear, ... for the center of intuition, ... for the telepathic center, ... for the power to remember past reincarnations.[9]

The temple activities were recorded on papyrus scrolls by initiate scribes. The scribes rode up the Nile on water chariots to hand deliver the notations and the daily journaling to the library at Alexandria. The temples were part of an elaborate training circuit for initiates. Magic rites, healing secrets, and multidimensional practices were systematically documented. Priestesses served as the Keepers of the Records, traveling to and from temples along the Nile. This knowledge was considered a great threat. The precious library at Alexandria was burned on three separate occasions, destroying the irreplaceable documentation. Yet all is not lost. The Hall of Records within the multidimensional chambers below the Sphinx still has secrets to reveal. We, as a humanity, have evolved to a state of readiness to receive the keys to unlock the mysteries.

Initiates were trained in the Temples of Isis through discipline, and after decades of training they achieved a tempering of unconscious and conscious processes. Isis was worshipped as the Mother of Tenderness during the second millennium BC. Mary Magdalene herself was a priestess of the Temples of Isis.[10] During the reign of Alexander the Great, ancient practices and teachings were institutionalized. The Cult of Isis spread into the African continent, Asia Minor, mainland Greece, along the Mediterranean, and north into Italy, Switzerland, and Germany.

> Maidens in the special line of the High Priestess were taught to journey through the realms of the soul, ascending in imagination to the seven levels of Heaven, gaining the blessing of each guardian planetary power at the 'gate' of that stage of consciousness, the key to a higher level of psychic ability. We committed to memory the powers of each level, for the mind creates reality; thus I can recite them to you:

- At the first level, initiates gained perfect recall of dreams.
- The second revealed the knowledge of other minds, living, dead, or yet unborn.
- At the third level, the soul reclaimed memories of past lives.
- The fourth and fifth levels revealed the whole history and purpose of the universe.
- On the attainment of the sixth level, the unity, or oneness, of all things would be fully realized in perfect compassion, unconditional forgiveness, and absolute love for all beings, living, dead, or yet to be.
- The seventh level of awareness, if it could be achieved, would be past the powers of language to describe the dissolution of the self in union with the One, *perfect bliss*.[11]

In the temples of Isis, focus was placed on past and future incarnations. The lessons that would be learned from the experiences of third-dimensional reality were sequentially organized in linear time, or third-dimensional reality. Initiates made karmic agreements to facilitate the development of earth plane consciousness and secured their intentions to their soul group, committed to the completion of karmic responsibilities.*

There came a time when it was understood that the balance between male and female energies, the human and the divine would be circumvented, darkened, and sublimated for five thousand years. Preparations were made and seeds were planted that would come to fruition in the next Age of Light. The cycle was to coordinate with the end of the 26,000-year processional cycle, the end of the 5,000-year Mayan calendar, and the change from the 2,000-year-long Piscean Age to the Age of Aquarius. All this was to occur simultaneously at the end of the millennium. A succession of unprecedented planetary alignments and astrological transits would precipitate the

---

*Karma is the sum of unprocessed emotions, thoughts, and desires that hold energy and the results of past actions that require repetition in this and other incarnations until they are clarified.

transformation,* allowing veils to be lifted on the planet and the new energies to penetrate the earth's grid.

Encodements were anchored in the Great Pyramid and in the sacred temples along the Nile, and their energies were held in the stone. When the ancient initiates reincarnated on earth in the twentieth century, their memories would be stirred and triggered. New energies would release the preprogramming. The energies embedded in the artifacts would remain intact until the consciousness on the Earth was renewed.

THE ISIS WOMAN

The Isis woman is a wise woman. Through tremendous soul-searching and self-discipline, the Isis woman finds herself. Highly experienced and internally motivated, she has become a spiritual warrior in her own right. Guided by the Angel of Cosmic Intelligence, the Isis woman understands the mystical. Isis represents the intuitive function and the heartspace that allows us to access ancient wisdom.

The Isis woman is fond of science and the occult, and she can easily become clairvoyant. Astrology and the study of mysticism all feed her desire for knowledge. She is broad-minded spiritually, which invites exposure to a variety of channeling phenomena, psychometry, palmistry, and the consultation of various oracles.** Her fertile imagination lends itself well to the development of visualization skills.

The Isis woman integrates the fresh innocence of the maiden, the nurturing containment of the mother, and the deep wisdom of the crone. Through the mystery of motherhood, which the ancients recognized as proof of Nature's omniscient wisdom and the Goddess' overshadowing power, the Isis woman touches divinity.

> The kernel of the Isis archetype is the consciousness of being the seat of life, as woman's awareness of her own function of beginner, nurturer, and medium for life to accomplish its means. This knowledge pervades through the character of the Isis woman, who owns the goddess-given gift of mastery of her own destiny. The Isis woman knows, in other words, that her life and her role of mother are part of the great mesh that forms the pattern of existence. Her motherhood reminds her of the flowers opening their petals to receive the light of

---

*Harmonic convergence was a time of worldwide meditation and astrological significance that occurred August 16 and 17, 1987. A magnificent love vibration was released then and veils were lifted. Since that time, it has been easier for humans to connect with psychic impulses and channeled material. According to José Argüelles, the activation of our solar system by a galactic synchronization beam began 5,100 years ago and entered its climax phase on harmonic convergence.[12]

**Oracles were games to teach spirituality to the illiterate in Pagan times, largely preserved and practiced by gypsy folk yet originating in pre-dynastic Egypt.

the sun, the moon, shining bright, of the stars and the whole Cosmos echoing her life.[13]

The Isis woman can function independently. Highly principled, she is not one to tolerate oppressive situations. She may find herself as a single parent. She is clear within herself and has much to offer her children. She is capable of providing a balanced home on her own.

> [T]he Isis woman may be perfectly at ease as a single parent caring for the child and providing all the comforts and sustenance herself. In this case, she will take on the role of father also, introducing the child into the unknown world of male mysteries in the same way as Isis in the myth where she undertakes the long journey in search of Osiris to the swamps of the Nile's delta.[14]

The Isis woman has endured the initiations of life and is fulfilled within herself. She takes the idea of spiritual discipline seriously and is willing to be of service to her family, to the community, and to humanity. Like her archetypal namesake, she knows that what is, is. She deserves to be honored.

ANGEL OF COSMIC INTELLIGENCE

The Angel of Cosmic Intelligence creates a point of contact with the Universal Mind. Tuning in to the vibration of this Angel allows the keys of the secret doctrines of the ancient philosophers to flow through us. The wisdom available to us through channeled material is increasing. Many are finding that they are able to access this information through automatic writing, visioning, or channeling. As we learn to access a deeper consciousness, we are receiving information of personal relevance and of relevance to the collective.

As priestesses in the mystery schools went through successive rigorous initiations, they were able to directly access Higher Intelligence through the grace of this Angel. The mysteries of Hermeticism [Hermes = Thoth = Keeper of the Records], the great spiritual truths, are hidden from ordinary consciousness.

> To those who are prepared she reveals herself as the Lady of Light. She points out the concealed path by the beams of her gentle lunar radiance, and gives freely her graces. She is Divine Inspiration.[15]

51

Incarnate on earth, we are meant to be divine instruments of Spirit. Spirit respects us and cannot interfere with us unless we request its assistance. The Angel of Cosmic Intelligence will be at your service for the asking. This intuitive relationship will grow with practice. The simplest way to begin is to ask a question that has a "yes" or "no" answer. The use of a *pendulum* or *divining rods** can assist you in picking up the answer. A "yes" answer is usually an opening of the rods or a clockwise circle on the pendulum. A "no" answer is a crossing of the rods or a counter-clockwise circle on the pendulum. When working with these instruments, it is customary to first ask three questions:

- "What is yes?"
- "What is no?"
- "May I ask some questions at this time?"

The ultimate goal for the spiritual warrior is to merge with the Higher Self. We can then allow the bliss of the infusion of Spirit into our physical bodies and become one with the pure radiating energy of the divine self. In that unity, the secrets of the Universe will be revealed. Two essential Truths emerge:

- With Wisdom we can have and be all things
- Wisdom from above is the only Reality, all else is illusion.

---

*Divining rods are pairs of L-shaped rods made of heavy-gauge wire or copper, held one in each hand. When questions with a yes or no answer are asked, they respond by either opening or crossing. Between questions, divining rods should be wiped with the fingers to clear the energy.

Hera

Large Vessels

Hera

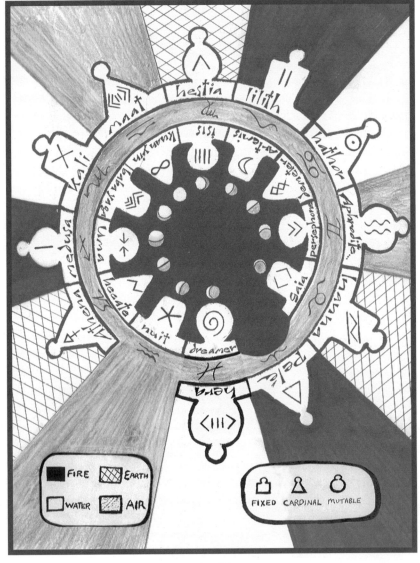

Sun in Pisces
Mutable–Water

CHAPTER VII

Ꮒera

3

In modern culture, Hera is the archetypal Wife. In ancient mythology, Hera is the guardian of the sacred marriage, the union between masculine and feminine principles. She symbolizes an ascent in consciousness, where the self is guided by the soul and by the emotions.[1] Embodied, she represents abundance, harmony, community, and relationship.

Hera vibrates to the number three, or the idea of creative synthesis.[2] The number three is embedded in the symbolism of many powerful trinities: the father, the son, and the holy ghost; the past, the present, and the future; the mother, father, and child; the beginning, the middle, and the end.

Connected to the Empress in the Tarot, Hera is sometimes pictured as a winged goddess or embracing a golden eagle.[3] This, as with all ancient bird images, represents the connection to spirit and the life force that soars beyond the physical plane. The Tarot Empress is in touch with the purest essence of femininity, with sensuousness, and with the love of beauty. She embraces the notion that the *power of love* is dearer than the *love of power*.[4]

> At her highest and brightest, The Empress illuminates the heavens, synthesizing all their powers: sun, moon, and the great wheel of the zodiac. In her lower, more earthbound aspects, the goddess' unbridled fertility can lead to overindulgence and stagnation.[5]

The Hera archetype manifests the energy of the Sun in Pisces that is imaginative and compassionate, tolerant and kind. A mutable water sign, it exemplifies the capacity to adapt readily to change and concerns itself with emotions and the welfare of others. This archetype is loving and can easily be influenced. There is an aversion to inflicting pain on others.

MYTHOLOGY

The word *hero* is the masculine of *Hera*. At an arche- typal level, Hera represents the heroine's journey, which is the inner pilgrimage to fully embrace and express feminine consciousness that has been wounded. The story of the marriage of Hera and Zeus appears in the context of the new patriarchal paradigm. This represents the onset of the double standard for female chastity and male freedom.

In early Greek mythology, we find that Hera's worship preceded Zeus, the infamous Olympian god. Hera is an emanation of the Mother Goddess whose milk nourished humanity. In some legends, she is reputed to have given birth to all the Angels.[6] There were many temples erected in Hera's honor, and she was greatly revered throughout ancient Greece. Greek poets referred to Hera as "cow-eyed,"[7] which could imply she had some association or origins with the Hathors. (See Chapter 23 for information on the Hathors.)

The pre-Hellenic mother of God, Rhea, condemned monogamy as a sin and insisted on her ancient law of group marriage. One of her sons was Zeus himself. Hera was Rhea's daughter. Zeus forced Hera into a monogamous marriage (though this meant monogamy only for her). Hera, the Goddess of Marriage, was expected to be faithful, loyal, and supremely tolerant. Zeus, on the other hand, was constantly adulterous. The idea here was that it was the male's privilege, right, and necessity to spread his seed. Hera detested his infidelities. Zeus had sex with all the Olympian females except the declared chaste virgins Hestia and Artemis. When Hera roused the other gods in a protest against Zeus's promiscuity, he punished her severely. This symbolically legitimized the forcing of wives into submission.[8]

Hera's environmental archetype, or ancient symbol that defines her, is the large vessel, or pythoi jar. This exemplifies her capacity for the psychological containment of another. It represents her ability to understand and to emotion- ally receive another without judgment, as well as her ability to measure and appreciate life, love, and truth.[9]

The History of Marriage

The word marriage came from the Latin "maritare," which meant union under the auspices of *Mary*. Psychologically, the "split" of the Marys has great signifi- cance to feminine consciousness. The Virgin Mary symbolizes all that is pure and chaste in the feminine soul. This is illustrated by the idea of the Immaculate Conception, the conception of Mary in her mother's womb without the stain of original sin. On the other hand, Mary Magdalene has been assigned all that is shunned in the feminine—sensuality and prostitution.

Originally, matrimony was a union with the goddess, with aspects of both Marys, an honoring and respecting of the sacredness of sexuality, fertility, and procreation. It also symbolized a marriage of two states of consciousness. The inner phase of the soul's activities symbolized an inner marriage or a welcoming of an inner spiritual teacher. The outer phase was symbolized by the wedding garment. It was important that "external thinking must be in harmony with the inner revelation before we can make complete union with the Christ."[11]

The rites and ceremonies were woven from the very fibers of matrilineal heritage where the children that emerged from the mother were her children. In peaceable early matriarchal cultures, land was not owned because it was thought to belong to the Creator. Later, land was owned and was transferred through matrilineal succession from mother to daughter.

In the Pagan tradition, the idea of fidelity and monogamy was abandoned each May for the all-important fertility rites that ensured the germination of seeds that would produce a bountiful harvest. In the *merry* month of May, a woman could make love to any man she chose in the name of the Great Mother. Any children that were conceived and birthed from these orgiastic activities were honored greatly, and these offspring were called *children of the goddess*. These children were special gifts, and not surprisingly, they stayed in the care of the mother not only because their paternity was uncertain, but also because women were and still are the primary biological nurturers of their offspring. What is certain is those matriarchal societies seldom permitted sexual jealousy.

When Christian fathers were reorganizing society, they were strongly opposed to the institution of marriage. They stated that the sexual passion of matrimony was unholy and impure.[12] The patriarchal fathers thought marriage was a crime against God. Their entire formulation for society, the church, and all citizens was to eradicate everything that resembled the culture of the goddess and that gave women control of their own destiny, their own bodies, their own reproduction, and their own spiritual connection to Mother Earth and each other. Therefore love and marriage became a sin, a moral crime, an obscenity, and a filthy practice. They then went on to say that only celibate men could become Christian, and no man who had ever been married could be baptized. In the 16th century AD, the Council of Trent declared that anyone who even so much as hinted that marriage could be more sacred than celibacy would quite simply be excommunicated.

It is noteworthy that the Christian Church did evolve to allow for marriage of the general populace while maintaining the rule of celibacy for its priesthood. Ruling against sexual union is a move against nature, the life force, and the feminine powers of procreation and regeneration. This ruling was meant to move the power center of the culture into the hands of the patriarchs. It would appear that this repression has had many repercussions.

Once the Church did permit marriage, the idea of monogamy for women later epitomized by the chastity belt was institutionalized. In this way paternity could be ensured and estates could be transferred from father to son. It became illegal for women to own land. Thus, the Hera woman became locked into the role of the wife in a patriarchal culture that saw God as the head of the Church, and man as the head of the household.

Many of these socio-cultural changes were enacted when the archetypal template of the Olympian pantheon established the notion of hierarchical power that endorsed the male as the heir to that power. It has often been speculated that procreation envy was at the root of the power struggle. When Athena, the original patriarchal daughter, was miraculously born out of the head of Zeus, the patriarchy mythologically achieved the right to that dominance. From this vantage point, women were superfluous. The rewriting of history was in full swing. This is among the distorted legends granting supremacy to men and encouraging a cultural devaluation of the feminine spirit, the female body, and the very womb of procreation. Yet as Cavander relates:

> Unofficially, the women of ancient Athens found ways, as their sisters have done in every age and culture, to undermine the barriers of male prejudice.[13]

For centuries, the role of wife was the only culturally visible role women were allowed. If a woman was to be a mother, she most certainly was expected to have a husband. Even if society has loosened its hold on traditional sex roles and accepts the variances of unwed mothers, single-parent families, and careers for women, the underlying meaning of the institution of modern marriage still holds energy in the collective unconscious. With 50 percent of first marriages and 65 percent of second marriages ending in divorce,[14] not to mention the high number of separations and loveless marriages, we must wonder about the viability of the institution as a whole. Yet as young girls, we are programmed to find our knight in shining armor, to set up households, and to live happily ever after. Even after they experience the devastation of a broken marriage, most women continue to feed the fantasy that the perfect relationship is on the horizon. But we have little understanding about why many marriages do not work.

Christianity accepted marriage only on the condition that the man and woman formed a master-servant relationship. Physical abuse and sexual coercion were so common in Christian marriages that the idea of "lover" always referred to love outside the marriage. This emphasized the accepted idea that no woman could love a husband due to the overwhelmingly sanctioned domination and control. The commonly accepted idea was that men were exhorted from the pulpit to lord over their wives, and the wives were "to kiss the rod that beat them." Until 1966 in the United States, it was legal for a man to strike his wife as long as the object had a diameter no larger than his thumb. This is still what is referred to each time someone utters the euphemism "rule of thumb."[15] American law upheld this maxim, stating that a woman could not sue her husband for assault because the suit might interfere with the "peace" of the home. Not until 1962 did a judge declare that wife-beating already destroyed this supposed peace and that this law was fundamentally unsound.

In keeping with the pattern established by the patriarchal church, it has also been declared that of all professional groups, the clergy have been the least willing or able to help battered wives. Of course, women were encouraged to seek counsel from priests. But then a woman would be instructed to be better at relieving her husband's tension and to examine how her wrongs brought the violence upon herself. By closely examining the legal system, we can see how firmly entrenched the patterns of blaming the victim still are.

Part of what sustains this patterning is that the Hera energy is the ultimate in forgiveness. Her openness and generosity soothe all who come into her midst. As soon as some kindness is restored, the Hera woman regains her balance and resumes her attitude of service to others. Hera gives of herself. Whether or not she is credited, the Hera woman is the Matriarch of her clan, and all who are nourished at her table are sustained.

Hera subscribes to the motto: *As you give to others you are giving to yourself, for there is only one self.* Hera is the ultimate container of emotion, the place where one can rest in the perfection of being contained. It is the sacrament of being received that touches the essence of the Spirit Self where the Great Goddess resides. For a man in love, the goddess shining through this woman can indeed be the light of his world.

Ancient Rites

The Hera archetype emerges from a powerful culture of women who honored the moon. These women would go into seclusion with their sisters during their *moon time*. Sacred traditions regarding menstruation are universal. During their moon cycles, women gathered in menstrual huts to pray together and to dream together. Huts were woven out of the lygus plant that was sacred to Hera.[16] The earth-honoring clans were well versed in herbology and plant lore. Flower distillations of the lygus plant were said to bring on menstruation.

The most sacred ceremonial time for young girls was the first menstruation. The arrival of this blessing would find maidens welcomed into the sacred moontime rituals that would be a rite of passage of the greatest significance in their life. Women who are close to one another will often find that their menstrual cycles will synchronize. Today, women have found that flying across the path of the moon can often disrupt the rhythm of menstrual cycles. This indicates the powerful influence of the moon on feminine biological cycles.

In ancient goddess-centered cultures, "moon blood"* was collected for the fertilization of plants to ensure a bountiful harvest of the essential herbs, flowers, and plants necessary to the well-being of the peoples. Women would also bleed directly onto the ground in the menstrual hut, returning the blood of life to the earth. During the sacred time of bleeding, women would pray, chant, commune with one another, and perform rituals and ceremonies. They would sleep together with their heads pointing toward the center of the circle. This bonding would culminate in the invocation of a collective dream.

The women were so in tune with nature and with the waxing and waning of the moon that not only would they bleed simultaneously, but it would occur at the new moon. After three days of honoring the dark phase of the moon and the psychic energies of regeneration, the women would emerge back to the clan rejuvenated, connected to the Great Mother and to one another, illumined by the collective dream, and renewed.

THE HERA WOMAN

The Hera woman in love brings with her a gentleness, a beauty, and the luxurious ecstasy of passion and rapture. She is tolerant, kind, generous, and harmonious. She engenders an emotional openness that heals the heart.

On the other hand, when she is crossed, there can be a spectacular storm. Hera has been promised monogamy, the good life, and to be provided for in exchange for her sacred service. In good faith, she accepts the bargain. She is steadfast and committed. She brings in the holy and creative energies that illuminate the household. She provides safety, warmth, structure, nurturance, and reliability. If she finds out her husband has strayed, there is hell to pay.

The Hera woman may seethe and express her rage. She may also go into years of denial. She may even appear to forgive and forget and make light of it. One day, she realizes that she has been repressing her anger. She contemplates the injustices and the price she has paid for the "bargain" in her marriage. She realizes that her husband has the power, and that the feminine energies that fuel the family are indeed not valued even though they are life-sustaining. She knows that if she leaves, the quality of the life of all involved, that she has worked fastidiously to preserve, is threatened beyond conception. The Hera woman eventually faces this outrage, and she erupts with the fury of a violent storm.

---

* Menstrual blood, or moon blood is the purest blood. It is highly oxygenated and carries decoded DNA. It is oxygen that decodes the strands of DNA and allows the restructuring of data.[17]

There is usually a calm before Hera storms, just as there are atmospheric pressure changes before earthquakes, tornadoes, and volcanic eruptions. When Hera's energies arrive at critical mass, the rampage begins. Hera manifests as insanely jealous of whoever is receiving the affections she so craves from her husband. In the end, Hera's outburst leaves emotional scars. The truth of betrayal, deceit, and denial wound her and disempower her. This contributes to a deep feeling of insecurity that erodes her well-being.

Channeling goddess energies makes the Hera woman energetically sensitive and psychic. When the Hera woman listens to her inner guidance, she can piece together the truth. When she realizes she has been deceived, her agony is overwhelming. When she speaks of her revelation, she finds her sisters are resigned. Incredulously, Hera listens to a myriad of stories of abuse and betrayal. After being immersed in the pervasive attitude and the cultural consensus, her heart is heavy. Her despair widens.

Facts show that most Hera women have endured more than one infidelity and sustained their marriages. The Lillith woman would not tolerate this disloyalty: she would indignantly turn on her heels and march right out of the relationship. Yet Hera fastidiously stays in the marriage. Her security needs take precedence over all. Typically, her longstanding co-dependency has limited her earning capacity that would afford her the sanctuary of independent living. After years of inadvertently reinforcing her husband's selfish insensitivity, she is trapped, stressed, and docile.

When a Hera woman is in her power, she is the epitome of love. She is generous, helpful to others, and in touch with the natural abundance of the Universe. She is secure in her relationship and benefits from the partnership. She is charming and likable and can be very good to others who are in distress.

THE ANGEL OF PROSPERITY

The Angel of Prosperity radiates the spiritual essence of abundance, beauty, luxury, and well-being. She is the vortex through which the energy of material prosperity and spiritual prosperity passes.

> The difference between spiritual prosperity and the material idea of prosperity is founded on understanding of the inexhaustible, omni-present substance of Spirit as the source of supply; the material idea is that the possession of things constitutes prosperity.[18]

Learning to notice that the Universe provides abundantly is an important step on the spiritual journey. In a society that promotes consumerism and materiality, it is easy to get caught in desire. Most of us have felt squeezed financially as we adjust to years of recession and inflation. Perhaps we know deep down that the Universe will take care of us. An essential part of the process is to remember to ask for help in an atmosphere of openness and to trust in divine timing. Even so, we have all experienced doubt, fear, and lack. But if we are clear on what we want, and if we trust deeply in the power of the Universe to provide, the Angel of Prosperity smiles upon us. This form of empowerment is not about greed and demands, nor is it about money per se.

It is about abundance. A common trap, and a naive one at that, is to learn about prosperity consciousness and affirmations and to expect to win the lottery. It is important to ask for what you want and take what you get, for the Universe provides that which assists us in learning spiritual lessons.

Part of trusting the Angel of Prosperity is understanding that if some goal we have does not serve our best interest for our ultimate growth, it may not be granted. Also, the clearer we are, the higher our vibrational frequency, and the greater our commitment to living a spiritual life for the greater good of all, the more appropriate the affirmations that come to fruition. When we focus on the plenitude abounding around us, we are empowering and acknowledging this Angel who has been with us all along.

Pele

Volcano

Pele

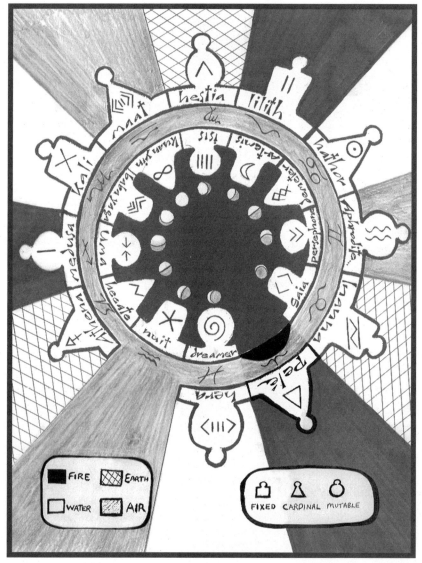

Sun and Moon in Aries – Open House
Cardinal–Fire

Chapter VIII

Pele

4

Pele is the archetypal Gate of Power through which we come forth from the invisible to the visible, and "it is through this gate that [we] must go to get into the presence of Spirit."[1] The spirit of Pele dwells inside the Kilauea Caldera, the largest active volcano on the planet located on the Big Island of Hawaii. Pele's energy is direct, volatile, and abysmal. On the physical plane, she erupts molten lava from the center of the earth. Emotionally, she can erupt material from the unconscious and bring it forcibly into consciousness. Pele is a force to contend with, and she can shake us to our very core. If we pay tribute to Pele, her energy will wrap around us, bringing clarity and assisting us in owning our personal power.

Pele is contained in the number four. She represents the four cornerstones of a stable foundation. There are four seasons, four directions, four corners of the earth, four archangels, four elements, four phases of the moon. Jung graced us with the knowledge of four ego functions: thinking, feeling, sensing, and intuiting.[2]

Pele is kin to the Emperor in the Tarot. The Emperor is a ruler wearing no armor, who brings perspective, stability, and permanence. The Emperor stands alone and is external to authority. "If he is harmed, the entire community suffers."[3] In the same line of thinking, if the fiery energy of Pele is repressed, the entire family system can be affected. It is noteworthy that the word "emperor" is closely related to the word *empower*. This is the "Holy Fire of Spirit" that seeks to illuminate the shadow both personally and collectively.

As depicted in the Astrological Template, Pele occupies an open house. She allows the powerful energy from the center of the earth to blast forth into the cosmos. Pele is the terrestrial portal exploding energy from the crystal core of the Earth into the cosmos, whereas Nuit, who occupies the other open house, ushers in Cosmic energy, showering it on the Earth Plane. Pele's Gate of Power and Nuit's Cosmic Gate allow an energy exchange from Earth to the heavens and from the heavens to Earth. These energetic portals release the yang energy from the earth to the heavens and the yin energy from the heavens to the earth. These portals allow the exchange of energy between the inner rim of the astrological template, containing the Moon Goddesses, and the outer rim, containing the Sun Goddesses. They are essential to an energetic understanding of the Angels and Archetypes system.

Pele's energy, then, harnesses both the extroverted energy of the Sun in Aries and the introverted energy of the Moon in Aries. A cardinal fire sign, Aries is primitive, dynamic, confident, ambitious, and courageous. The Moon represents the past of the entire soul, with all its subconscious programming and memories.[4] The Sun is the future and the fulfillment of potential. The process of growth occurs between the internal, or Moon influences, and the external, or Sun influences. Within the archetypal Zodiac, Aries represents the search for a separate identity. Interestingly, this manifests in Pele as breaking free of the collective unconscious.

MYTHOLOGY

The goddess Pele is revered in Hawaiian mythology. She is a vital spiritual force. Pele's consort is half man and half wild boar. She manifests the supreme energy of the eternal grandmother. Natives pay tribute by making prayers and offerings to appease her glory and her wrath.

It is known that Pele's energy is big energy. Pele is directly connected to the power of Mother Nature. She is penetrating and intense, and reveals the secrets from the crystal core of the earth. She is a personification of the Gate of Power, the portal through which we pass as we claim our birthright to our own divinity and our own empowerment.

Pele probes into individuals. She manifests in various intensities. According to the natives, she can either caress you or shake you to your core. If you are in your power and shining your own light, she will wrap herself around you and bathe you in her fire. If you are hiding from yourself, she will confront you and scorch you with her fervor.

All existence is said to have begun with the statement, "Let there be Light." This was not referring to the sun's light, but motion, dynamism, and rhythmic change. Aries is the initiating will to be, the Light of Life itself. Breathing is the first act of independent existence within the open environment of the Universe, and is symbolized by sunrise. Pele knows every individual can be reborn at any moment.

Volcanoes become dormant. Tourists love to take the risk of walking into a crater. Yet when the geological plates shift, and Mother Earth shrugs her shoulders, the rumblings of earthquakes can make volcanoes potentially active. Similarly, when our deep self rumbles with Truth, and the tectonic plates of our consciousness shift and grind, our own internal volcano brews. Pele becomes an instrument of confrontation.

The Tarot Empress and Emperor are a wedded pair that are bonded in power and in instinct. They can function creatively with the other. Nichols states:

> ...when we develop ego consciousness, we think of ourselves as *one*. But as we grow in awareness, we gradually come to realize we are *two*—conscious and unconscious, ego and shadow (the one who rises early and the one who prefers to lie abed). If we are to reconcile these opposing aspects of ourselves, we must discover an inner mediator, a number *three* which can correlate these two so that they can work harmoniously. When this happens, the 'out of the three'—through the activity of this third factor—comes 'the one as the *fourth*', an emergent feeling of wholeness, a unified personality that can again function as one, but now at a new level of awareness.[5]

The word "individual" means "not divisible" or not able to be divided. Pele's motto is: "Selfhood is indivisible." This means that the Self is not available to be categorized, minimized, compartmentalized, or limited to any existing view. Pele thus keeps us whole.

THE PELE WOMAN

The Pele woman is powerful, direct, and volatile. She resents being controlled or dominated. She resists external authority. The Pele woman readily expresses anger and moral outrage. She is disturbed by the condition of the planet and the oppression of one group by another.

There is a cultural tendency to leave deep in the Underworld all that which seethes, in the shadow of our consciousness and in the shadow of the culture. The Pele woman is a strong woman. She is somewhat of a role model who can express her outrage in a matter-of-fact fashion. She is willing to confront facts and to express her concerns.

Sometimes the topic that needs to be confronted is locked so deep in the unconscious that the emotional body becomes filled and overflows the trauma into the physical, manifesting as disease (dis-ease). In many women, rage has been repressed so thoroughly that physical or emotional malaise manifest. Unexpressed rage can be the root of psychosomatic illness and has been linked to headaches, cancer, pre-menstrual syndrome, arthritis, depression, and boredom.

The Pele woman has learned that she pays a high price if she does not identify the emotional root of her discomfort. If she is operating in an atmosphere of secrecy and denial, she may delay her response or feel guilty for her feelings. Ultimately, she knows she can no longer be complacent. She knows she must speak her Truth regardless of the reaction it causes. Otherwise her communication will be awkward and apologetic.

For the Pele woman, the first step of the journey beyond oppression occurs when she speaks out, confronts the facts, and says "no." In saying "no," she protests what would be unacceptable for any person to experience. In this fashion, she stands up for all women, not only for herself.

Sometimes, oppressive psychological patterns drag us so deeply into self-doubt that our vision of what is acceptable treatment becomes veiled. When Pele's energy is out of balance, guilt runs wild and we feel ultimately disempowered and undervalued. We feel guilty for speaking up and guilty for not. We feel guilty for serving others and guilty for not giving more. We feel guilty for needing so much while we are repressing our needs. We long to be more accepting, while we are being taken advantage of. Thus we are immersed in the swirling, molten material of the unexpressed. We know we have been disempowered, yet we become incapacitated when it comes to standing up for ourselves.

Pele's energy can assist us in becoming vigilant. She helps us to know what is acceptable behavior and what is not. Pele assists us in blasting through the conspiracy of silence. Culture constantly provides images of women that are oppressed, silenced, boxed in, and controlled. Pele invites us to be individuals who are whole and free and who have separate identities. Then, like the volcano, we can be seen as forces to contend with. This is not to suggest that we will be consumed by constant emotional explosion, generating fear in those around us. We can deal with and express, rather than repress, our emotions in a graceful yet firm fashion.

When Pele's energy is released, the result may be intimidating. Women expressing themselves with fortitude and clarity are often judged as "militant." Interestingly, this term is not used to describe men fighting in a war. It is time to break through the cultural programming that has dictated that women are to be the peacemakers and the tolerant ones while injustices and oppression reign supreme.

The Pele woman refuses to invalidate herself. She clearly expresses herself and she maintains her power. She does not engage in co-dependency. She walks securely through the Gate of Power. In changing her style of communicating, she establishes her strength and does not give her power to others. The Pele woman is a woman living fully *in* her power.

THE ANGEL OF EMPOWERMENT

The Angel of Empowerment is a fiery propellant reaching from the inner depths of the Underworld and blasting through into the Upperworld. This Angel is a vitalizer and a dam breaker. She gives us a voice.

Indeed, it may seem at first that she is speaking for us. Her strength and fervor is compelling. She assists us in changing our style of communication, and through this we establish new ground. The initiative of the Angel of Empowerment opens the door to clear boundaries, direct communication, decisiveness, and inner security.

With her assistance, we suddenly become visible. We release that which seethes in us, and that which seethes in the collective shadow of culture. As we allow the Angel of Empowerment's divine defiance to ignite us, we are freed. We can now harvest the treasures of living consciously in both the Underworld and the Upperworld.

In the presence of the awakened soul, an awesome power is released. It is an inner authority that is not controlled by the ego. Our lives can now be ruled by a connection to the spiritual power from within.

We are immersed in a time of profound change. Most people are well aware that the world structures are tremendously strained, that leadership is not what it was, that governments are not representing the populace. As external walls crumble, internal paradigms are also shifting.

Law and order refers to the laws of the Universe that support Truth and Light. The Cosmic forces of the Universe are constantly pulsing and throbbing. The vigor, vitality, spontaneity, and purpose here allows for joy and a fresh start. The ultimate surrender is to the Divine Fire of Spirit that penetrates to the ultimate Truth. The experience is like passing through the eye of the needle.

We are here. We have arrived at the forefront of a new mythical era. The significance of this is simple. The Age of Light is about illumination and power from within. It is the resurgence of ancient traditions that have been denigrated and eradicated. The Angel of Empowerment helps us understand that the only true power is from within and that all healing, depth, meaning, and soul are generated and accessed from within an individual.

Inanna

Stairway to Heaven

Inanna

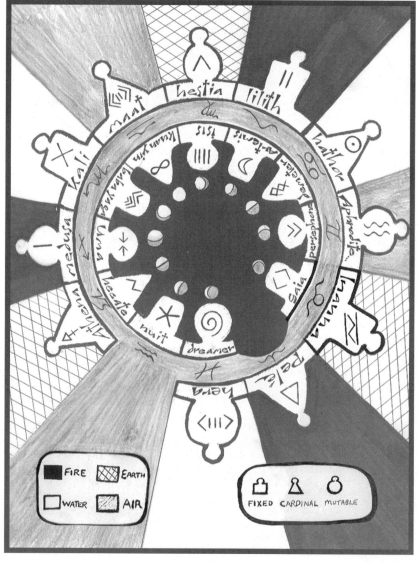

Sun in Taurus
Fixed–Earth

Chapter IX

Inanna

5

Inanna is the archetypal Queen who has dominion over three worlds: the spirit, the body, and the soul. Inanna first descends from heaven to Earth. Next, she descends into the deepest caverns of the psyche, is stripped bare, and sinks into the primal, dark vortex of the Underworld. Finally, she integrates the shadow, comes into her power, and ascends back to the Upperworld. She is at once fascinating and compelling, terrifying and repelling. Inanna demonstrates elasticity of character and has dominion over the entire scope of human experience. She is, all at once, Queen of Heaven and Earth, and Queen of the Underworld.

Inanna harnesses the energy of the number five, a symbol of the human condition and the level of human evolution.[1] The number five can be seen as a trinity—god, goddess, and holy spirit—immersed in duality (3+2=5). Five is the number of the fully awakened self, the number of Christ consciousness.

Inanna also represents the Tarot Hierophant who has mastered all the tests of life. This represents the inner spiritual phase of being when true light shines throughout consciousness.[2] There is open dialogue between consciousness and the instinctual powers of the psyche. In Tarot images, the seekers are kneeling figures, who "have not yet had the strength to stand up to the supra personal power."[3] By embracing the Inanna archetype, we stand up to these powers.

Inanna's energy is rooted in the Sun in Taurus. A fixed earth sign, it archetypally functions in the now, reacting from a balanced, grounded position. The energy of Taurus is persistent, determined, cautious, and retentive. It is steadfast and rarely scatters forces. There is an inner drive to build from the foundation. This position is slow to anger, but when frustrated, there is fury. This position makes for a faithful friend and an implacable enemy. It is sympathetic and understanding. It loves splendor, possessions, and status symbols, all well suited for a queenly scenario.

MYTHOLOGY

The origin of the story of Inanna, as translated from cuneiform tablets, dates up to 500,000 years ago. In reviewing sacred texts, we see that Inanna was a goddess from a royal family of Pleiadians who had off-planet origins, but was born on Earth.[4] She was the great-granddaughter of the god An, who was a "numinous power of the sky" and "lived in the highest heaven and never came down to earth."[5]

The Descent of Inanna from Heaven to Earth

Sitchin has done extensive research, examining some 5,000 ancient Sumerian cuneiform tablets. He concludes that An and his family were the Anunnaki, a race of superhuman beings, and "the highest heaven" was referring to an unknown planet within our solar system. The Anunnaki first came to earth from their planet 445,000 years ago. The term translates from Hebrew as "Those Who from Heaven to Earth Came." They are spoken of in the Bible as the *Anakim* and, in Genesis, as the *Nefilim*. They were described as "a gifted, energetic, innovative people, technically inventive and ideologically resourceful."[6]

Sitchin cites a 4,500-year-old cuneiform tablet, kept in the Near Eastern Section of the State Museum in Berlin, that accurately depicts a map of our solar system including this otherwise unknown planet.[7] Sitchin definitively describes this planet as Nibiru, which has a huge elliptical orbit that passes between Mars and Earth every 3,600 years. Between the Tigris and Euphrates rivers, where the city-states of Sumer were located and where the story of Inanna unfolded, there is ample evidence of sudden technological advances and genetic transmutations in this area each 3,600 years.[8] This area was a portal, or entry point, for the extraterrestrial visitors. There were also other portals used by the Pleiadians, notably Machu Picchu in Peru and Tihuanaco in Bolivia.

Ferguson relates that Nibiru is an artificial planet that is home to Inanna's family who were originally from the Pleiades, a group of seven stars neighboring the constellation of Taurus.[9] Due to nuclear activity and high levels of radiation, Nibiru was in a state of ecological deterioration. When it made its passage close to Earth, the Anunnaki would send crews to mine minerals and gold. For eons, gold particles were scattered into the Niburian stratosphere to preserve a life-sustaining balance of the atmosphere of Nibiru.[10]

Sitchin's research indicates that some 300,000 years ago, the Anunnaki workers assigned to the African mines mutinied. It was then that the chief scientist and the chief medical officer of the Anunnaki used genetic manipulation and in-vitro fertilization techniques to create primitive workers, called the "Lulus," to take over the backbreaking toil in the mines. Besides the artificial insemination and genetic manipulation, male Anunnakis mated with human females to pro-duce genetically enhanced strains of human offspring. The Lulus were the first Homo sapiens.[11]

The Anunnaki were a male-dominated race who visited the earth when peaceable matriarchal cultures flourished. The Anunnaki came to view Earth as their genetic experiment. According to Sitchin, it is the Anunnaki themselves who caused the world flood in order to wipe out the genetic anomalies that were created during the experimentation.

It is into this context that the goddess Inanna is introduced. She functions as a feminine deity and influences a civilization reflecting new technologies and social structures that would lead to patriarchy. Yet, as she descended to the earth plane, Inanna was thrust into her emotional body, characteristic of this third-dimensional reality. Here she was to feel the full range of human emotion. After she endured the emotional travail of the earth plane, she would become wise and thereby activate her divine powers.

When we meet Inanna we see a woman who is initially unsure of herself, her budding sexuality, and her responsibilities as Queen of the land. Her story is a tender, erotic, love story with shocking passages into the Underworld.

Inanna and the Tree of Life

The story opens with the "seeding" of the world, the beginning of life, in the form of the "huluppu" tree, which is also referenced as the Tree of Life or the biblical Tree of Knowledge. The tree was the axis of the three worlds, connecting the Underworld, the Earth, and the heavens.[12] To establish herself, Inanna must "rescue the tree of life from the world flood." She plants it in her garden and "wants to make a shining throne and a sacred marriage bed from the growing tree," thus claiming her queenship and her feminine consciousness.[13]

Inanna's first task is to rid the tree of a serpent, the dark-maid Lillith, and the "anzu" bird with a nest of young chicks. At first Inanna is powerless because she cannot charm the serpent into leaving. Serpents in mythology always represent feminine, sexual energies. The dark-maid Lillith, or the independent one, and the "anzu bird," or nurturing one, will not willingly vacate the homes they have made in the tree. The "hero-king" Giglamesh, reputedly Inanna's "earthly" brother, is summoned. He violently evacuates the snake, the dark maiden, and the mother bird by cutting down the tree. Thus the Tree of Life, a symbol of the wholeness of nature, is destroyed.[14] In an emerging patriarchal climate, it is appropriate that Inanna could not rid the sacred tree of the symbols of female sexuality, freedom, and spirituality. Her developmental task was to preserve the feminine principles and her feminine power.

Inanna Outwits Enki —the God of Wisdom

As the drama unfolds, Inanna encounters her next situation that teaches her about feminine power. Having been granted the power to rule the populace, Inanna sets out to visit Enki, the Great Anunnaki Shaman and God of Wisdom. Enki and Inanna drink together and, in a state of inebriation, Enki becomes excessively generous and offers Inanna his many secrets that constitute the knowledge necessary to rule her kingdom. These *me*, or ordering principles of civilization, include one especially vital principle that activates the rest, referred to as the "gift of making decisions."

When Enki sobers up, he becomes abusive and enraged and demands the return of the gifts. Recognizing the dual nature of the god, Inanna, with the help of a temple priestess, tricks Enki and manages to return safely to her city. Her people benefit from the treasures and she becomes all the wiser for the experience.

The Courtship of Inanna and Dumuzi

The story continues honoring Inanna, who has earned her throne and is gaining stature and wisdom. Yet the sacred marriage bed is still empty. Inanna's brother selects a husband for her. Inanna protests and seeks the freedom to marry a farmer. Surely we would expect her, as Queen of Heaven and Earth, to have the right to freely choose a mate unless patriarchal imperatives and the ultimate control of the feminine were creeping into the existing culture.

The conflict rises to the surface between existing Goddess cultures and the new patriarchal domination. We begin to see how "the free expression of [the] feminine instinctually had to be restrained and reduced, subjected to patriarchal breeding purposes."[15]

Inanna is described as "dynamic, fierce and independent; embodying the playful, self-willed, never-domesticated aspect of the feminine."[16] Sumerian poems express her irrepressible vitality and state that "she claims her needs assertively."[17] Even so, after a time, Inanna submits to her brother to avoid a quarrel, and she agrees to marry the shepherd Dumuzi. Gadon alerts us:

> Behind this family quarrel is the historical reality of invasion. The shepherd represents the pastoralists from the north who have overcome the people who farm the rich alluvial plains.[18]

Inanna bonds with Dumuzi who becomes her "honey man, the one her womb loved best,"[19] and their passion explodes with sensual pleasures and joy.

Inanna functioned as an initiate priestess in the Sumerian culture where sacred sexuality was the key to life. As a hierodule, temple priestess, and sacred prostitute, Inanna is well versed in mediating the "mystery of existence through body and sexuality."[20] "Her receptivity is active ... and she celebrates her body in song."[21] Inanna is an uninhibited, irrepressible woman who is described as loving, jealous, grieving, joyful, timid, exhibitionist, thieving, passionate, ambitious, and generous.[22]

In the temples where the worship of the goddesses was fundamental to culture, the sacrament of sex was central to the functioning of the populace. Later, when honoring the feminine was negated, distortions to texts, stories, and laments redefined sacred priestesses as harlots and prostitutes. Their function in society was debased and redefined according to the new patriarchal morality. If we take a closer look, we begin to see the links to the biblical story of Jesus and Mary Magdalene. Mary Magdalene was a sacred prostitute and a temple harlot whom Jesus loved and honored. It is only later that the negative labels drove the misinterpretation into the Bible itself along with the general view of women as soiled and tainted.

Nevertheless, for two thousand years, sacred marriage rites were performed in Mesopotamia[23] to ensure "luxuriant vegetation and a bountiful harvest."[24] The king in the fertility drama penetrates the goddess in the sacred temple of Inanna at Uruk. In bonding with the exalted goddess, he gains power.

> Through marriage the Goddess gives her husband the strength to provide leadership, guidance, and fertility to others. She gives him the throne, scepter, staff, crook, and crown, as well as the promise of good harvests and the joys of her bed. Sadly, when the honeymoon is over and Dumuzi takes on the prescribed role of father and king, he asks to be set free.[25]

Inanna's Descent to the Great Below

Once Dumuzi is empowered by Inanna's love, he rebels and seeks the freedom to rule the people independently. This action damages the sacredness of their union. Inanna feels ravaged and moves into a deep despair. When "love is gone,"[26] Inanna begins to descend, slowly at first and within herself, but ultimately to the depths of the Underworld. She is on a journey to retrieve the aspects of herself and of feminine consciousness that have been lost. She leaves a message that she is going to the Underworld, alerting Enlil, the God of Air, Enki, the God of Wisdom, and Nanna, her supportive friend, to come to the rescue if she does not return in three days.

In this light, the story of Inanna begins to make some sense, and we see how her descent into the Underworld is a response to the deep wound gouging into the feminine as the changing order takes power. In earlier goddess cultures, the Underworld represented the unconscious, yet in the new patriarchal order, it was a place of "horror and dread."[27] Here we meet Ereskigal, who is known as Inanna's dark sister. It is instructive to also consider her as the shadow side of Inanna herself, the part that she must fully integrate to become whole and in her full power.

Upperworld, conscious processes have begun to be pitted against Underworld, unconscious processes. The new patriarchal imperative thus speaks.

> We believe in order, reason, and progress and assign change, destruction, and transformation to the unconscious. We prefer not to look too closely at the awesomely dissolving and destructive, yet also dangerously attractive, abyss of the dark side of the goddess. Hence, of the vast range of feminine qualities, only the life-giving and protecting motherly qualities came to be acceptable to the patriarchal ego.[28]

Ereskigal, who embodies this dark shadow, is jealous, demanding, vengeful, vindictive, angry, and punitive. She governs everything that is opposed to life—death, non-being, annihilation, and emptiness.[29]

As Inanna descends, she comes upon seven gateways at which she is asked to relinquish an aspect of her power. Interestingly, in Clystra Kinstler's interpretive novel, Inanna gives up the "crown of the High Priestess to the Anunnaki"[30] at the first gateway.

At the second gateway, she relinquishes a lapis lazuli rod, the sign of her earthly queenship. At the third gate, the gatekeeper demands her lapis necklace, representing the power and privilege of feminine grace and beauty. Dismayed, she wanders through the archetypal Underworld.

At the fourth gateway, she meets a demon who claims the talisman of her heritage, the safety and love of her family. She is entirely without comfort. She continues to descend.

At the fifth gate, the gatekeeper violently claims the breastplate of the Goddess that included the protection Inanna derived from her spiritual guides and angelic companions. This leaves her utterly abandoned on all levels, devoured by the forces of the dark Underworld. Trembling, panicked, and forlorn, Inanna is subjected to the atrocities of the sixth gatekeeper, who claims a gold ring. This makes her even more vulnerable and symbolizes the rupturing of her ego boundary.

Demons are now free to fondle and caress her, mocking her, provoking obscenities. Inanna is molested and humiliated. She is stripped naked and depersonalized. Here she is dead in the presence of her rival sister.

> It is the place of powerlessness of chaotic and numb unchanneled affect, the lonely grief-rage of powerlessness and unassuaged loss and longing, a hellish place where all we know to do is useless (thus

there is no known way out of the despair). We can only endure, barely conscious, barely surviving the pain and powerlessness, suspended out of life, stuck, until and if, some act of grace with some new wisdom arrives. Such raw, impersonal, though potentially initiating miseries are Ereshkigal's domain.[31]

The relentless tortures continue. Rejected and ravaged, Inanna is cast aside and left for dead. Ereshkigal, the shadow sister, is victorious. The Anunnaki are there to pass judgment on Inanna.

> The pure Ereshkigal seated herself upon her throne. The Anannaki, the seven judges, pronounced judgment before her. They fastened their eyes upon her, the eyes of death. At their word, the word that tortures the spirit. The sick woman was turned into a corpse. And the corpse was hung from a stake.[31]

It is equally fascinating that Inanna is also "dead" to Dumuzi, who remains in the Upperworld. He carries on, having power over the populace, and he scarcely gives Inanna another thought. Inanna is not missed by Enlil or Enki either. It is the god Ea who notices the people, the land, and the animals are sterile in her absence. Inanna's energy is no longer fueling the fertility of the land. Through prompting by Ea, Enki realizes that Inanna must be rescued if the land is to provide for its people. Enki arranges for her release, but there is a ransom fee.

> Inanna was about to ascend from the nether world, when the Anannaki seized her. No one ascends from the nether world unmarked. If Inanna wishes to return from the nether world, she must provide someone in her place.[33]

The Return of Inanna

She returns to find Dumuzi gloating in his newly attained power, utterly unconcerned that she has been missing and in danger. When she realizes that he did not act to defend her, she is enraged. Incensed, Inanna takes action. In retaliation, Inanna consigns Dumuzi to be her replacement and sacrifices him to the Underworld. There he will wrestle with his unconscious feminine, the denied aspect of himself. Returned to her power, she dooms her husband to the Underworld for his failure to show her proper respect.

Dumuzi, like Inanna, takes time to descend, losing virility, status, and strength as he makes his passage. He roams directionless, without power and without comfort. He grasps the enormity of his loss, feels trapped in the inescapable forces, collapses in a heap of tears, and falls asleep. He awakens with a dream.

Dumuzi seeks out his little sister, Geshtinanna, who listens to his dream and takes pity on him. Geshtinanna consults Inanna and offers to take Dumuzi's place in the Underworld for half the year. Thus, Dumuzi is temporarily liberated. Relieved, he returns to the Upperworld and the blessings of the union with Inanna.

Upon his return, there is much left to reconcile. In order for Dumuzi to re-enter the sacred marriage bed, the betrayal must be healed. With this, the cycle of the Tree of Life is now complete. Both Inanna and her "honey man" have faced their shadow selves. Returning to the Upper Realms, they have added the knowledge of darkness and death to the knowledge of life and love. Inanna has made a shining throne and a sacred marriage bed from the huluppu tree. As Queen of Heaven, Earth, and the Underworld, she can now rule over the entire fertility cycle of birth, death, and rebirth.

THE INANNA WOMAN

Inanna's journey represents the gaining of feminine wisdom and power, the surren-dering of the worldly self, the death of the ego, and a return to innocence and purity. The Inanna woman embraces the primordial abyss and emerges reborn, wiser, and unafraid. She stands tall in the power of the conscious feminine.

Inanna women are faced with immeasurable grief and loss due to a life trauma, which usually involves betrayal, loss of a loved one, or severe loss of health and mobility. Women in abusive marriages, those who have been molested as children, who have been raped and dishonored, invaded, judged, stripped bare, and cast aside have all sadly done time in the Underworld. Like Inanna, they have lived in isolation, without comfort, and have been thoroughly disempowered. If they have tried to confront their perpetrators, they have likely been subjected to denial and witnessed a Dumuzi-like attitude. When others are unconcerned for our pain, it cuts deep. If they have pressed charges and involved themselves in the legal system, they have likely been re-victimized, judged harshly for their part in the trauma, and been wholly disenchanted. They have thus been delivered to the despair of the Underworld. It could be that they roam there abandoned and in excruciating pain for years. Who can soothe these troubled hearts?

In real life, some act of grace, some new wisdom, someone who can vali-date the Inanna woman's experience arrives, and she is able to crawl out of her desperation. After such a descent, she rebuilds and regains her power one stage at a time, ascending back through the gateways rung by rung. They have to rebuild their self-esteem and confidence, reconstruct their careers, rekindle friend-ships and family relationships, and reacquaint themselves with the workings of the Upperworld. The deeper the descent, the less meaning past successes have.

Again, this powerful story parallels a collective desperation. Ereshkigal wants Inanna to feel what it is like to be immobilized, rejected, and incapable of rela-tionship. At the depth of depression, disorientation, and loss, many of us have experienced the utter insensitivity of a "dark sister" who "kills us" by withdrawing friendship because they judge us and think we are "too angry." There may be the slow erosion of our support system when others feel uncomfortable with the depth of our despair and can no longer tolerate seeing us in pain. These dark sisters abruptly "kill" us by telling us it is time we "got over it," and turning away in disgust. When a woman is abandoned, the intensity of her suffering and her loss is devastating, and it multiplies with the realization that, as she festers in the Underworld, life in the Upperworld continues without her.

Inanna embodies the notion that the seeker of truth must search farther and deeper. Having command of the Upperworld requires the psychological growth that is offered by descending into the Underworld to face the shadow self. These are the trials and travails of Inanna's initiation.

THE ANGEL OF DESCENT

The Angel of Descent moves us to a deeper, more eternal soul-place. It invites us to grasp, interpret, and thus appreciate the meaning of all things, including our purpose for incarnating on the earth.

Everyone has a curiosity about the nature of our mission here on earth. Some are content to distract themselves with third-dimensional reality while others are stumped by the mysteries of life.

> The birthplace of true understanding is right within our consciousness. As that dynamic energy begins to work in our minds, we first develop an intellectual understanding of our divine constitution, and as it seeps into our emotional nature, a sense of knowing is registered subjectively. We are beginning to realized the Truth of our nature, but realization is by degrees and it is not until we have elevated understanding to its highest spiritual level that we move into Knowingness—where *we know, and we know that we know.*"[34] [emphasis mine]

The energy of the Angel of Descent invites us to be conscious of the spiritual principle of Selfhood—the Truth that the Spirit of God is expressing as individuality, the divine Self, which in turn expresses through the personality on the lower plane.[35] When we know who we are, a gentleness and a harmlessness is born within us.

Aphrodite

Entwined Lovers

Aphrodite

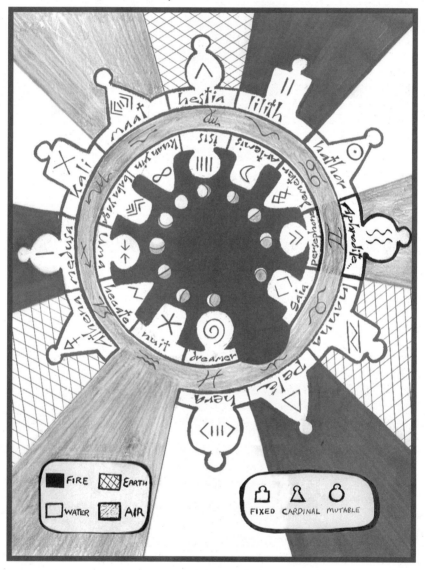

Sun in Gemini
Mutable-Air

Chapter X

Aphrodite

Aphrodite is the archetypal Beauty who is known as the Goddess of Love. She connects us back to the sexual passions and charm of the magnetic feminine. Aphrodite governs the soul qualities of love, beauty, and sensuality. She impels women to fulfill both "creative and procreative functions."[1] Aphrodite helps to learn about ourselves through romantic involvement with others. Aphrodite represents the faculty to discriminate between human love and divine love. She introduces us to the Realm of Roles.

Aphrodite is associated with the number six. Six, in Latin, means sex, and *sexen*, in Egyptian, meant to embrace or copulate.[2] The origin of the number "666" originally was a sexual charm sacred to the *triple goddess* Aphrodite.[3] The term "triple goddess" refers to the three states that can be contained within the feminine: the virgin, the mother, and the crone. Later, when sexuality and the honoring of the goddess were denigrated by church fathers, 666 became a symbol of evil and of the devil. Also, the number six was symbolic of initiation in Europe and the Orient.

As Tarot Lovers, the Aphrodite archetype has mastered sensual and sexual mysticism. Through divine love and an open-hearted state, initiates were able to touch Spirit. Man was able to touch the reality of life and achieve the power to deal with it through a physical union with the feminine.[4]

> It was a general rule in the East that shamans, priests, sages, and other holy men required a spiritual/sexual marriage before they could come into full possession of their powers.[5]

Represented by the Sun in Gemini, we see that Aphrodite personifies the twins within. Anchored in a mutable air sign, the Aphrodite archetype is adaptable. She will be able to keep alert to the many possibilities that are presented to her. What will ultimately be important is the integration of the experiences she so avidly seeks. This merging motivates a dissolution of ego boundaries and opens us to the experience of ecstasy. The Aphrodite archetype is eloquent, sensitive, and talkative. She loves to socialize. Although she loves to be in love, she tries to avoid deep emotions. She is optimistic and flexible and she is a good communicator. She can be vague and irresponsible and needs constant change. Her restlessness can cause her to vacillate. She will be either impartial and self-reliant or arrogant and domineering.

MYTHOLOGY

According to Homer, Aphrodite was the daughter of Zeus and Dione, the sea nymph. Hesiod tells a violent story of her origins. He suggests that Cronos cut off the genitals of his father Uranus and threw them into the sea. Aphrodite was thus conceived in the sea foam, and was born in a seashell as a full-grown adult. She achieved the status of *Queen of the Sea* who ruled by the "natural law of the maternal clan."[7] It is significant that Aphrodite was raised both motherless and fatherless. Denied a natural childhood with adequate and healthy role models, she emerged seeking completion in relational bonding.

Aphrodite was the goddess of the "oldest continuously occupied temple of the world" and was referred to as "the ancestral mother of the Romans."[8] Her connection to sensuality and sexual mysticism precipitated the Christian belief that all descendants from the island of Cyprus, where Aphrodite's temple flourished, were demon-infested.[9] During the Christian era, this temple was rededicated to the Virgin Mary, and many still see the Goddesses as related in purity, peace, and femininity.

Bolen refers to Aphrodite as the alchemical goddess who governs a woman's enjoyment of love and beauty, sexuality and sensuality, and who impels women to fulfill both "creative and procreative functions."[10] According to Bolen, she was associated with: "doves, those billing and cooing lovebirds, and swans, noted for their beauty and pairing; with flowers, especially roses, traditionally the gift of lovers; with sweet fragrance of fruits, especially golden apples and sensual, passion-red pomegranates (a symbol shared with Persephone)."[11]

Aphrodite is associated with the power of sexual surrender that is equivalent to giving oneself wholly to the goddess. In so doing, we face the unknown. When two lovers come together in mutual respect and reverence for the sacred energy of divine love, they touch the true loving nature of the universe. Man was able to touch the reality of life and achieve the power to deal with it through a physical union with the feminine.[12] Thus there was a step toward individual awareness through an involvement of the heart.[13]

> In its origin, all love is divine, but in passing through the lens of man's mind it is apparently broken into many colors. Yet, like the ray of white light, it ever remains pure.[14]

Aphrodite also represents an internal marriage, the unity of contra sexual aspects. On a psychological level, the indivisible self simultaneously contains anima and animus. According to Carl Jung, anima is the feminine side contained in the male. Animus is the masculine side of the female. The sacred marriage of the initiation mysteries refers to the union of opposites, the internal marriage of the archetypal masculine and the archetypal feminine within.

Aphrodite represents self-knowledge and multidimensional learning. Aphrodite's influence is compelling and irresistible, and the connection is both psychological and spiritual. When Aphrodite focuses her attention, the impact is dramatic and enamoring.

> Whenever growth is generated, a vision supported, potential developed, a spark of creativity encouraged ... then Aphrodite is there, affecting both people involved.[15]

On a psychological level, this union involved a balance of contra sexual aspects. In Truth, the Self is indivisible, simultaneously containing anima, or feminine qualities, and animus, or masculine qualities. Until we give validation to the masculine, active aspect of ourselves, our internal masculine remains unconscious. We run the risk of projecting these characteristics onto a man. We know that opposites magnetically bond together, and we seek wholeness in a relationship, instead of within ourselves. When our internalized masculine comes out of the shadow, we can have relationships that are grounded in reality rather than immersed in projection.

Eros, or love, was defined by Plato as *"the desire and pursuit of the whole."*[16] Thus the anima and animus, or feminine and masculine natures, strive to form a unified whole within the integrity the individual. It must be understood that the pursuit of completion in a relationship can lead to an imbalance within the self.

This understanding led her to educate and inspire others. Legend has it that Aphrodite, in her wisdom, set Psyche to four labors that, through the rich symbolic content, transformed her.[17] In the first she was asked to sort an enormous pile of seeds. This is symbolic of the endless values and bits of pertinent information we sort each day. Overwhelmed, Psyche allowed herself to be guided by her higher self. As she sorted, she asked for guidance in the hugeness of her task and worked until she fell asleep. Birds, symbolic of the connection to the divine, came and assisted in the sorting of the seeds. Upon awakening, Psyche was pleased to find the seeds sorted into appropriate piles. This provides a lesson in trust and illustrates what can brew and be sorted through in dreamtime.

Psyche's second task was to retrieve golden fleece from horned sheep that roamed the meadows. This is symbolic of all forms of retrieval of self. Where is the "gold"? How can we integrate the valuable lessons as we roam through the treacherous domain of the psyche? Psyche positioned herself in the meadow. Each time she attempted to grasp some fleece from a horned beast, they would startle, attack, or run. Frustrated, Psyche waited beyond the meadow. As dusk fell, she realized that the sheep would fall asleep. She determined that she could collect fleece from the branches where the sheep had rubbed. The lesson here is that retrieval of lessons is often indirect and requires a certain degree of cleverness.

Psyche's third task was to fill a crystal flask at a cascading stream guarded by dragons close to the mouth of the Underworld. Psyche perches herself close to the cliff. Just when Psyche ascertains that the task of filling the flask is impossible, an eagle flies by, scrutinizing her circumstance. This is symbolic of the importance of the Aphrodite woman assessing her relationships, so she can see them for what they are.

The fourth labor Aphrodite set upon Psyche was to take a box to Queen Persephone in the Underworld, the domain of the collective shadow. This box contained the secrets to understanding beauty. Both Persephone and Aphrodite commanded copious amounts of this treasured quality. In her descent to the Underworld, Psyche confronted her own shadow, the aspects of herself she had hidden from consciousness. Upon the integration of these unfamiliar fragments, Psyche developed an understanding of the secrets of internal beauty.

The challenge of this task was further complicated by the imperative that she was not to save the drowning man she would meet along the way. The warning was an important message to all women in modern culture. Because we have been raised as nurturers and sometimes get caught being rescuers, this task is psychologically challenging. Taking a deeper look, we have the opportunity to examine how we sidetrack our own growth because of the emotional difficulties of the men we are enamored with. We decide not to take care of our own development because of co-dependent relationships. A common psychological hook for women is the "need to be needed." We question ourselves, the depth and quality of our love, if we consider leaving a man in his pain. After a fight, we attempt to repair the damage by apologizing. We have come to think that it is our *responsibility* to save the drowning man. This is a powerful archetypal lesson going against the grain of our socialization as women.

Aphrodite's concern is the thrill of passionately relating to her man, not with the social responsibilities implicit in being a wife and mother. Aphrodite was a woman who *belonged to herself*. She was accountable only to the goddess and the "ecstatic Dionysian darkness within."[18]

> She did not submit herself to any man but sovereignty bestowed upon the supplicant the renewing power of divinity through sexual union.[19]

THE APHRODITE WOMAN

An Aphrodite woman thrives on men's adoration and devotion. She will never be long between relationships, even though she will perceive it as an unbearably long time since she had a passionate affair. To the Hestia woman committed to single life, the Aphrodite woman appears to be always searching for, waiting for, or getting over a relationship.

An Aphrodite woman sees having men fall in love with her as something of a contest. She seeks approval and she longs to be found attractive, but she will not put away her love potions until her prey is hopelessly hooked on her. A man in love with her is the prize, even if the consequence becomes his unwanted persistence. Being essentially kind-hearted, she often feels obligated to the man she has manipulated into loving her.

The Aphrodite woman is usually physically beautiful. She is often athletic, will be in her glory working out at the gym, and will inevitably be a good dancer. Because she is centered and deeply sensuous, her movements will be natural, free, and magnetic. Her beauty is more than skin deep. She is often well developed spiritually, beautiful from within, with undeniable charm and grace. Men watch her and easily fall in love in love with her image. They are not in love with her, but have projected their internalized idealized feminine, or anima, onto her.

Culture does not encourage men to embrace their *animas*, or the receptive, emotional, nurturing side of their natures. It becomes a delicate synthesis for men to gain more awareness of the feminine, because they usually feel this may threaten their masculinity. As a consequence, many men seek to connect with Aphrodite women to touch the subtle feminine within themselves. It is important not to allow this to become emotional co-dependency.

Because of their success with men, Aphrodite women inadvertently neglect their relationships with women. Invariably, women envy her, which makes it difficult to develop camaraderie with them. This isolates her from feminine company and the comfort that comes from being understood by women. Her relationships with women become secondary, and when she needs the support of women, she often finds it sadly lacking.

The modern Aphrodite is confident in her beauty. She is well versed in the charms of love, has known great passion, and loves the delirious ecstasy of giving oneself over to the magnetism of a lover. Yet this can turn out to be a curse. Media image tells us that beautiful women get the *crème de la crème* of life. The Aphrodite woman will assert that this role can sometime turn out to be a burden.

The Aphrodite woman, left to her own devices, will leave herself little time for reflection. Deeply internal Baba Yaga is the Self she fears. The rugged, practical protests of Baba Yaga are precisely what Aphrodite needs to appease her preoccupation with finding love.

If Hestia and Baba Yaga invited Aphrodite to a pajama party, Aphrodite might appear quite flat and uninterested in the conversation that amuses Hestia and Baba Yaga. Oracles divining future loves will enliven Aphrodite and keep her awake until the wee hours. The next morning, when Aphrodite dresses to rendezvous with her prospective lover, she will ask the others if she looks alluring. Hestia and Baba Yaga would not attempt to impress a man. They are far too independent. Hestia will go write, and Baba Yaga will crawl under her rock and return to her deeply internal state.

Not surprisingly, since approval and continued affection are her primary goals, the Aphrodite woman is apt to stay in touch with lovers from the past. She may be married yet have secret affections that endure for decades. Unrequited love is Aphrodite's specialty. In her own heart of hearts, the Aphrodite woman savors the embellished remnants of past loves in her rare reflective moments. When she is "between men," she romanticizes about past amours and rationalizes an occasional call across the continent to rekindle a flame.

If all this preoccupation with loving relationships is not enough, the Aphrodite woman will usually project on a male movie star or two. She will go to any movie he is in. She will read everything she can find about him, notably in the magazines that promote her insatiable appetite for the beautiful. The star is romanced in her daydreams as she pins her fantasies to this image of her ideal man. When he comes to her in dreamtime, he has officially attained a prominent place in her psyche.

When the Aphrodite woman is in balance, she can withdraw her projections, be less focused on external approval, and integrate the masculine aspect of herself. When she is whole, she can cherish the magnificent master-being that Aphrodite represents. Then divine love is made manifest and the primary relationship is with Spirit.

THE ANGEL OF LOVE

The Angel of Love is the first angel in the Realm of Roles. In this realm, we are infused with the spiritual qualities of love, focus, peace, sagacity, and magnetic resonance. Thus fortified, we can embrace the challenge of the Realm of Renunciation that ultimately prepares us for the Realm of Cosmic Consciousness.

The Angel of Love brings lessons through relationship. In our primary relationships with lovers, the depth of our psyche is processed. Family patterns are acted out. Conflicts are resolved or they come to a stalemate.

The Angel of Love brings us new partners to reveal the next stage of development. If we have not fully integrated past lessons, we repeat the old patterns. As we clear our Karma, the Angel of Love may give us back to ourselves, so we can strengthen in self-love before we venture into our next healing context.

The first relationship to focus on is that with the Self, for we cannot totally love another if we do not love ourselves at the core. Jesus taught us to love the Self with heart, soul, mind, and all of our might. We are instructed to love, adore, and cherish the magnificent master-beings that we are. We then establish a solid sense of esteem, and a friendly approval of ourselves.

Rest assured, the Angel of Love is a tough taskmaster who brings the pain of love along with the joys.

Medusa

Warrior Women

Medusa

Sun in Sagittarius
Mutable–Fire

Chapter XI

ℕedusa

7

ℕedusa is the archetypal Amazon Woman. She was a beautiful African Queen and an elegant priestess. She is sometimes depicted with graceful golden wings.[1] Her association with snakes signifies feminine divine wisdom dating back to the Minoan Snake Goddess in Crete in the sixteenth century BC and to the *uraeus*, or cobra, of the ancient Egyptian goddess cults.[2] The name Medusa actually means *rulerless*.[3] Amazon tribes were solid, self-assured, spiritual warriors who fiercely defended values of freedom and independence for all. At one time, Amazon tribes existed on every continent.[4] These tribes, or clans, were comprised of women and children who were conceived at yearly mating rituals. They were masters of healing arts and of training horses. Freedom was the highest value for the Amazons who instinctually knew it was their privilege to be as free as the birds, the trees, and the flowers.[5]

Medusa is associated with the number seven. Though restless in its nature, seven represents good luck, focus, and mastery. Seven is a mystical number of completion and accomplishment. There are seven notes in a scale. In the Hindu system, there were seven chakras, or energy centers, in the body.* The number seven also rules the planet Saturn that teaches patience and restraint.[6]

Associated with Tarot Chariot, the Amazon archetype is the drive to reach our destiny. Sensitive yet outwardly dynamic and assertive, she is directed by her own inner ambition.[7] A release of energy allows us to transcend human limitations. This is the archetype of the *heroine* who carries an impulse toward higher consciousness, conquering inertia and displaying courage, strength and awareness.

---

* It has generally accepted that there are seven vortexes of energy, or chakras, in the body. As we evolve, an eighth chakra is being recognized. It is called the *thymus* located between the heart and the throat. This is a psychic center which has 4 concentric rings around it, filtering electrostatic energy and converting it to electromagnetic energy. There are also 4 chakras outside the body that connect us to the moon, the sun, the galaxy, and the Universe.

Medusa's energy is anchored in the Sun in Sagittarius. A mutable fire sign, the archetype functions through the intellect, is strongly principled, and adapts readily to change. Her enthusiasm is high and her fervor is intense. She is honest and tolerant, yet can come across as blunt and impatient. She cheerful and optimistic yet hates to be fenced in and restricted.

MYTHOLOGY

When Aryan tribes were encroaching on matriarchal cultural boundaries, the Amazon warriors protected their rights and fought for their survival. Medusa was a wise woman and a High Priestess who mentored the maiden Athena while she lived among the Amazons. Their stories are closely linked, and together with Athena's mother Metis, they form a virgin-mother-crone triplicity.

Patriarchal mythology later claimed Athena had been born from Zeus' head in full armor. This was a crowning glory for the patriarchy, for if a woman could be born from a man's body, it would pacify the male's *procreation envy*. (To those who rewrote history, it was simply incidental that Athena was a fully mature woman and that she had already trained as an Amazon priestess.) The legend went on to elaborate on how fierce Athena was as a warrior, and how she led the persecution of the last of the Amazons, notably the Gorgons and Medusa herself, and what a victory that was for all to behold. The connection between Medusa and Athena is well represented in Whitmont's work:

> Mcdium and Amazon can be seen as personalizations of Medusa and Pallas (Athena) respectively, the abysmal strife and civilization-generating, transformative aspect of the Feminine.[8]

Medusa and the Gorgons wore masks during interactions with outsiders. This reputedly masked their beauty, and they were, as a consequence, seen as fierce and frightening. The Medusa archetype is representative of the animus, the aggressive, active, focused, masculinized aspects of the feminine. A Medusa woman is a career woman and can function aggressively in the marketplace. She is steadfast, focused, energetic, aggressive, bold, and determined. She may be beautiful, especially because she is usually fit and her energy is moving, but her femininity is underground so she is seen as defeminized. She may be domineering, tyrannical, authoritarian, or just plain impenetrable. When she goes to bat on an issue, she is often right, but her surge of aggression is often so unbalanced, she creates enemies.

> Medusa is the abyss of transformation, the seemingly chaotic riddle that woman is to herself and to the puzzled man she leads to the dread of unpredictability and seeming emptiness and depression and annihilation. Hers is the way of medium priestess or healer, the inspired artist, or an erratic, hysterical devouring borderline personality. A *femme fatale,* and *belle dame sans merci* or witch. At her best, she connects with the abyss, she challenges and inspires. Hers is a realm to which every woman and anima must descend for renewal, like Inanna to Ereshkigal.[9]

Medusa is typically depicted with a grotesque face and with snakes in her hair. She is known to have turned men to stone which she accomplished through the use of magic spells. She gained her reputation from the fierceness of her actions yet needs not be feared.

THE MEDUSA WOMAN

The Medusa woman is focused. She has the impetus to complete a major project. She has stamina, fortitude, and motivation. In this state, an Medusa woman looms larger than life.

She is often muscular and large in stature. She has a large energy field. When she walks in a room, she is a force to contend with. She is direct, self-assured, and present. Like Pele and Kali, her energy is powerful and strong.

Her goal is to achieve greater control over unconscious processes and not to lose her focus. The Medusa woman has analyzed her relationships. She knows when she is being invited to give her power away. She stands firm and fiercely defends her own honor and her personal space. She is not prone to be solicitous.

The Medusa woman is adventurous. She is philosophically oriented and can make a devoted teacher. She is expansive, and she will always search for wisdom and an understanding of the greater whole. She maintains a personal code of ethics based on humanitarian principles and the empowerment of the feminine. Her beliefs and convictions are unshakable.

THE ANGEL OF FOCUS

The Angel of Focus illuminates the achievement of our goals and offers us assistance in overcoming obstacles. This Angel gives us the initiative to persist, fortitude when we falter, and the determination to complete our endeavors.

In dealing with this Angel, it is important to know what we want. The closer we are to accurately defining our purpose, the closer we are to staying motivated and task-oriented. The more attuned we are to our Higher selves, the more we will receive instructions and guidance pertaining to our ultimate purpose in this incarnation.

> You will not need to fight in this battle; take your position, stand still, and see the victory of the Lord on your behalf.[10]

"Stand still" refers to the state of serenity and trust that allows us to surrender to the Presence within and to have faith in the activity of the Spirit.[11] It also means that when we are attuned to our higher purpose, we enter a *being state* that facilitates a state of effortlessness in our work. Instead of forcing ourselves to achieve, we are so perfectly suited to the activity that it no longer seems like work. This is divine grace in action that paves the way to immense productivity. It is this accomplishment that prepares for the energy of peace that the next Angel brings.

Kuan Yin

Temple at Sunrise

Kuan Yin

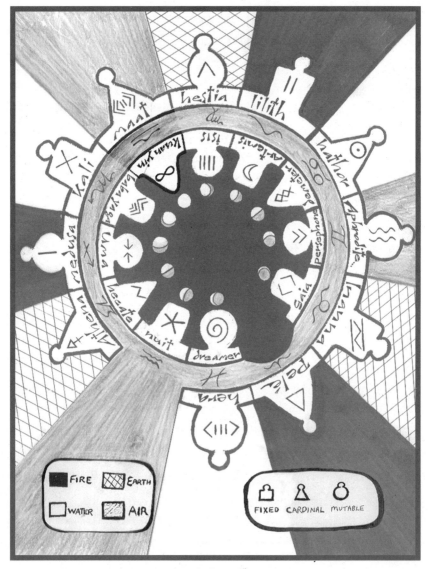

Moon in Libra
Cardinal–Water

Chapter XII

Kuan Yin

Kuan Yin, the Holy Mother of Compassion, is an eternal source of comfort and peace. Kuan Yin's roots are in Buddhism,[1] and she is the archetypal Meditator. For Kuan Yin, peace comes through stillness and in hearing the silent melody of the soul.

Kuan Yin is connected to the number eight, which naturally forms an infinity symbol depicting balance and harmony. Eight represents philosophic thought, spiritual devotion, and concentration of purpose.[2] It is the number of dynamic, ongoing adjustment and crystal clarity.

Kuan Yin is connected to the balance, order and form of Tarot Justice. Justice, by definition, is the administration of law. Our modern legal system is adversarial in nature, pitting one side against the other and winning by finding loopholes in the law. Criminals are routinely defended, and the law bends to those who use it. Truth does not necessarily come into question. Kuan Yin champions the principles of Universal Truth and has compassion for all who have been violated and wounded. She establishes order and harmony in a higher court.

Kuan Yin manifests the energy of the Moon in Libra, which champions cooperation, sharing, and partnership. A cardinal air sign, it is highly sensitive and aware. The search is for balance and harmony, and intuition is relied on.

MYTHOLOGY

Kuan Yin is an ascended master who was conceived as a savior having infinite life, whose task was to save sentient beings.[3] She was a principal teacher in Buddhism, and in some teachings, she was Buddha's consort. Kuan Yin is a *bodhisattva*, who has postponed full ascension until all sentient beings have achieved enlightenment. According to Diana Paul:

> It was at this level that this subset of bodhisattvas, often called "*celestial bodhisattvas*", became autonomous or semiautonomous deities who

were endowed with countless miraculous and psychic powers to help those in distress.[4]

Buddhism emphasizes meditation and moral virtue as a means of overcoming suffering in the material world.[5] In order to achieve levels of consciousness, "tremendous self-exertion was not required, but rather an act, usually requiring visualization or recitation, acknowledging the externalized powers of the object of faith."[6] Buddhism promotes the achievement of higher levels of consciousness. In the Buddhist tradition, desire is the root of all suffering. Meditation, balanced living, and moral conduct are said to release us from worldly pain. "First, the spirit cannot be liberated by torturing the body; for a person is not two things, a soul or a spirit trapped in a body, but a single organic whole of many dimensions."[7]

> ...Buddhists assumed that most beings die and are reborn innumerable times, sometimes in human form, other times in plant or animal forms, and sometimes as Gods and Goddesses.[8]

Meditation assists us in developing the *objective witness*, which allows us to see ourselves in a balanced, non-judgmental fashion. This is the beginning of the path of the initiate, who perceives through the dimensions of reality beyond the entrapments of the material world.

Meditation is a discipline. Its purpose is to quiet the mind from spontaneous and incessant inner chatter. Concentration on a word (or *mantra*), a geometric mandala (*yantra*), a physical position (*mudra*), or a sound (*bija*) offers a focus. The mind will naturally wander. Meditation is the art of repeatedly returning consciousness to the object of concentration. When we realize our focus has strayed, we simply return, return, return. With practice, the breathing slows, the brain waves change to alpha,* we experience deep relaxation, and we experience transcendence.

Kuan Yin asserts that the seed of enlightenment must be watered by the Self. No mentor or methodology can do the work on our behalf. The arduous task of becoming conscious is our challenge on the earth plane. Kuan Yin graces us with infinite compassion and assists us in coming to consciousness.

Countless spiritual leaders have requested the participation of individuals to join group meditations visualizing world peace. This tradition continues and

---

* Alpha is a state of brain-wave activity that is induced while falling asleep, when waking up, while under hypnosis, while in a trance, or while meditating.

meditators around the planet have to substantiate the tangibility of grace and harmony that is integrated by the participants of such an event.

THE KUAN YIN WOMAN

The Kuan Yin woman is easy and gracious, charming and diplomatic. She is contemplative and sweet, affectionate and good-natured. She has a feeling for humanity, and a concern for the welfare of all. She likes beautiful, peaceful, uncluttered surroundings. She knows how to be alone.

The Kuan Yin woman is a meditator. She practices mindfulness and concentration in both sitting meditations or moving meditations such as yoga and tai chi. Even though this discipline may take many years to achieve, the Kuan Yin woman pursues it with diligence and daily practice.

The Kuan Yin woman is compassionate. Tuned to the Underworld of emotions, the Kuan Yin woman is a blessing to a friend in need. Consider a woman coming to terms with childhood sexual abuse. A woman tuned to the Upperworld will approach her in a matter-of-fact fashion. They will urge her to stop wallowing in self-pity and get on with her life. They will question her. They will want her to be productive, to forgive and forget. On the other hand, the Kuan Yin woman will be finely tuned to the vast amount of emotional material that is stirring in her friend. Being highly intuitive, the Kuan Yin woman will understand the scope of the trauma. She will exude empathy. She will be able to embody Kuan Yin's radiant, compassionate heart. She will offer her friend the safety she needs and the comfort she deserves. She will give her as much time as she needs to heal.

This is a woman who rests deep within herself. She is mature, centered, and sincere. She is a hard worker and a generous soul. She enjoys harmony in her relationships. She is secure within herself.

THE ANGEL OF PEACE

The Angel of Peace regulates a perfect balance between polarities. She is poised and radiates a serenity and a tranquillity. Joy is the byproduct of this balance. The greater the joy, the greater the flow of energy.

> This is the perfect balance between head and heart, will and love, inner and outer, work and play, stillness and action, impression and expression, listening and speaking, receiving and giving, radiation and attraction.[9]

A Buddhist teaching was reflected in the idiom: "Neither this, nor that." We are in perfect balance on each continuum and live at neither end of the polarities. We are neither lazy nor active, neither messy nor neat, neither fat nor thin, neither smart nor dumb. This Angel of Peace is beyond judgment. She makes room for what is. She stands in full acceptance.

When this Angel is free to function, divine order reigns supreme in our lives. Thus when plans are unexpectedly changed, we can relax. We know that a problem is a disguised opportunity. We wait patiently for evidence of the perfection of the moment.

Ꜧꞓꞇꞟꜳ

The Hearth

Hestia

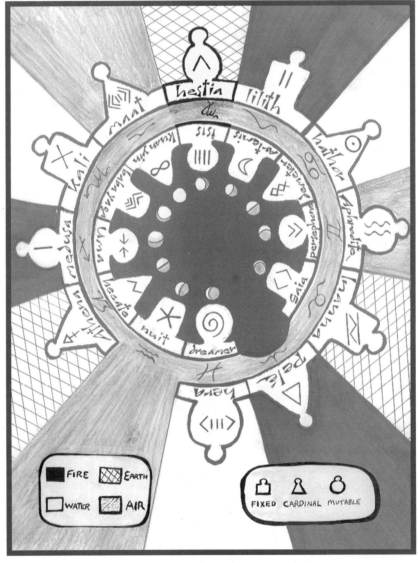

Sun in Virgo
Mutable-Earth

Chapter XIII

ῌhesτia

9

Ͱhestia is the archetypal Vestal Virgin, the goddess of the hearth and of the home. The Hestia woman is an internal woman who nurtures herself and exemplifies the joys of solitude. She represents the flame within, that is, the sacred flame of the essential self. The flame purifies and balances and ultimately leads to individuation.

Hestia is associated with the number nine, the master completion number. Cheiro states that those ruled by the number nine are "resourceful and excellent in organization, but they must have the fullest control."[1] Nine is the ultimate number of fulfillment. In ancient Egyptian mystery schools, there were nine levels of initiation. The Eleusinian Mysteries were nine days long. Gestation lasts nine months. Nine is mysterious numerologically in that any number multiplied by nine, when digitally added together, becomes nine (2 x 9 = 18; 1 + 8 = 9). It is thus the height of power attributed to a single digit.[2]

Hestia is complemented by the Tarot Hermit, the wise old sage who is the *way shower*. The Hermit shines the light of the Holy Spirit and returns the holy fire to its source.

> As the lighted lamp does not need another lamp to manifest its light, so the Soul, being Consciousness itself, does not need another instrument of consciousness to illumine Itself.[3]

The Tarot Hermit is a master of transmutation and refinement. The process takes place when the individual consciousness makes union with the higher self. It contains the insight of the mystic, the light that is not externally driven. It is the sacred flame that illumines from within and cannot be extinguished due to external influences. This is the light that dispels spiritual chaos.[4] The experience of being connected to one's own light is the essence of soulfulness. It brings an immense sense of meaningfulness to a human life.

Hestia is astrologically anchored in the Sun in Virgo. A mutable earth sign, Virgo is methodical and adaptable. The energy is modest, discriminating, conscientious, and meticulous, and enjoys routine. There is a high regard for beauty, health, and hygiene. There is determination and endurance.

MYTHOLOGY

Hestia was the eldest child of Rhea and Cronos. By birth-right, she was an original member of the twelve Olympian gods and goddesses. As first-born to Rhea and Cronos, Hestia was a first-generation Olympian and the maiden aunt to the second generation. Hestia was later replaced in the Olympian Pantheon by Dionysus as he grew in charm and popularity as the God of Wine.

Hestia was honored in the temples of all the other gods and goddesses. Her energy was made manifest in the flame that burned in the hearth within the temples. Hestia manifests the energy of pure devotion to spirit and the transmutation that occurs within from that focus. It is noteworthy that *focus* is the Latin word for hearth. As the hearth-flame, she was venerated by the Greeks.

In Homeric hymns, there are references to Aphrodite weaving seduction magic to cause Poseidon and Apollo to fall in love with Hestia. Hestia adamantly refused them both, pledging to her unshakable virginity. Hestia was a Vestal Virgin who lived a monastic life dedicated to the Great Mother Goddess. She and her fellow priestesses were unequivocally chaste and saw this resolve as an honoring of the Goddess. To lay with a man would desecrate the Goddess and break a solemn oath and was punishable by death.

Hestia is nonetheless likened to Hermes, not as a partner, but rather as a representative of the masculine energy in balance with feminine principles. As patron saint of travelers and thieves, Hermes was invoked by planting a pole or a tall stone, called a *herm*, in the yard of a home, just as Hestia's flame protected the home at the round hearth.

To honor Hestia, the ancient Greek matriarchs carried a torch to light their daughter's hearth the day she moved away from home to settle with her new mate. This symbolizes the mother's warmth and protection vitalizing the new home. The eternal flame originated at the temple of the Vestal Virgins, was protected as sacred for thousands of years and was only extinguished in the 16th century AD.

The passing of Hestia's sacred flame sanctified new homes and villages. It is the basis of the honored tradition of the Olympic torch relay that is central to modern Olympic Games. Brought from the original site of Olympia in ancient Greece, the flame is passed from one human hand to another. Upon its arrival at the Olympic site, the opening ceremonies are graced by the official lighting of the flame. The honoring of the eternal flame symbolizes the essential fire of the soul, and the commitment to excellence.

THE HESTIA WOMAN

The Hestia woman is grounded, centered, and wise. She delights in the meditative and the soulful activity of caring for a home. As she puts the house in order, she herself feels cleansed and balanced.

The Hestia woman leads a monastic, introverted life. She could live in the far north in the tundra. She could be a lighthouse guardian or a forest ranger. She could be widowed or divorced, and spends years living in her own company.

A Hestia woman does not necessarily maintain separateness from the outside world. She has achieved a sense of inner security and, like the Hermit, seeks her own counsel. She is soothed by her internal process and does not fall prey to the unconsciousness in the commercial world.

When the world presses in, the Hestia woman knows she can make a cup of tea, have a bubble bath, and snuggle up with the cat and a book. When friends are out and gregarious, the Hestia woman is content deep inside her soul. If the Hestia woman is married with a family, she will incorporate time alone into her life or it will be her undoing.

The Hestia archetype is also often scholarly and well-read. She endures in the domain of self-study and may be a perpetual academic enjoying the scholastic life. She will have her own way of nurturing herself, whether that be through creativity, dance, music, or meditation. These activities will be her respite, her replenishment.

The Hestia woman cultivates her own rituals and reflective practices. She builds an altar of precious objects, sacred symbols, candles, crystals, and aromas. These are archetypal symbols of her internal process. She consults runes, cards, and oracles. She cultivates an inherent strength and an intuitive fortitude. Her active inner life radiates out to touch others.

Guided by the Angel of Discernment, the Hestia woman spends time processing and contemplating elements of her life. She carves out precious routines for herself that she holds as sacred. She sorts through and discerns what needs to be recycled, what needs to be enlivened, what needs to be cleansed or repaired, and what needs to be enjoyed more.

In the lucid moments of contemplation, she resolves issues and regroups. She illumines her intentions and plans for the future. In this way, when she re-enters the work-a-day world, she is clear, decisive, and self-assured. She knows her internal timing is essential to her well-being. The Hestia woman is in her glory luxuriating in self-care and in the care of her environment.

The essence of the Hestia archetype is a woman without a relationship, and as an archetypal Vestal Virgin, she is not waiting for a man. Hestia is unlike her sisters Hera and Aphrodite, who would consider themselves to be between relationships were they without a man.

THE ANGEL OF DISCERNMENT

The Angel of Discernment[5] is a wise sage who visits periodically to help us assess our lives. When this Angel appears, we are encouraged to sort through our values, attitudes, friendships, and possessions. The Angel of Discernment carries a keen, farsighted judgment. This Angel evaluates with ruthless scrutiny that which is soulful and that which is soulless in our lives. This instills high perception and deep discrimination to keep us clear and on track. In each decision we make, the Angel of Discernment can assist us to ascertain whether our motivation contributes to the highest good for ourselves and for all concerned.

It is in the inner sanctuary of the sacred feminine that we individuate and learn to express our essential selves. We reckon with ourselves not because of external approval, not because of a reward that will follow, but because of the developmental step that individuation entails.

> The art of individuation, of becoming one's unique self, is (as the name implies) an intensely personal experience and, at times, a lonely one. This is not a group phenomenon. *It involves the difficult task of disentangling one's own identity from the mass of mankind.* To discover who we are, we must ultimately withdraw those parts of ourselves which we have unwittingly projected onto others, learning to find deep within our own psyches the potentials and shortcomings which we had formerly seen only in others. Such recognition is facilitated if we can withdraw from society for brief periods and learn to welcome solitude.[6] [emphasis mine]

In the tranquillity of this inner sanctuary we see our true selves. Guided by the Angel of Discernment, we consciously own our projections, take stock, and feel the eternal flame burn within us.

Athena

The Parthenon

Athena

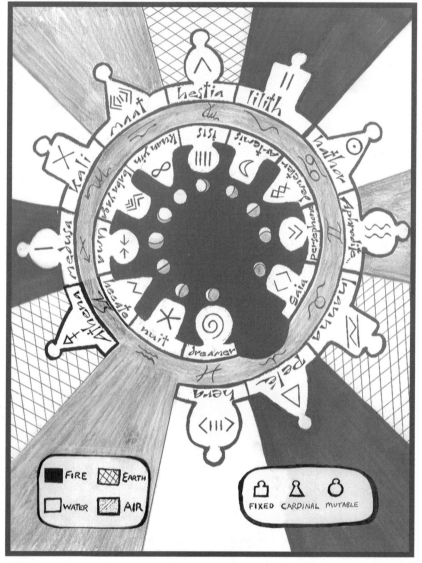

Sun in Capricorn
Cardinal–Earth

Chapter XIV

Athena

Athena represents virtue, firmness, strength, and intellect. She yearns to know the unrevealed spirit. Athena is known in modern history as the Goddess of War. Her purity and true character have been distorted, and she has become the archetypal Animus-Driven Woman.

Athena is number ten in our journey, and in this manifestation, the self (1) is no longer alone: she now has a vehicle (0) to propel her on her path. An expression of ten, Athena will be a leader and a forceful figure, yet she runs the danger of being more concerned with her ego than with her soul.

An embodiment of the Tarot Wheel of Fortune, Athena grasps the idea of the Great Round, the cyclical nature of life, and the essence of fate. The wheel is an energy system whose essence is in motion.

> With the revolution of the Tarot Wheel and the impact of its number ten, the hero, too, experiences a similar psychic revolution. For the first time, (the) ego, disengaging itself from the circular prison of endless trivia, stands aside to observe the pattern of [her] life as a whole—to view the unique mandala of [her] individual being against the infinitely expanding circle of the cosmos. [S]he begins now to discover in the jumbled chaotic events of [her] life a consistent thread of dramatic patterns. [S]he begins to experience [her] personal fate as a kind of myth, and to connect [her] individual myth with those of the archetypal gods and heroes whose stories are immortalized for all time in legend, and whose names are forever emblazoned in the constellations in the sky.[1]

The Athena archetype is rooted in the Sun in Capricorn. A cardinal earth sign, it features the natural leader and is grounded in practicality and material sensibility. The Athena archetype is ambitious, serious, and dedicated to duty. She is responsible, self-disciplined, and has a strong purpose and direction. She is willing to work hard for what she wants, and owing to this attitude that perseveres, she is usually triumphant. She will also prove to be a steadfast friend.

MYTHOLOGY

The mythology of Athena reads like a modern espionage novel of intrigue, deception, and betrayal. Athena is said to have been birthed from her father Zeus' body. This was the crowning glory of the patriarchal forefathers, a symbolic victory that alluded to the superfluousness of women in society. It was considered incidental that Athena was full grown when she was born out of Zeus' head. Older legends have it that she was born to Metis, one of the very Amazon priestesses her father sought to eradicate. Being born of the father and participating in the murder of Medusa, the mother figure, is at the root of the Athena archetype.

Athena becomes the father's daughter. In her over-identification with him, she seeks to emulate him and thus becomes masculinized herself. She manifests in modern culture as the professional woman who has learned to think like a man so she can compete with men in the patriarchal arena. We can see clearly that the Wheel of Fortune is an ideal projection holder that allows us to act out the dynamic roles the Athena archetype contains.[2]

> Athene, in a sense, represents just this: the repression of the feminine and the undoing of the repression as a soul task. Really to understand Athene demands a courageous examination of our own participation in misogynous self-denial. To recover the Athene who is mothered by Metis and not only fathered by Zeus is to recover ourselves. We need to begin by recognizing that Athene's separation from her mother is not hers alone, and that we delude ourselves about ourselves if we self-righteously condemn her for it.[3]

Athena is a virgin goddess, not a goddess of procreation like Hera and Demeter, but of creation. At a psychological level, this may resonate from the original wound between her mother and her father. After all, her mother Metis was swallowed by Zeus when she was pregnant with Athena. Symbolically, for a woman to be swallowed by her husband is an explicit enough metaphor. This represents the many mothers and grandmothers that have been overpowered and silenced by their husbands. Athena's mother offered much that profoundly affected Athena, even if she could not acknowledge it.

> Metis represents, and bequeaths to her daughter, a "watery" wisdom—intuitive, attuned to subtleties and transformations, sensitive to nuances of personal feeling, poetic rather than abstract, receptive rather than commanding.[4]

From another perspective, by being born again from the head of Zeus, Athena is metaphorically being released from being contained by the masculine. It is her task to reclaim her true self, her feminine soul. Athena is a reminder of how much easier it is to forgive our fathers and to judge our mothers, another example of how Athena pays homage to the masculine at the expense of the feminine.

In Jungian terms, when Hera and Athena are caught in the grip of the ego, Hera is *anima* possessed while Athena is *animus* possessed. In other words, Hera errs by being excessively focused on her feminine attributes, while Athena is overly focused on her masculine traits.

Women are collectively becoming wise to themselves on this issue. Culturally, women are beginning to honor the feminine in themselves and are learning to value vulnerability. The patterns are emerging and are being brought into consciousness. Women are understanding how easily they have, in the past, given their power to their fathers and to the masculine.

It is in the shadow of this archetype that we can contemplate the exchange of power, and, as Downing describes, the *latently incestuous element* in the attachment to the father.[5] In Downing's words:

> (Athena) defends against Zeus's potentially overwhelming masculine power by assimilating it in her own being, by being *so like him that in many ways she becomes the female Zeus.*[6] [emphasis mine]

This identification with the aggressor is exemplified in the situation between Persephone and Hades as well, but in marrying him, Persephone is embracing a creative relation to the dark. She *joins* him, but in contrast, Athena *becomes* him. In order for her to be released and whole within herself, the Athena woman must come to terms with her relationship to the father. She must release him, and, that is not to say, hope to change him. She must leave him to his own opinions and values, and see how they are well suited to him. Then she must release herself and honor her individual differences, her femininity, and her own personal process within a culture that has systemically devalued and disadvantaged her.

In considering the shadow of the Athena archetype, we must understand the hidden truths embedded in the myth. As difficult as this may appear, the interpretation of myths often requires a reclamation of what has been projected. Athena has been presented as an agent of Zeus, dependent on him as the source of her power and prowess in the public arenas of her life. Yet the power of her father over her is really Athena's fantasy. She has colluded with him by attributing to him aspects of herself that are really her own. Even if this realization is met with powerful resistance, it is crucial to the reclamation of a lost part of her essential self.

Ironically, Athena is the goddess who has enjoyed the highest profile in Western culture. It is common knowledge that the Acropolis is an ancient temple to Athena, yet she was represented as the Goddess of War. This has supported the false assumption that the feminine that procreates life also endorses war. This is a patriarchal invention that has flourished since the goddess tradition was eradicated.

The Greek pantheon of gods and goddess can be seen as a template for the psychology of modern culture. Athena has been the patron saint of war; as a patriarchal goddess, she legitimized its inevitability in a culture that sanctions power *over* another. Perhaps Athena was catapulted to the status as goddess of war to normalize the institution of war that still plagues the planet. Many people believe that there has been war since the beginning of time. In actuality, there has been war since the beginning of the recorded history of the patriarchs who endeavored to eradicate all physical evidence of goddess worship and of peaceable cultures. There is a saying, *"History began when the soldiers came."*

THE ATHENA WOMAN

The Athena woman is the perfectionistic patriarchal daughter. She, like her father, is the master of controlled emotions. She is strategic, intelligent, strong, and self-confident. Because she is task-oriented, she will drive herself to completion. This incessant activity is adequate distraction from self-examination and does not mirror Hestia's contemplation or Persephone's emotionality. She is rewarded by the patriarchs for her diligence while her more emotional sisters are judged as hysterical and unproductive.

> Pallas (Athena) creates and strives; she is ready to fight for her own needs and rights, for cultural achievement and human dignity and causes. For the sake of her convictions and needs she is willing to disregard relationships and destroy old patterns that have outlived their usefulness. She inspires the career and pioneer woman.[7]

The Athena woman may not have easy access to her inner world. She is exemplified in the woman lawyer who wears a business suit with a buttoned-up collar and a tie. David Givens is a researcher who studied primate courtship behavior and its relationship to human courtship behavior. He explains the custom of men wearing a knotted tie at their throat is a protection from vulnerability. He goes on to state how femininity is emphasized by the exposure of women's throats through an open collar or a low-cut bodice. This is well illustrated in advertising and in the media. In his thought-provoking and entertaining book *Love Signals: How to Attract a Mate,*[8] Givens examined human behavior in singles bars and compared them to the instinctual activities of gorillas. His conclusion is nothing short of fascinating.

Sexual attraction is governed by the oldest part of our brain, the brain stem, or the reptilian brain. Givens concludes that whom we are attracted to is therefore beyond our conscious control. Not only that, the four stages of establishing sexual attraction occur in a mere four seconds. It can be disconcerting to think that this type of instinctual decision-making can occur almost at a glance. If morality interferes because someone is already spoken for, this chemistry will never be acted on.

The big issue in the instinctual domain of both gorilla and human males, if contact is to be established, is for the female to be readable, to be non-threatening, and to give off the message that she will not refuse the male. Givens ascertains that by exposing her throat, a woman is showing her vulnerability. When a woman wears a buttoned collar and a tie, she is consciously or unconsciously covering her vulnerability and thereby expressing her sexual unavailabilty. This can also occur through weight gain, as women who have repeatedly lost and gained the same ten or twenty pounds will attest to. Not surprisingly, this tack in itself often does not ward off attention from men.

The Athena woman makes sure she is not prey for the opposite sex. She is loyal, independent, and achievement-oriented and takes pleasure in struggle and challenge. She finds that passionate relationships with men can be entanglements that distract her from her goals. If she is to befriend a man, she will join with him as "one of the boys." Athena women over-identify with men even on the friendship level.

If we examine the archetype of Athena at its depths, a paradox is uncovered. Athena represents a valuable dichotomy for women who are reclaiming themselves and their feminine nature. Traditionally, Athena has been somewhat scapegoated when she has been described as the defeminized woman. The implication has been that she has betrayed her femininity, the very essence of her being. Figures like Margaret Thatcher, often referred to as the "Iron Maiden," have spearheaded this very prototype. Both men and women alike can feel a certain discomfort when they watch such a woman in action. Athena offers a more complex image of the creative woman than the other archetypes, and the template of our sociocultural context and the consequent expectations for women are rooted in her mythology.

The nature of the father-daughter relationship is, of course, at the very pinnacle of understanding the depths of Athena. A major breakthrough occurs when the daughter realizes that the power the father has over her is the very power that she has *given* to him herself. The way is paved by the unconscious collective agreement in patriarchal culture that sees the daughter belonging to the father. The complex is initiated when the daughter, in turn, also feels herself to belong to him.[9] Consistent messages infiltrate from the collective unconscious that would have daughters try to emulate the wishes of the father or suffer greatly in their attempts to rebel against these imperatives. The very rebellion is proof of the power that the father holds in the psyche of the daughter.

For the patriarchal daughter, individuation requires a sincere examination of the values that dominate her. In order for the reclamation of self to occur, we must see how the father has fostered identification with him and the insidiousness of the cultural support for this. Until this can occur, the personal freedom of the Athena woman is in bondage. Major growth often occurs after this illumination.

THE ANGEL OF MAGNETIC RESONANCE

The Angel of Magnetic Resonance offers a cosmic tune-up to our physical bodies. As we continue to focus on our internal journey, we become aware of the many physical changes that accompany the spiritual, mental, and emotional growth we are undergoing.

We feel as though we are on a roller coaster ride. We experience energetic surges, then we are overly fatigued, napping for days on end. In truth, as our spiritual bodies tune in, our physical bodies are evolving, our DNA is mutating, and our emotional bodies are undergoing immense clearing. Whenever we enter into periods of seeming inactivity, we are gathering a force for a mighty leap. We are making an electromagnetic frequency adjustment. In other words, we are vibrating at a more refined or faster frequency. We pass through a dimensional gateway. This reveals a new cycle of experience and growth. It is none other than the Angel of Magnetic Resonance that shows us the width of our band of illumination.

120

Your divine consciousness, the Reality of you, has its own beat, vibration, and rhythm. By adjusting your mind and feeling nature to your own particular soul pulsation through meditating, listening, and living the spiritual life, you can rise above the hill-and-valley experiences. There will continue to be periods of intense activity followed by interludes of going within in order to assimilate the divine impressions, but you will soon move beyond the sense of duality with its highs and lows of health and sickness, abundance and lack, harmony and conflict, joy and sorrow.[10]

The Angel of Magnetic Resonance advises us to assist our physical bodies through cleansings, drinking copious amounts of purified water, and bathing in luxurious baths laced with oils, salts, and bubbles. At the same time this Angel cautions us against over-exposure to the electrostatic frequencies of electric lights, appliances, televisions, and microwaves. This Angel loves candlelight, fires, and quiet. Allow her to soothe you as you transform and become prepared for the next realm in the spiritual journey, the Realm of Renunciation.

Lillith

Restless Sea

Lillith

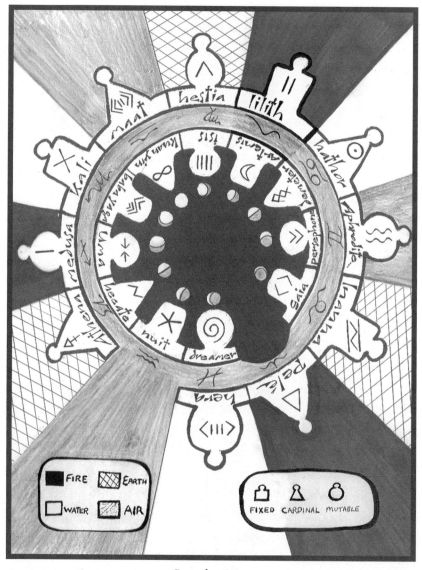

Sun in Leo
Fixed–Fire

Chapter XV

Lillith

Lillith is the archetypal Unshackled Woman who refuses to be controlled. Lillith passionately claims her personal power, stands firm on her convictions, and is driven by an internal motive. She was considered a Divine Lady in Sumerian texts.[1] She is also referred to as Handmaiden to the Goddess Inanna and is woven into her mythology and the story of the sacred *huluppu* tree, or the Tree of Life. She is a largely misunderstood archetype who has been called Poetess of Darkness, Imp of Impetuosity, and Occasional Serpent of Seduction. Lillith is the personification of the *restless sea*. She is deeply committed to her personal freedom and keeps her moral strength alive.

Being governed by the number eleven, a master number, suggests leadership through struggle, sacrifice, and even martyrdom.[2] The number also symbolizes an archetypal gateway through which Lillith passes as she claims her individuality and takes charge of her own Self. Numerologically, Lillith is connected to the sensitivity of Isis and the wisdom of the Priestess (since one plus one equals two, but also because Isis' glyph is 1111 and Lillith's is 11).

Symbolized by Tarot Strength, she turns to her instinctual nature and sacrifices ego strength for a different type of strength. Lillith is both fearless and untamed and she roams freely in the wild. In Tarot symbolism, she is seen taming a lion. In the Thoth deck, Aleister Crowley calls her *Lust*, indicating that the Lillith archetype is in full command of the female sex force.[3] She is an enchantress living in the undiluted multiplicity of the spiritual force. She has a mysterious power that is permanent, direct, and instinctual. We learn that "strength and experience are required in dealing with instinctual drives if one is not to be overwhelmed or carried away."[4]

Lillith's energy is anchored in the Sun in Leo. Fiery and fixed, her energy is deliberate and dramatic. She is unabashedly self-possessed. She functions from a place of personal dignity. Lillith has many qualities. She is generous, youthful, self-assured, and affectionate. She is emotionally exuberant and displays a dramatic approach to life. She is willing to express herself and is active in her endeavors. She is fond of children.

MYTHOLOGY

Lillith is referred to as a Great Mother of settled agricultural tribes who resisted the invasions of the nomadic herdsmen.[5] Her name is fashioned after the "lilu", or lotus, the Great Mother's flower-yoni, the feminine gateway to sexual union. Yoni is a Sanskrit term that is the basis of the word Uni-verse.[6]

In the literature, she is also referred to by a host of names that suggest that she was feared. She is called Mother of Demons, Consort of Satan, Demoness of the Dark, Evil Semi-incarnate, and Evil Which Lurks in the Shadows.[7] This tainted image of Lillith reflects a socio-cultural climate in which women were expected to be subordinate, submissive, passive, and compliant. The impetuousness of Lillith shows independence and strength, which was unpopular and unacceptable to patriarchal fore-fathers.

In Hebraic tradition, Lillith was Mistress of the World who was married to Adam. She refused the submission he expected of her, sneered at his sexual crudity, cursed him, fled from the Garden of Eden, and made her home by the Red Sea.[8] The Red Sea is archetypal in itself representing a "fixed sea of universal thought that has become part of the very world in which we live."[9]

> There is a universal life force, which moves upon a universal substance. This combination of life and substance is the matrix in which all mind force works; symbolically it is the Red Sea or life sea. Human thoughts, which form part of the race consciousness, have impregnated this sea. The Red Sea represents the sum of all the thoughts about life with which the race has impregnated the universal ether.[10]

The Red Sea also symbolizes a sea of moon blood, the essence of procreation, the feminine elixir. There is a major distinction between the male and the female when we considered blood. Menstrual blood, or moon blood, was sacred to the pre-patriarchal ancients. In matriarchal cultures, moon blood was utilized in sacred ceremonies and was connected to an intuitive, feminine power that was revered and to the genetic matrix that links us to cosmic influences. When the feminine was repressed and men began conducting similar ceremonies, blood was obtained through the sacrifice of animals. Male blood can only come through killing or injury. The patriarchal obsession with bloodshed is still readily apparent in male-dominated wars. It suggests that if men had menstrual cycles, their connection to the earth would necessarily be augmented, and a value system that supported the cyclical nature of life would be ensured. Because this is not the case, it is no secret that men rely on women to keep their connection to the earth.

Lillith's separation from Adam was a contentious issue for the biblical forefathers. In the patriarchal version of the story, there are two trees, one of life and one of knowledge. Lillith's banishment from the Garden of Eden is the beginning of separating life from knowledge and replacing renewal with sacrifice. The issues of cyclical life and reincarnation are challenged. Forced obedience to externally imposed law is introduced, and Lillith is scapegoated. The passion and lust of the feminine are thus repressed. Fear, punishment, and misery are introduced. The story of Lillith was thus removed from the canonical Bible, and Eve is introduced.

> The tragedy of the male, as he aspired to the heroic ideal, was represented as a faltering in his resistance to wily woman; letting himself be deceived or seduced into accepting from her hands the forbidden fruit of desire, passion, and bodily urges. The more the patriarchal culture came to stress the life-denying ascetic ideal, the more were the repressed passions—the vulnerable as well as the lustful sides of existence—projected upon women.[11]

The Metaphysical Bible Dictionary refers to Eden as "a pleasant, harmonious, productive state of consciousness in which are all possibilities of growth. When [we] are expressing in harmony with the Divine Mind, bringing forth the qualities of Being in divine order, [we] dwell in Eden, or in a state of bliss in a harmonious body."[12]

It is into this context that Adam himself was created. His name finds its origins in the word "Adamah," which means female magic and "bloody clay."[13] The suggestion is that Adam was formed from clay moistened with moon blood. He did not produce the Mother of All from his rib, he himself was fashioned from hers, as early Mesopotamian stories indicate. The reversal of the order of myths is common. Original stories have undergone immense distortion. Christian theologians and Persian patriarchs held the idea that heaven was closed to all women except those who were submissive and who worshipped men as gods.[14] As women were disempowered, their roles began to shift.

> Consequently, women needed to be kept in subordinate positions, if not quarantined in harems or hidden beneath disguising or disfiguring clothes, veils, or *sheitels* (wigs worn by Orthodox Jewish women).

Femininity was to be limited to obedient passivity, domesticity, and maternal nurturance. Women themselves had to learn to distrust the tides of their emotions and to suspect the voices of their bodies.[15]

The Lillith archetype so adamantly retained her sexuality and her passion that she was popularized as the "harlot of hell" and was reputed to be able to seduce men and young boys in their sleep. If a male smiled in his sleep, it was thought that Lillith was fondling him. Well into the Middle Ages, amulets were made to protect men from this plight and from the wet dreams that were supposedly brought on by Lillith.

It was also thought that Lillith could steal children. Chalk circles were drawn around cradles and symbols were carved into doors to protect the young. The power of Lillith extended into her female offspring. Hence, the Daughters of Lillith could also execute such mischief. They were called Night Hags and were greatly feared.

THE LILLITH WOMAN

Though Lillith is an archetypal personage, she is not a goddess, but a human being with the strength to be herself. She is mortal, but she is no ordinary woman. Lillith's strength can be both energizing and debilitating. Filled with vigor and defiance, she is a veritable *Wild Woman*[16] unto herself. The Book of Urantia claims that Lillith bore Adam twenty-three children before she fled to the Red Sea. Thus the *Angels and Archetypes* system respects Lillith as the Mother aspect of the Wild Woman, Artemis as the Virgin aspect of the Wild Woman and Baba Yaga as the Crone aspect of the Wild Woman.

Psychologically, Lillith represents an archetypal journey in three stages. She begins as a female fully expressing her passion: lusty, connected to her bliss, strong of body, free in spirit. A young girl who is not repressed is naturally in touch with this freedom and physical bliss. Eventually she is judged, repressed, humiliated, and oppressed by those who are afraid that she will "get into trouble" if she is free and open. She is thus labeled precocious. Yet the essence of Lillith remains and she carries strong medicine for women who wish to invoke her independence.

Picture an adorable four-year-old girl. She feels secure for the moment and ventures into a family function. Her light shines as bright as her patent leather shoes, her party dress is fresh as a spring morning, and she begins to interact. Who will stop her? Eventually she will be reprimanded. If Lillith is activated in her, she takes a stand, upholds her own integrity, and marches off pouting: "Why can't I be strong? Why can't I hang upside-down? No, I am not hungry!"

The battle begins. The Lillith girl may get even by being rebellious. She learns to play dumb and hear what she wants. She retreats into her own world, and puts herself in exile. Her self-esteem is eroding. Who are these people she is trapped with? She begins to plan her escape. This could get worse. They may resort to hitting her if she does not submit. They may send her away. They may withdraw all affection. She begins to starve emotionally. Who are these people?

Internally or externally, Lillith begins an exile of despair. She is not free. Her family does not like her. She must be terrible. She plots her escape.

The Lillith woman thinks to herself: "I could leave. I would go everywhere alone. No one can stop me. One day, I will travel. I will go on a journey where no one can control me. I will go as soon as I can."

Years pass. One day, she does get away.

In later years, if a Lillith woman grows up to marry a man who controls her, he will be surprised at her indignation. Because the culture endorses the domination of one group over another, and because she is a woman, the control seems so culturally sanctioned and nonchalant that she is incensed. All around her, she sees women being controlled. She sees women who have deadened themselves, who no longer seem animated and alive. She vows to not be like them.

To the Lillith woman, married women seem trapped. Lillith, in her indignation, is all too willing to compromise her relationships to maintain her integrity. She reacts by destroying her relationships to preserve herself and is perplexed by women who destroy themselves by preserving their relationship. Lillith could perhaps learn a valuable lesson from Hera, whose top priority is to preserve her marriage. Perhaps Hera would do well to learn from Lillith's courage and conviction.

The Lillith woman is not patient. She needs to learn discipline and emotional fortitude to tolerate the emotional intensity that can cause her to bolt from relationships. She is strong and self-indulgent. She has a desire to express herself in a way that reflects authenticity. She has immense creativity and personal power and the stamina to execute large projects. She is ambitious and wants to be appreciated for her uniqueness and for her talents.

THE ANGEL OF COURAGE AND CONVICTION

As we enter the Realm of Renunciation, we are challenged to release our attachments in order to further evolve spiritually. The Angel of Courage and Conviction is there to give us fortitude and steadfastness as we walk the Red Road. All those on the spiritual path can attain the stamina it takes to process the past, deal with karma, and face the challenges of life. There is a vortex of divine energy that gives us the spiritual determination to persist through the continual tests.

We experience a loss of power when we are betrayed, invalidated, or taken advantage of. Enormous grief and loss can cause an internal meltdown, and it feels as if we lose our strength. If we reach out into the cosmos and ask for assistance, we are inevitably fortified. Of course, life challenges always push us beyond our capacity to cope, and in many situations we simply do not feel strong enough. The Angel of Courage and Conviction offers us the determination and the resolve to go on and to meet the demands at hand.

Even if we are shaken to our roots, we are re-established in our own power. The Angel of Courage and Conviction offers one more treasure. When we appeal for assistance, we enter into an energy that remolds and recasts the situation into a divine scenario for the good of all concerned. By facing our fears and standing up for what is right and good, we participate in the evolution of consciousness and break the mold of oppression.[17] This Angel energizes us and assists us to stand in the Light of our Master Self. It is that power that is our courage and that helps us be firm in our convictions.

Tarot symbolism, and the Strength card to which Lillith is related, tells us more about this Angel.

> The young woman in this major trump represents spiritual strength, and the picture shows her with her hands on the mouth of a lion. The lion here is symbolic of the one mentioned in 1 Peter 5:8 ("Your adversary the devil, as a roaring lion, walketh about, seeking whom he may devour"). This is a direct reference to the ego-dominated personality, which must be controlled and mastered before the advent of the Christ Consciousness. This card implies liberation, achievement gained at considerable risk, and a capacity for accomplishment.[18]

Being on the path involves many tests and challenges. Growth always has a high price attached. When we realize that there is a cosmic force that can assist us for the asking, we can often accept the trials with greater ease and grace.

Baba Yaga

Mossy Forest

Baba Yaga

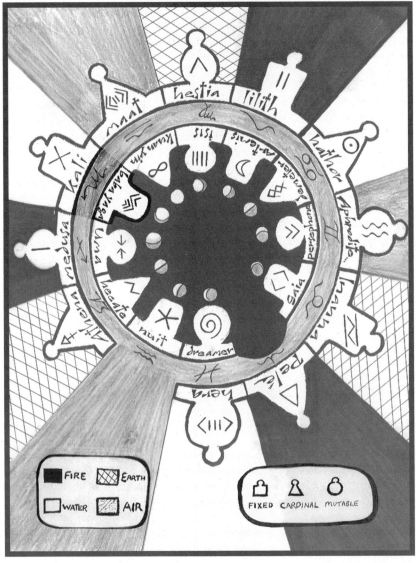

Moon in Scorpio
Fixed–Water

Chapter XVI

Baba Yaga

12

Baba Yaga is a strange and powerful character in Russian, Slavic, and Hungarian folk tales whose name means "old woman." Baba Yaga is the archetypal Hag. She is an aged, ugly crone who has a horrifying appearance and a curt disposition. Some say she is the guardian of the frontier between the territory of mortals and the spirit world. Baba Yaga's energy returns us to our savage selves and the dark recesses of our psyches.

Baba Yaga is a powerful archetype connected to the number twelve. There are twelve hours of day and twelve hours of night. There are twelve months and twelve signs of the zodiac. The evolved human will access twelve strands of DNA. We now can connect to twelve chakras, or energy centers, eight inside the body and four in the light body outside the physical. As we break through limitation, we are beginning to grasp that we can access twelve dimensions.

> As four times three, the number twelve connects the trinity of spirit with the foursquare reality of earth. Transfixed now at the mercy of the wheeling stars above, the hero experiences [herself] in this expanded dimension of twelve.[1]

The twelfth trump in the Tarot is the Hanged Man, who is depicted hanging by one leg from a tree. Closely connected to the energy of Baba Yaga, he is temporarily incapacitated and disconnected from the ordinary world. In this state, there is the possibility of communing with a power superior to ego consciousness. On the basis of tarot symbolism of the Hanged Man, Manly P. Hall says,

> To attain the heights of philosophy ... man must reverse (or invert) the order of his life. [She] then loses [her] sense of personal possession because [she] renounces the rule of gold in favor of the golden rule ... This refers to the reversal of thought.[2]

Baba Yaga's energy is rooted in the Moon in Scorpio. She is curious and wants to learn about the occult and life after death. She can probe into an issue, but because she is secretive, she often knows more than she chooses to disclose. As a fixed water sign, she is deep with shrewd insight. She is dark and savage, and grounded. She can wallow in emotion.

MYTHOLOGY

Baba Yaga was emaciated like a skeleton with long sharp teeth, a crooked nose that curved down, a pointed chin that curved up. Her face had warts, and she had disheveled, greasy hair. Her eyes would glow red.

Baba Yaga lived deep in the forest in a hut that was suspended on scaly, yellow chicken legs. Her house could walk around all by itself, and some say it would sometimes spin round and round. It was surrounded by a fence made of human bones and skulls that would glow in the dark. The latches on the doors and windows were made of human fingers and toes. The house is brimming with life and has a mind of its own. Even though the parts could be interpreted as morbid, the house is personified and animated.

Legend has it that she would fly around in a cauldron shaped like a mortar, rowing herself along with a pestle.[3] She would brush away the traces she left with a broom made of the hair of a person who had long been dead.[4] Baba Yaga can make magic, and she brings to life that which is inanimate.

Psychologically, images of perfectionism lock women into a sterile life. They attempt to be too good, too normal, and too sweet. It is a developmental task to let this aspect die back a little and to embrace a rudimentary, savage, brazen self. When Baba Yaga is depicted as impatient, argumentative, and blunt, she is inviting us to loosen up, to shake up our complacency and hyper-politeness. As Baba Yaga is expressed, a new, more authentic woman is born.

> Baba Yaga is fearsome, for she is the power of annihilation and the power of the life force at the same time. To gaze into her face is to see *vagina dentata*, eyes of blood, the perfect newborn child and the wings of angels all at once.[5]

Baba Yaga teaches us how to take care of the psyche of the wild feminine. She has a voracious appetite for life, for magic, and for all things that stir culturally induced complacency. Her legends describe, in mythological form, ancient initiation rituals. The heroine seeks out Baba Yaga when she has a query or a problem. She

134

undergoes trials to find her in her house in the mossy forest at the frontier of the realm of death, and she returns with magical gifts, wisdom, and maturity.

In almost all Baba Yaga tales, the seeker is offered some magical food or drink, potions and substances that are intended for secret initiations and rituals. Baba Yaga often administers magic mushrooms. These are often hallucinatory, and the soul experiences extraordinary perceptions of the self that restores inner harmony.[6] Modern culture has forbidden chemically induced inner journeys, judging them as indecent and improper. Yet indigenous peoples all over the modern and ancient world use plants as sacraments in shamanic rituals and initiations. We can count on Baba Yaga to shake up the status quo and confront commonly accepted cultural ideals.

Another common theme in these legends is the purification of the heroine through a specific task outlined by Baba Yaga. She will be asked to sort seeds, to sweep the floor of her house, and to clear her yard of debris. Psychologically, this translates as the soulful work of sorting through the material of the psyche, of clearing space for oneself, of keeping one's private time in order. Within this, the mature woman can process her internal self and achieve a balance.

In other tales, the protagonist is asked to cook for Baba Yaga. First she must build a fire and burn within herself. She must examine what burns her, what she has neglected to address, that which pains her. She must also attend to what she is passionate about, what makes her hot. Otherwise her life is lukewarm. She needs to "cook." Then she must nourish her own wild self. As Clarissa Pinkola Estes says: "The Yaga must be fed. There's hell to pay if she goes hungry."[7]

After the heroine has sorted the seeds, cleansed her psyche, fired herself up, and nourished her soul, she receives part of Baba Yaga's goddess wisdom. Through these trials and tribulations, she loosens the bonds of culture and is free to be her authentic self.

THE BABA YAGA WOMAN

Many would like to turn the Hanged Man around, to put him on his feet and get him productive again, and perhaps to avoid the pain of growth. The Baba Yaga Woman knows better. She knows that it is old behavior patterns themselves that turn us upside down and disconnect us from the richness of the Renunciation. Viewed from the perspective of the unconscious, this Realm is rich and casts auspicious shadows. It is difficult for the Western mind to tolerate inactivity. By visiting Baba Yaga, we have the great privilege of escaping ordinary time and entering into the sacred timelessness of the goddess. In this state, if we are very, very quiet, the goddess will speak to us. It is up to us to heed her call.

The Baba Yaga Woman temporarily withdraws from her outer life and explores the hidden realms within her psyche. Undistracted, this energy is very

135

grounding. It is a deep, internal, restful, outwardly unproductive time. Baba Yaga is the force that takes over when we cannot get dressed all day, let alone comb our hair. Inwardly, we roam our psyches and howl, we dig in, we sleep, and we stare into space. By spending time with Baba Yaga, we temporarily renounce the world. We spend the day, quite delightfully, in the Underworld, shades pulled down. When our housemates arrive home, we appear to them as though we had just crawled out from under a rock.

The Baba Yaga woman is willing to have the "uglies." She champions Bad Hair Days. Not surprisingly, her favorite time of month is moon time. Pre-Menstrual Syndrome (PMS) delights her, because it so easily allows for uncried tears to flow and unexpressed resentments to surface. She knows that this monthly release keeps the system clear.

We know a sleepy day is restful and is better than getting sick. Depending on how hard we drive ourselves, we may only spend time with Baba Yaga when we are absolutely forced to. She may only visit us when we fall into our beds with antibiotics in one hand and Kleenex in the other. We know we understand the importance of Baba Yaga's energy when we begin to voluntarily book time off completely away from demands. But nature does have her way with us. If we do not sign up for time with Baba Yaga, she will come and get us wherever we are.

This persistence may be the very quality that has us succumb to our dark friend. After all, if the moon can disappear for three days in twenty-eight, why can't we? If we join with this energy, we, like the moon, emerge renewed.

There is a rationale for this advice. As the planet evolves, we too evolve. At this time of planetary shifts, we are subject to energetic shifts and changes of vibrational frequencies. Physically, we need sleep at unusual times when we are changing rapidly, coming into alignment with the moon cycles, and getting ready to contain greater energies. Drinking plenty of water, taking many baths in epsom salts, staying clear of television and electrically powered lights and appliances, and taking a hiatus from newspapers and magazines can give us a break from culturally imposed images and release us to the care of the crone of wild women, Baba Yaga. Rejoice, for she will prove to be a valuable, liberating friend.

Many women are afraid that if they are temporarily unproductive, they will become Bag Ladies. Baba Yaga represents the uncensored aspect of the psyche of a woman. If you should invite the Bag Lady in for the night, and if you listen carefully to her, you will hear a profound story of renunciation. She is a loner. She abhors confinement, lies, lack of integrity, and control. This could be how she became homeless. She may even have had a mental breakdown because of the strain from all the trauma she has endured trying to survive. You are meeting a woman who has no doubt endured chronic poverty, rejection, and lack of support before she took to the streets.

When we allow Baba Yaga her due, we withdraw from the third-dimensional world to nurture our essential selves. Otherwise, we will be swallowed by the collective unconscious. There is a confrontation of the "monstrous chaos"[8] of the unconscious and a recognition of our karmic burdens, or the *cross* that we bear. We accept an initiation that represents a voluntary surrender to the death and resurrection process celebrated in shamanism.

THE ANGEL OF REVERSAL

The Angel of Reversal invites us to let go of the ego-driven personality and identification with the "I" of ourselves. The spiritual leap here is to function in intimate association with the Higher Self. The quest in life that builds ego, that accumulates material possessions for the sake of status and prestige, that needs to be right, falls away.

> To awaken to our true destiny, we often have to give something, often at a sacrifice. But once we break out of the dream, we see that it was not a sacrifice at all, only a replacing of the lesser with the greater.[9]

The Angel of Reversal is shown pouting. At first, self-restraint feels like deprivation. There is an important transition that occurs when we master non-attachment. For in Truth, *when you have nothing, you possess everything.* When we hold on, we have the tendency to hoard our possessions; we feel immense threat and loss when we relinquish materiality. It is the state of thinking that there is never enough and that we must save "for a rainy day." The ego projects fear of loss and deprivation, and we can develop a suspicious and jealous nature, and a feeling of being everyone's prey.

> The Tibetan master Djwhal Khul says that "to hold, one must detach, and to keep, one must release. Such is the Law. Life, for the disciple, becomes then a series of detaching processes, until [she] has learned the lesson of renunciation."[10]

Connection to Spirit in all things begins a life-changing process. We often leave jobs that do not support spiritual values and leave relationships that hamper our spiritual growth. In changing our value system, we make firm convictions regarding what we will stand for and what we will not. The price we pay is often dear, yet it paves the road to connecting with our Higher selves.

137

We begin by giving up our mortal sense of existence. We detach ourselves from what we consider the *personality* and becoming identified with the Higher Self within, our divine consciousness. We have been socialized in a manner that supports ego structures. In this process of changing identities we surrender all that has been acquired by the personality. We give up the entire inventory of the lower nature to the higher because the higher cannot infuse the lower until the lower is empty of all that it was. The lesser must be sacrificed for the greater, otherwise the spiritual rebirth cannot occur. Consider the following list of characteristics compiled by Price.[11] We are asked to give up:

1. *The tendency to criticize*

2. *The tendency to assume the responsibility for others that is not yours to assume*

3. *The tendency to surrender to someone else the responsibility for your own welfare*

4. *A feeling of needing to be cared for and protected by another person, which seldom relates to point 3 above*

5. *Spiritual pride and the tendency to prove your spirituality by giving unsought advice or spiritual counseling*

6. *Selfish personal ambition*

7. *Personal self-pity*

8. *Sensed personal power*

9. *A sense of futility*

10. *A tendency to find release in alcohol or drugs*

11. *The tendency to play the "misery loves company" game*

12. *Emotional controlled relationships of any kind, including those with spouse, children, parents, and friends*

13. *Deception and dishonesty*

14. *Fear and guilt*

15. *Feelings of unworthiness*

16. *Identification with the body as the Self and a preoccupation with the physical form and its needs*

17. *An emphasis on personal security*

18. *A Feeling that "my truth is higher than your truth," that "my mission is grander than yours"*

19. *A Messiah complex*

20. *A spiritless consciousness—no vitality, fire, light, animation—living without inspiration*

The great renunciation, the final step before regeneration, takes place after you have recognized every personality characteristic and complex, focused on each one, and disengaged it. This requires conscious awareness, an awakening from denial. It takes discipline, but with every detachment more Light moves into the Self.

> Coming up from the dark cellar of the lower nature is not always a smooth, upward glide; it can be a tough and strenuous climb ... You are here to be reborn in Spirit, and then to share that blazing infilling Light for the benefit of the world.[12]

Baba Yaga exists within the Realm of Renunciation. Bonding with her precipitates a deep cleansing, a break between the old and the new. This requires a constant refining process, and there is a perpetual ascension of matter to mind and mind to Spirit. This is an initiation that requires trust, courage, persistence, and above all consciousness.

A period will finally come when the whole Universe will be resolved back into its original essence in God.[13] Those who are involved in personal transformational work are involved in the process of reassessment of what is important and what we can no longer support.

The Angel of Reversal guides us to renounce our attachments to material possessions. As we purify our intentions, Spirit comes in to do regenerative work.[14] This makes us strong enough to live by new values.

Kali

Women Touching the Void

Kali

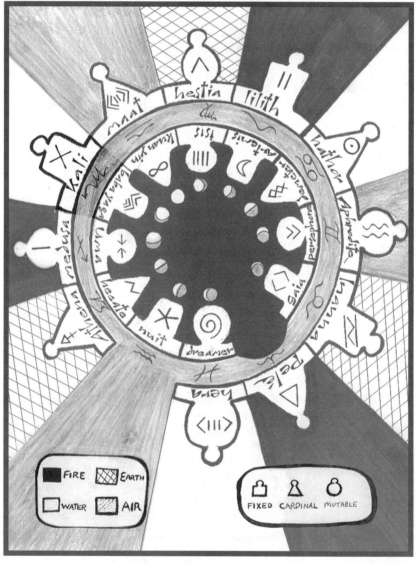

Sun in Scorpio
Fixed–Water

Chapter XVII

Kali

| 13 |

Kali is an ancient Hindu goddess whose best-known aspect is the archetypal Destroyer. She is depicted standing naked with blood dripping from her mouth, wearing a necklace of skulls and earrings of dead babies. She proudly displayed remnants of her prey and "filled the skies with her roar."[1] Kali is also the ultimate creatrix so ancient that Hindu tradition claims she is the mother of us all. She is said to have given birth to us from her unfathomable depths.[2] As we embrace Kali, it is this depth that transforms and renews us.

> She is full breasted; her motherhood is a ceaseless creation. She gives birth to the cosmos parthenogenetically as she contains the male principle within herself. Her disheveled hair forms a curtain of illusion, the fabric of space-time which organizes matter out of the chaotic sea of quantum-foam.[3]

Kali is number thirteen in the evolutionary journey. Thirteen was a sacred number to the ancients as there were thirteen lunation cycles in a solar year. In repressing feminine, reflective lunar consciousness, the number thirteen has been feared and is considered unlucky. Thirteen connects Kali to Pele (13 is 1+3=4). They share an explosive quality and the need to confront and express that which has been repressed.

Kali represents the Death card in the Tarot. Death is the most misunderstood concept in the twenty-two stages of conscious development in the Tarot. Through Kali we affirm that everything in nature lives to die, and dies in order to be transformed and reborn.

Kali's energy is anchored in the Sun in Scorpio. A fixed water sign, the archetypal energy reflects our attachments and emphasizes the emotional climate. The energy is shrewd, deep, and secretive. It can be jealous, aggressive, and vindictive. Yet her recuperative powers are remarkable. She has keen judgment, penetrating insight, and willpower. She is expressive and direct. The Kali archetype characterizes how we feel about our attachments to people and possessions in the world and how we react when we are threatened with losing them. Scorpions themselves teach us this:

> The stinging experiences that beset one who has given way to the sensations of the flesh; they goad [one] on to seek a higher expression of [their] creative forces, that [they] may enter an abiding consciousness of life, health, peace, and harmony—the Promised Land.[4]

MYTHOLOGY

The symbolism of Kali is profound and provocative. Kali is invariably depicted with many hands. In one hand, she carries the club of physical extermination with which she releases us from bondage. Another hand holds a miniature staff to dispel fear. Another holds a bowl, a receptacle for spiritual strength, signifying the balance of the Universe. The freshly severed head indicates the annihilation of the ego-bound evil force. When this energy is released, a shift is possible.

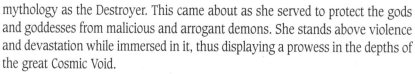

In the Devi Mahatyma,[7] a sacred Hindu text, Kali is subordinate to Durga, and is not the controller of the universe, but has been incorporated into the shadow of traditional Hindu mythology as the Destroyer. This came about as she served to protect the gods and goddesses from malicious and arrogant demons. She stands above violence and devastation while immersed in it, thus displaying a prowess in the depths of the great Cosmic Void.

Kali is intoxicating, arousing the primal vibrations of the Universe that bring creation into existence. She is depicted as a cosmic dancer, creating and destroying, as she pulses with life.[8] She is often shown dancing on the body of a man. In the original myth, the man is Kali's husband and he places himself under her feet. Kali's energy is thus transferred to him, through her feet, *bringing him to life*. He raises his head, and his penis becomes erect, making him ready to join with her in the creation of the world.[9] This represents the ultimate in the blending of the masculine and the feminine principles. It marries control and surrender and is a sacred interaction between two souls, two physical bodies, and two light bodies. Mookerjee states:

> In this form she is changeless, limitless power, acting in the great
> drama, awakening the unmanifest Siva (masculine principle) beneath
> her feet.[10]

Kali embodies a paradox. She traditionally presents her ravaging side first, leaving her benign, renewing side in the background. She is a dark goddess depicted as devouring and bloodthirsty. She engenders a primordial fear of the power of the unrepressed feminine. At the same time, she encompasses the purity and tenderness of the primordial mother.

It is characteristic of Kali to be portrayed with many arms and hands. Some are to slash away the old and the dead aspects of our lives. The others are principal instruments of work. Good and evil actions are created by them and are the manifestations of karma itself. They represent the wheel of cause and effect, a principal tenet of the Hindu philosophy. Ultimate freedom is attained through the release of such bondage. The full embodiment of the Kali archetype represents the freedom that is available when we can step off the wheel of karma and onto the ascending spiral of evolution.[11]

Through the Tantric tradition, Kali is a representation of a world beyond duality. The cyclic nature of the Universe and its inherent unity illuminates the principals of spirit and matter. The idea here is that the male and female, or the Shiva and the Shakti, energies are contained within the whole of each individual. Tantric tradition involves the recognition and reunion of primal consciousness (Shiva) and primal life forces (Shakti) through discipline, through meditation, and through the ultimate control of sexual energies. In Whitmont's words:

> The endless cycles of the Great Round, the merging of the death of
> the old with the birth of new life were celebrated in sacrificial festivities
> in which violence and destruction merged with sexual ecstasy and
> drunken intoxication.[12]

At the core of Indian mythology is the idea of reincarnation. When the Christian church outlawed belief in reincarnation, it was replaced by a belief that we only live once, which led to a collective phobia of death. The ultimate goal is the liberation from the cycle of death and rebirth through the transcendence of ego impulses and through the realization of the illusions of earthly reality. Kali's role, then, is to shatter the delusions of the ego. Her destructive influences, seen in context, are an opportunity for salvation. True transcendence is the death of death. In fact, nothing can be destroyed, only transformed.

Kali manifests beyond space and time. Beyond time, she dissolves into the cosmos. Dishevelled, she flies free, going beyond the bonds of physicality and karmic influences. Kali is the liberating power that breaks through all illusion, destroying the finite to meet with the infinite. Kali transcends dimensional realities and reveals the spiritual truths that go beyond earthly reality. When fear is released, there is perfect freedom and divine bliss that overflows into the universe in an all-affirming love. Beyond form, she dissolves into blackness.

> Just as all colors disappear in black, so all names and forms disappear in her.[13]

Kali's gift is neither morbid nor stationary; it is momentum through the dark hours, the dark night of the soul. Standing in a ring of fire, the black side of Kali is unlocked from the unconscious, and repressed emotional energy is released. The Kali energy can be fierce and searing, and we cringe a little when she appears. She is a force to contend with, but without her we stagnate in the winter of ourselves, deadened yet not renewed.

THE KALI WOMAN

The Kali woman knows how to sever attachments in order to release the self to rebirth and revitalization. She is vital, strong, direct, and unattached. The Kali woman knows when it is time to move on, and she has the courage and fortitude to follow her truth. She knows when a relationship is over, when it is time to move, when it is time to clean out the closets, when it is time to leave a job. She honors within herself that which is no longer vital, that which she has outgrown. She knows the way to the dump. She also knows the termination of one phase of her life is a launching pad for her next endeavor and for her renewed self.

The Kali woman is a master at expressing intense emotions. When an emotional charge can no longer be contained, she is an emotional volcano unto herself, perhaps fashioned after Pele. She relishes in a Kali rampage when she needs to release pent-up energy.

The Kali woman wears her shadow on her sleeve. She cannot function if emotions are lurking beneath the surface or when people are afraid of upsetting the apple cart. She calls a spade a spade and gets on with it. This can be disconcerting to those who are well-versed in emotional repression and in keeping the peace.

Because men have been trained to compartmentalize information and emotions, they are quite able to continue functioning while issues fester beneath the surface of a relationship. A man is traditionally committed to repression and denial. The Kali woman will petrify him. This may put her in danger because he will, no doubt, stop at nothing to repress her explosive rage. The more he represses his shadow, the more she will push to unleash the dark, unconscious material—both his and hers. The two, no doubt, will polarize on another, and the clash between them can lead to violence. With such tension, the man may maintain his composure, but the Kali woman will go wild.

For a time, the Kali woman may collude with the oppressors and remain silent. But she will be frustrated. She knows she will not engender sainthood by participating in the repression of the dark goddess. Women are clearly socialized to be passive and unexpressive. In extreme cases, the Kali woman can crack, and a psychotic episode can take the place of directly expressed rage. Picking up the pieces after such a trauma can be devastating. In this intensity and torment it is important to recognize and honor that the energy is, nonetheless, Kali's own.

When someone dies, the Kali woman is usually ready to assist the soul of the deceased in their passage to the afterworld. When others shed a polite tear at the funeral, she will be sobbing. She will process her grief as she feels it, and maintain a strong connection to the soul making its passage. Kali herself will be lurking in the background, encouraging this transition.

When the Kali woman's energy is out of balance, she can become the *terrible mother*. She can be critical, controlling, and abusive of her children, flying into a rage without warning. This is self-defeating and indulgent. As unpopular as Kali's energy can be in a climate of denial, it by no means sanctions abuse. When Kali's power is misunderstood or unconscious, it can be a dangerous and destructive force. When harnessed and clear, Kali's power can be a saving grace.

THE ANGEL OF ULTIMATE RELEASE

The Angel of Ultimate Release ushers us through the portals as we let go of possessions, relationships, and outmoded ideas. Seen standing on the body of the Devil, the Angel of Ultimate Release liberates us from denial and from the confines of the earthly plane. With a huge swoop of radiant light, our sights turn from concern with material gain to cosmic ideals, to ultimate release, and the ecstasy of freedom. We open, fly a little, and ascend. A new vitality springs forth from our souls.

This is no doubt preceded by a difficult time, and we may have felt that our progress was at a standstill. In welcoming and honoring the Angel of Ultimate Release, we emerge from the dark night of the soul. When we fully embrace the natural cycles that are the Law of the Universe, we can be still, and let the heroic task of allowing rebirth to unfold. This is the energy of spring itself and is represented by a metamorphosis, pregnant with new potential.

We are conditioned to believe that we are only born once. We are cut off simultaneously from our instincts and from information about our purpose for being here. As a consequence, we have difficulty living spiritually fulfilling lives. When we contemplate death, we become fearful, partially because we know we have never truly "lived" and partially because we have no concept of life after death and the splendor of cyclical process in the Universe.

Because of death being driven into the shadow of the culture, we have been saturated in images of death and dying. The media embellishes our obsession by constantly showing images of real and fictionalized deaths, violence, and disrespect for life. There are cultures who celebrated death as an opportunity to return to divine origins and as an opportunity to return to earth renewed, reborn, and recycled. We recycle everything else; why not embrace the notion of recycling our souls?

> In Truth that which we call death is but an entrance into a more glorious life of joy, fulfillment, peace, and freedom, whether the experience is physical or mystical. In each case it is an unceasing flow of sentient life, but with a difference. Except for the immediate uplift of consciousness derived from the experience of being freed from the corporeal body, physical death is nothing more than a change in form. We maintain the awareness, understanding, and knowledge gained during our visit on earth and carry our tendencies and interests with us as we move from one plane to another.[14]

When we voluntarily revoke our incarnation, we can be released into the light. Yet aborting an incarnation through suicide has consequences in the cosmic scheme of things if we perceive life on earth as an opportunity for spiritual development.

The initiates in ancient times and those who have participated in monastic incarnations in the more recent past were not meditating, chanting, and praying so they would appear "holy" to some external God. They were seeking freedom from the bondage of the physical world so that they could remain in this world and participate in its transformation Consciousness begins within each individual.

As we pass through the spiritual birth canal guarded by the Angel of Ultimate Release, many of us experience our own "crucifixion." We feel forsaken, sacrificial, and betrayed. Symbolically, the crucifixion of Jesus was about the lower nature dying in order for the higher nature to manifest fully as the Resurrection.

When we finally stop focusing on outer reality and realize that we have been fostering a mental illusion, we break through to a place where we can experience living as heaven on Earth. At first, we only get glimpses of the manifest perfection. We notice the miracles of life on earth in a sunrise, the song of a bird, a gentle breeze, or abundance in our lives. Undoubtedly, we will embark on a new cycle of learning until we can perceive the perfection of all. The more we surrender, the more we learn how to surrender.

Uma

The Cave

Uma

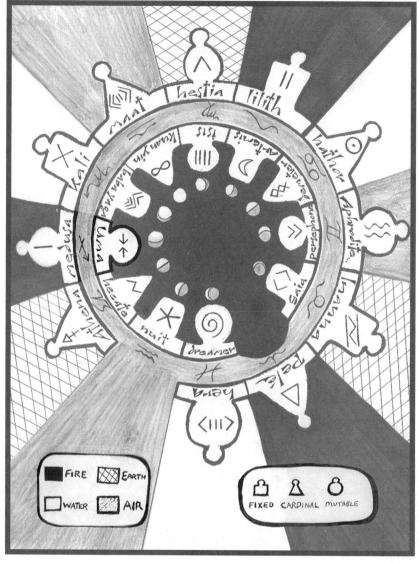

Moon in Sagittarius
Mutable–Fire

Chapter XVIII

Uma

Uma is the archetypal Ecstatic Dancer. She was an ancient cave dweller who would dance into a trance bringing spiritual energy to her clan. Her role was to live in service and to ground cosmic energy. Whenever the clan ritualistically honored the cycles of nature, praying for fertility and for communion, Uma would function as a human transmitter. She would bring down the raw energy of the cosmos and ground it deep in the earth. She would also raise up the energy of the Earth and shoot it out into the cosmos. Through her, the cosmos and the earth conjugate and embrace.

The number thirteen gives way to a new psychic being, to Uma, and to the number fourteen. Fourteen is a pivotal number in the lunation cycle. In a twenty-eight day cycle, the moon waxes for fourteen days and then wanes for fourteen days. Fourteen days is the duration of lunar directional flow. Numerologically, Uma is connected to Inanna. Uma and Inanna both partake in heavenly and earthly realms and seek to balance cosmic energies and earthly energies. In the goddess tradition, the sexual energies were the elixir of magic, connected to the Universal life force and to Christ consciousness (also associated with the number 5; 14 is 1+4=5).

As Tarot Temperance, Uma harnesses the desires of the soul. She balances energies and is a healer. She is in touch with Divine Law, and establishes inner knowing and the deep resonance of Truth within her being. She harmoniously adjusts the electromagnetic currents in the physical body. She is sometimes depicted as a woman with wings, alchemically balancing opposing forces.

Uma is an intuitive goddess whose energy is rooted in the Moon in Sagittarius. A mutable fire sign, the energy is dynamic and dramatic and thrives on the internal flow of energy.

MYTHOLOGY

In the Yoruba tradition in Africa, the *orisha*, or the uma, are conceived as divine personalities who are manifest in the external world through ceremony.[1] Clan members would depend on the powers, grace, and energies of the orisha to meet the problems of life. In turn, the *uma* would depend on the nourishment of the clan for survival. The role of Uma is highly spiritualized and highly charged with energy. The rays of cosmic energy flow directly through her. The ancient cave-painting ancestors understood our divine purpose for incarnating on earth. They understood the path of human consciousness to be a continuous interaction of biological and spiritual evolution.

Uma's function is to ground cosmic energy into the earth and release earth energy into the cosmos. Energy, like lightning, must be grounded. She visits the interior parts of the earth. Electromagnetic currents pulse through her body and soul. Being an electromagnetic conduit is a responsibility requiring clarity, focus, commitment, and purity. If she is unprepared, the tremendous forces and energies may simply be too much for her body and may overload her nervous system.

Uma's preparation is the culmination of a number of shamanic initiations that have opened and cleansed her physical and emotional channel. She is a human transmitter who cosmically balances the earth's forces. Uma functions at this level because she has transcended all fear. She has brought all opposing forces, all duality, all polarities into physical balance. It is as though a tantric fusion has occurred and the physical being is in perfect balance. In this state, latent physical nerve and brain centers are opened allowing the *Christ-current,* or the energy of Christ consciousness, to vibrate through the body. This upgrades the physical body and allows a superior consciousness to flow through. Thus, the link to the divine world is enhanced and we are released from earthly limitations.

> Every cell can be alive and vibrating as if one were electrical or indescribably blissful, and it seems to fluctuate of its own accord until there is a gradual stabilization. Basic to this is an inner kind of balance that cannot be described and must be learned moment by moment. Physical symptoms such as tremor, weakness, extreme sensitivity to heat or cold, and muscle spasms may occur. Yet if one

comes into harmony with the current, the sense of strength and vitality is nearly superhuman. But even when there is an inner peace the initial energy can simply be too much for the body—something like putting too much current through a wire.[2]

Uma is a cooperative character who unites the energy of a gathering, a community, a family, or a clan. Conjoined and united, there is a communion of souls bonded in their humanness, their equality. A state of divine balance is thus achieved. The poise leads the way to perfect expression of all the faculties and powers of the conscious human.[3] Uma's dedication to the clan and her sophistication in working with energy have earned her dominion and mastery."[4]

> The relation of poise to mastery and dominion is this: the consciousness of dominion through divine principle gives a state of poise, and a poised state of mind adds to the realization of dominion and mastery. The realization of mastery is attained by unifying the consciousness with Divine Mind as its one source, by prayer and meditation, thus attaining Christ consciousness.[5]

The favorable conditions that enhanced the rituals and ceremonies are drums and songs that were celebrated at the *guemilère*,[6] or clan gathering. Specific rhythms, dances, and "emblematic accessories"[7] would trigger the trances and call in the cosmic energies through the complex codes of the rhythms. This energy or healing medicine is referred to as *um.* The shaman-healer receives it in a successful initiation.

> *Um,* residing in the belly, is activated through trance dancing and the heat of fire. It ascends or *builds up* the spinal column into the head, at which time it can be used to pull out the sickness afflicting others.[8] [emphasis mine]

Released from the mundane world, she can soar up to heaven riding on cosmic currents. Bonded to her higher self and to the Angel of Temperance, Uma successfully contains both worlds by moving to the multidimensional realm beyond time and space. Here, she is blessed with patience and acceptance knowing that all things are perfectly orchestrated and divinely timed. Uma is incarnate on earth and will deal with mundane reality, and it can be confusing when the rational ego of the Upperworld and the symbolic impressions of the Underworld intrude upon one another. One can get entangled and unable to consciously differentiate between these two worlds. Some dramas are inner dramas while some are best acted out externally. If they are confused, it is impossible for the issue to come to resolution.

Uma has fully come to terms with her shadow and fears nothing. She is relaxed, and she trusts herself. The Uma energy is mentally balanced. Uma knows how to execute an exact proportion between idea and action. In other words, if she has an idea, she understands the scope of her goal. If she carves out her conviction and makes a plan, she will be determined to match her energy to the demands of the project.

THE UMA WOMAN

The Uma woman is fiery, spirited, unencumbered, strong, and free. She needs activity, thrives on physical exertion, and passionately expresses herself through dance, movement, individual sports, or physical disciplines like yoga and tai chi. Her orientation will be expansion: expansion of consciousness, expansion of horizons, expansion of capacity. She is a born traveler both on the earth plane and through the Cosmos. She is receptive to superconscious realms.

She has keen prophetic sense, is highly spiritual, and has strong psychic abilities. Her judgment is acute, she can be very focused, and her mind resents confusion. She is always searching and can even be seen as restless in her undying need to find wisdom and the deeper truths about life. She is a natural teacher, is philosophical, and likes to help others. The Uma woman reacts to others as though they were a part of herself. She can merge and melt into many situations.

The Uma woman is a compulsive dancer. When there is music playing, it is difficult to keep her still. She relishes in wild abandon as she writhes and screeches her way to ecstasy. She is uninhibited, exuberant, and physically expressive. She is fully in touch with her body. She could be an exotic dancer, and is likely to be trained in African dance, belly dancing, flamenco, or the tango.

THE ANGEL OF TEMPERANCE

We all sense intuitively that we have a purpose for being here. In recent decades, insight on our true purpose has been limited owing to the veils that were placed around the planet.

Evidence of these veils is that in the 1980's training to become a channel* took five years of intensive work. More recently, psychic abilities were enhanced, and people with keen interest are learning to channel in one sitting.

*channel: The skill of bringing information from disincarnate entities forward. Trance channeling involves the channel stepping aside and allowing the entity or ascended master to speak while the channel is not conscious of what is spoken. Automatic writing is the act of listening to words from an entity or from the higher Self and writing them. Kinesthetic channeling occurs when the body receives signals and the spirit moves through as in trance dancing.

It is said that the veils were lifted at Harmonic Convergence on August 16-17, 1987. At that time there was a major planetary alignment and new energies were henceforth made available to seekers and doubters alike. This energy introduced the new energies five years before the entry into the last 20-year slice of the Mayan calendar that will bring us to completion in our mission on this planet. This energy was described by Price as:

> The divine process of individual reawakening and the realization of divinity of every soul on every plane of existence everywhere. Its destination: the Fifth Kingdom of God, the realm of Pure Being where Love and Peace are absolute, its time of arrival: at the flash signifying the Christing, or spiritualization, the collective consciousness and the healing and harmonizing of Planet Earth.[9]

The Fifth Kingdom of God is synonymous with the fifth dimension, or a vibrational frequency beyond space and time, where heaven is experienced on earth. This state of realization is one of confidence, trust, and acceptance of all that is. There is no fear of the future, no impatience, no anxiety, and no anger. There is a balancing of the body, the mind, and the emotions.

Even though third-dimensional reality continues to demonstrate violence and promotes the addictions of our dysfunctional popular culture, we can develop an inner world of equanimity. We can be:

> Divinely protected ... [T]he invisible world behind the appearances is gathering force and Power and will soon come crashing through the veil of matter to reveal the Truth of Being.[10]

The Angel of Temperance is the energy that allows us to trust in the divine process and live in total acceptance of that which is good, true, and beautiful. "Become aware of me, and through the channel of your awareness I will demonstrate to you that the Will, plan, and purpose of God is the only activity taking place in your life."[11]

The idea is that the energy and force will lead to a complete readjustment of values among the people and a revelation of the purpose behind every difficult experience of life.

> Live with patience—not an attitude of long-suffering but one of perseverance and tenacity, for the good will surely be revealed in this world; it cannot be held back. Live with acceptance-not of things as they appear to be, but in the context of consenting to order, beauty, and freedom, for they will certainly be manifest.[12]

This is the sense of proportion in life, of Temperance. It is represented by the rainbow, which can be seen as the activation of the chakras in the body, the light body in all its multicolored splendor.

In ancient Mystery Schools, it was the power of persistence, perseverance, determination, and resolution that allowed the initiate to progress. It was the exacting proportion between idea and action, and a balancing of the inner and outer worlds. Acceptance is the ultimate surrender to the power of the divine. Temperance here is the mastery that allows the initiate to choose the middle path between extremes. This energy gives way to intuitive perception and true optimism.

> The bottom line is that when we truly commit to Spirit, then Spirit is in charge of our lives and there is nothing to worry about regardless of how difficult the situation appears. And how can we tell if we have given everything up to the Lord and Master Self within? By the measure of our patience, knowing that every activity is divinely timed, and by the degree of acceptance, which means to accept our good *even when it is not yet visible.*[13] [emphasis mine]

Hecate

The Gateway

Hecate

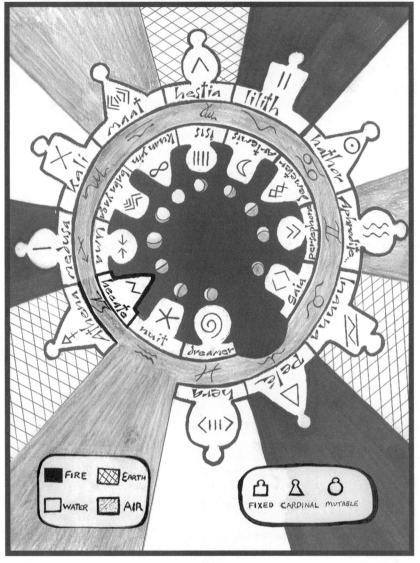

Moon in Capricorn
Cardinal–Earth

ḥecate

|15|

Ḥecate is the archetypal Crone, or wise woman. She was the Queen of the Dead, who understood physical immortality. Hecate's story dates back to ancient Egypt where she was an original "Holy Woman," or *heq*. She was a "predynastic ruler who knew the words of power, or *hekau*."[1] Hecate's ritual practices were connected to the earth energies and were performed in sacred groves and temples in ancient Egypt and in ancient Greece.

Hecate is a powerful figure who is represents the number fifteen. Numerologically, this links Hecate to Aphrodite (1+5=6). Ultimately both were connected to the reverence of the feminine and the honoring of feminine beauty. Aphrodite, a dynamic sun goddess, has her energy honored in the Upperworld, whereas Hecate's feminine energies have been driven to the depths of the Underworld

The Devil card in traditional Tarot is connected to Hecate. The Devil can be viewed as the collective shadow, or the part of culture we live in denial, unidentified, unprocessed, and unconscious. Evil is that which does not honor life. The word devil is d "evil." It is also "lived" spelt backwards. From this vantage point "denial" is the "devil." To understand Hecate's role with the Devil card, it is helpful to recognize that Lucifer means *light bringer*. When the matriarchy was under siege, Hecate was standing watch, filled with grief.

> The Devil represents the repression of this free spirit by Church and State, to which it poses a threat to authority and order ...The outcome of this repression of the wildness within us is robotism—dull, mechanistic, monotonous way of living. And the extreme reaction to such servitude and lack of meaning is violence and aggression, often 'unexpected' and often misunderstood. When the free spirit makes itself felt through a normally well behaved individual, it feels as though the *Devil made me do it*.[2] [emphasis mine]

Hecate's energy is rooted in the Moon in Capricorn. This is a cardinal earth sign exemplifying practical, grounded energies. There is a natural leadership and an avid interest in changing social structures to further promote the conscious feminine.

MYTHOLOGY

As Crone of the Underworld, Hecate carries the grief of the sublimation of the matriarchy. Being pre-Olympian, Hecate witnessed the flourishing of peaceful, agricultural, spiritual, vital societies that honored the Goddess. We imagine her to have lived at Knossos, which still survived on Crete a full three thousand years after the Aryan tribes began to devastate Amazon fortresses and matriarchal villages. Eventually, interruption of the peaceable civilizations at Mycenae and Knossos occurred through natural disaster and invasion, and the last vestiges of Goddess traditions were driven into the Underworld.

Symbolically, Hecate is like the Phoenix rising out of the ashes. Her original untamed spirit is yearning for freedom from the confines of patriarchy and the greed for power and material wealth. The Metaphysical Bible Dictionary states that the Phoenix itself was a "haven of Crete."[3] Crete signified the material, sensual, and worldly aspects of matriarchal consciousness. Blood-red temple pillars signified a degree of conquest and power, the renewal of life activity, and an expression of carnal consciousness in the individual.[4] The ideas of conquering power and resurrection into newness of life denote victory over error and the ultimate resurgence of the feminine.

> It [feminine energy] must be lifted to a higher plane of understanding, realization, and use before it can become abiding in the consciousness of the individual and work for harmony and true upbuilding in [the] mind, body, and affairs.[5]

The energy of Hecate thoroughly imprinted the ancient ways of temple priestesses. It is through her that we remember the lifestyle of the temple maidens at Knossos. They luxuriated, draped in shallow pools, and rested after the morning activities of making music and dancing to honor the Goddess. The exquisite comfort, the regal serenity, the abundance, and tranquillity would rival any modern-day spa for the rich and famous, yet it was commonplace for the culture of the Goddess.

Neumann, in his essay entitled *The Moon and Consciousness*,[6] examines the linguistic roots to *moon-spirit* and the "totalities of the soul's inner-most sensibilities and feelings." Herein he finds Germanic words linking the ideas of inclination, tendency, feeling, disposition, recollection, and consciousness with material, sensuous, voluptuous, sentient, headstrong, and willful.[7] He draws a clear distinction between matriarchal consciousness, which is contemplative instead of goal-oriented as is patriarchal consciousness that contains the knife edge of analytic power.

Moon consciousness is a fermentation, a process, that involves the entire personality and is beyond justification and fact. It is the inner experience of deep knowing that is neither abstract nor stripped of emotion. Matriarchal consciousness preserves the connection to the Realm of the Underworld.

If one were to travel to Knossos today, a tourist would find references to "King" Minos and be offered a view of the excavation slanted through the patriarchal eye. There is no visible evidence of matriarchal culture or of the sacred grove freely revealed. Yet buried deep within the recesses of the Simone de Beauvoir Library at Concordia University in Montreal exists a document with a map of the original site at Knossos. This map includes the location of the sacred grove, high on a hill that overlooks the entire temple complex. The trees were destroyed, but the energy remains. Putting oneself into a receptive state, one can be drawn into the original energies and cognitions, and experience the magnificence of the once-flourishing temple life at Knossos.

Hecate has been roaming in the Underworld for so many millennia that she is expert on the recesses, maps, and delights of an existence in Shadowland. She illuminates the shadow of the collective. As the Rolling Stones would say, she has "sympathy for the devil." Hecate has an understanding of the devil himself and the temptations that materiality can bring. Each of us is caught in various attachments vis-à-vis the material world. It is through our reckoning with our own internalized devil that we reconcile our desire for the material.

It takes an enormous effort to free ourselves from the forces symbolized by the Devil card. We must mobilize both personal and collective power and break free of the socialization and enculturation that keep us stuck in ineffectual ways of thinking. There has been an air of defeatism as we confront the cultural institutions that promote dominating ways of being and thinking and selfish egoism. Patriarchy has detached itself from spirit, and it is this fact that has devastated Hecate.

> Without connection to what is spiritual, the human ego becomes immersed in the unreal; and since it pays attention to nothing else, the ego dismisses any other way of thinking as *unrealistic*.[8]

Through Hecate we learn that we can have everything if we possess nothing. Possessiveness indicates greed and attachment and is fueled by an assumption that there will not be enough. Sometimes this inherent reaction has its roots in our early infancy when we were fed on a schedule. Our reaction to being left hungry was precisely as serious as it sounded, yet our parents persisted in letting us scream it out. We thus became hoarders, psychologically and materially.

THE HECATE WOMAN

The Hecate woman is a wise woman unto herself, a Crone in her own right. She has lived independently and not been a slave to cultural expectations. She has much life experience and has been through a mid-life crisis, even if she is only nineteen years old. The Hecate woman dances to the beat of her own drum.

She can be touchy about certain issues. She wants to be recognized as an important and powerful person, though she can be insecure about her own worth. She may act with personal dignity, or she may be crass and short. She is down-to-earth, but she can be reserved and shy. The Hecate woman is introverted and emotionally profound.

The Hecate woman is concerned about achievement and success. She has great ambition to succeed, but on her own terms. She seeks the truest path of duty that connects with her higher purpose. She has a need to feel socially useful. Her reputation is important here, so when she is judged, or society does not share her values, she can feel rejected.

If the Hecate woman can maintain her integrity, she has the potential to make a significant impact. Her developmental task has been to illuminate her own shadow. Hence, "Pollyanna" types, or those who have relegated their shadow material to the unconscious, tend to project their shadows onto the Hecate woman. As the Hecate woman becomes more conscious, she begins to feel it when someone projects their shadow onto her. She will experience this as a weight, which can cause her to brood. It certainly fuels her internal process. As she communicates her experience, she is assisting others in owning their projections. By standing up for what she believes, even in the face of unpopularity, the Hecate woman makes inroads in her social circle and builds spiritual fortitude.

ANGEL OF THE ILLUMINED SHADOW

In days past, yogis who were attempting to achieve enlightenment renounced the world. They lived in caves in the Himalayas and were able to meditate from morning to night. Modern spiritual warriors are challenged. We are being asked to live a spiritual life in a material world. Living a spiritual life on earth is not about renouncing all people and material possessions. It is about being able to maintain our equilibrium in relationships. It is about enjoying modern conveniences without attachment.

In ancient Mystery Schools, Lucifer was known as a *spiritual monitor*. At first, this was simply a measure of the spiritual development of the initiate and their level of detachment from possessiveness and materiality. To the initiate, Lucifer was not a manifestation of evil, but a representative of causal power. The challenge was to be able to live, love, laugh, and be happy without the torment of fear, guilt, greed, competition, and sorrow.[9] We are, then, in the world but not of it.

> Know all things while recognizing that we know nothing, to do all things with the understanding that we are not doing anything. We are to be materially satisfied yet not spiritually complacent, to love right action without being fanatical about it, and to meet responsibilities without overemphasizing a personal sense of duty.[10]

When the energy of the Angel of the Illumined Shadow is blocked, we lock our shadows in the recesses of our psyches and project negative aspects of ourselves onto others. Then they become the ones who are invasive, rude, negative, obsessive, or greedy. We live in bondage to outward appearances. We become fearful that we will not get enough. Our desires to "keep up with the Jones" can overwhelm us.

The Angel of the Illumined Shadow is a sophisticated friend. Connecting with her requires a great personal courage, but we then are able to see the aspects of ourselves that are manipulative and controlling.

Demeter

Tall Tower

Demeter

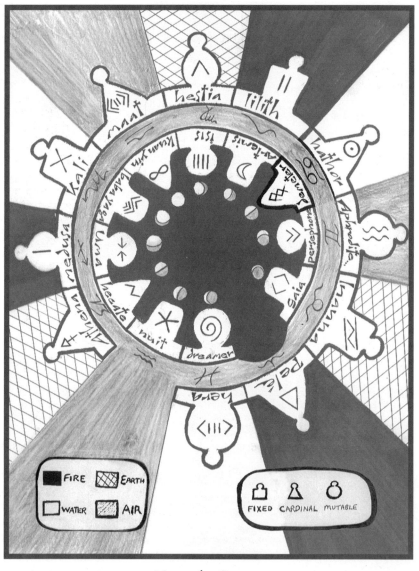

Moon in Cancer
Cardinal–Water

Chapter XX

ᗪemeter

16

$\mathcal{T}$he goddess Demeter embodies the archetype of the Great Mother. She was honored and revered in ancient Greece and was the tower of strength in the extended community. In prehistoric Greece, the mother-daughter bond was the most sacred of all relationships. In the characteristic matriarchal culture, mothers and daughters had a fierce loyalty to each other and a sweet intimacy that allowed for the passing of the sacred feminine secrets from one generation to another.

Demeter, the archetypal Mother, is represented by the number sixteen. One and six are both materialistic numbers, but when added together they produce seven, the number of spirit. Again, our evolutionary task is to spiritualize the material. Sometimes that change comes as a lightning bolt from the heavens. Numerologically, Demeter is connected to Medusa, the Amazon Queen, a mother and a mentor herself who had fierce loyalty to the young maidens in her clan.

As the Tarot Tower, Demeter contains the purifying eye of self-awareness and the promise of creativity restored. She manifests as the tower of strength. In traditional Tarot, the Tower is being struck by lightning, symbolizing the fertilization of the abysmal womb by Zeus (who fathered Persephone) and "the blood of all living creatures was made of female waters warmed and reddened by his fire."[1]

Demeter is anchored in the symbolism of the Moon in Cancer. A cardinal water sign, the energy is nurturing, dedicated, protective, responsible, maternal, and courageous. Her home and family are her primary attachment, and she has a deep need to dominate her home. Demeter's reactions can be slow and uncertain. She picks up negative emotional energy from others and can emerge moody and unhappy. She is intensely aware of other's moods and reactions. She is easily imposed on and can be unnecessarily generous and selfless.

MYTHOLOGY

Persephone, Demeter's beloved daughter, was abducted by
her uncle and disappeared into the depths of the Underworld. The intensity of Demeter's lamentations alerted
Hecate, a crone goddess who lived in the Underworld.
Hecate assisted Demeter in retrieving Persephone, who
emerged from the Underworld at Eleusis. This gave way
to the Eleusinian Mysteries, marking the pain of domination
by the male on the matriarchal spirit.

> In the prehistoric women-centered Goddess
> culture, the primordial relationship was
> between mother and daughter who formed
> the nucleus of the female group. In the early
> patriarchal period the male is often an alien
> who comes from without and by violence takes
> the daughter from the mother. Separation and
> reunion, the restoration of the primary relationship
> to the mother, is the great motif underlying the Eleusinian Mysteries.[2]

The Great Goddess was venerated and celebrated in Greek temples until the
fall of the Roman Empire.[3] For over a thousand years people traveled from far
and wide to be initiated in the Eleusinian Mysteries. The sanctuary at Eleusis is
22 kilometers from Athens. Each fall, lavish processionals of initiates made a
sacred pilgrimage to Eleusis for nine-day rituals. These rituals, which were referred
to as the Greater Mysteries, involved gratitude for the harvest, purification, prayers
for the collective, and individual initiations. Springtime festivities were three
days long and were referred to as the Lesser Mysteries. The sanctuary and the
initiation rites at Eleusis persisted until it was burned by the Goths around 400 AD.[4]

There is much speculation about what transpired in the Eleusinian Mystery
Schools, partly because they were experientially based and partly because participants were sworn to secrecy. Surviving artifacts reflect the key events of the
mythology and the ritual associated with these mysteries. Cicero said, "The
mysteries of Eleusis mellowed people's hearts, transformed barbarian natures
into being truly human."[5]

The Mysteries themselves were comparable to a modern psychodrama, or
the ritual enactment of a myth in a structured situation. This essentially con-
sisted of descending into the Underworld, confronting grief, oppression, and
death, and resurrecting back to an enhanced life. Initiates were transformed and
became ecstatic. This fulfilled a spiritual need that civic religions could not, and
it was available to all citizens whose *"hands were free of blood,"* meaning that
they had not taken human life.[6] The Eleusinian Mysteries were more than rote

religious activity: they provided a great service to the populace by bringing the initiate into harmony with the divine.

Central to the Eleusinian Mysteries was the overcoming of the fear of death.[7] The dead were referred to as the *Demetereioi*, or Demeter's people. She was said to preside over all who lived, and to restore life to the dead by receiving them into her bosom.[8]

> Immanence of the divine and the continuity between life and death were core ideas of the Goddess religion, part of the common world view. Suppressed by the Olympians, the mysteries preserved and made this wisdom accessible only to those initiated.[9]

The Mysteries dramatized, and therefore normalized, two fundamental realities in the natural cycle of life: the natural intimacy of the mother-daughter relationship and the primordial relation between life and death. On a yearly basis, the initiates were led through a series of intense emotional rituals lasting for nine days that legitimized and formalized the intensity of grieving and the value of life.

The dramatization of Demeter's arresting agony when her precious daughter was abducted ritualized the grieving process and emphasized the power of the mother-daughter bond and the potency of this primal bond. This is much the same as the ritualized grieving that was represented in the Mystery schools of Ancient Egypt that reenacted Isis's grief when she was separated from her brother-lover-husband Osiris. Again, the legitimization of lamentation and the ritualization of the emotional turmoil provided a valued service to the populace. The formal reenactment literally increased the emotional capacity of initiates and was seen as training for the eventuality of grieving in everyday life. It also expanded the arena of support within the populace. This is in sharp contrast to our cultural imperative to not be excessively emotional. Crying in public is taboo, and we are taught to choke back our tears even at funerals. In current culture, when a loved one dies, we are expected to instantly recover and complete our grieving within a limited time. This denies the profound process of grief and loss that has us reckon with the meaning of life.

During the yearly Eleusinian Mystery Rituals,

> Pilgrims came for the emotional experience, their mood shifting from anxiety to rapture as they re-enacted the passion of Demeter, the descent of Kore [Persephone] into the Underworld, and the fate of the dead.[10]

This lent itself to the second part of the ritualized mysteries, facing the realities of death. As in all goddess traditions, emphasis was placed on the inevitability of rebirth after death, the idea of the soul being recycled into new form. Facing one's own death brought one closer to the essence of life. The facing of fear led to a deep personal transformation. These revelations illuminated the natural mysteries of life and death, the idea of immortality and eternal rebirth. The rituals included a purification ceremony and a "crossing over" in which initiates experienced the magical realms of heightened senses and deep knowing distinct from ordinary, profane life.

Research on the Eleusinian Mysteries respects that details were to be held secret, and this mysteriousness is obvious in commentaries and documents. Although the burning question of exactly what occurred in these rituals is held dear, scattered literary testimonies, excavated remnants, and symbolic artifacts provide clues and allow us to reconstruct the sanctity of the rituals and the elaborate preparations that preceded them.

On the evening before the first day, the cult symbols and sacred objects, or *sacra*, were transported the 14 miles from Athens to Eleusis by priestesses who walked in solemn procession carrying the sacra on their heads or dancing in the procession. These processions followed ancient *dragon lines*, or powerful earth currents, from one holy site to another.

> The sacred processions were grandiose. With them one came to understand the Great Mysteries and the supreme descent of the Spirit toward matter. This was a grandiose event that was anticipated with as much eagerness as when we look forward to the ascent of man toward the superior worlds today.[11]

The initiates that were to participate in the rituals were selected on the first day in Athens. On the second day there was a procession to the Aegean Sea, which borders the Temple complex, for purification. The third day was given over to prayers for the city. The fourth day was for the integration of latecomers. The fifth day, the *mystai*, or the initiates, were crowned in myrtle and carried torches from Athens to Eleusis and the sacred grounds of Demeter, enclosed in high walls to preserve the secrets within. As in all ancient traditions, there was singing and dancing in honor of the Goddess. It was written that on this night, "even the goddesses in the stormy heaven of Zeus danced to honor the golden-crowned maiden and her holy mother."[12]

On the sixth day the *mystai* fasted and offered sacrifices. On the seventh and eighth nights, the actual initiations took place. Initiates drank *kykeon*, a fermented mint-flavored drink that was intoxicating and promoted a "seeing," or an "opening of the eyes." This substance contained ergot derivatives, a psychedelic substance.[13] A ceremony followed involving a replica of the womb, a phallus or a snake, or cakes in the shape of genital organs.[14]

One of the hidden secrets was the sexual nature of the Mystery Schools around the world. According to Woer:

> In the unfathomable depths of time there were powerful civilizations and magnificent mysteries. There were always priestesses of Love in the temples. Those who practiced Sexual Magic with them became the Masters of the White Lodge. The Master must be born within us with Sexual Magic ... All systems of intimate, self-education have Sexual Magic as their ultimate practical synthesis. All religions, all esoteric cults, have Sexual Magic as a synthesis. In the Eleusinian Mysteries there were nude dances and ineffable things. Sexual Magic formed the fundamental basis of those Mysteries.[15]

The *mystai* were said to look skyward and to cry as "rain" fell to the earth, and they proclaimed "conception." After the sound of a thunder-like gong, the goddess acquired another name that means "the strong one." New life is Mother Demeter's gift to humanity. The goddesses, as mother and daughter, belong together in their transformation from one to the other. The daughter becomes a mother who has a daughter who becomes a mother and so the cycle continues.

> Usually the maiden is characterized by the flower she carries, the mother by the fruit. Flower and fruit, narcissus and pomegranate, represent their respective roles. The redness of the pomegranate symbolizes the woman's womb, the abundance of seeds, its fertility. The narcissus expresses seduction to the sexually awakening girl.[16]

When Persephone is abducted by her uncle, she is stooping to pick a narcissus, symbolic of her virginity. Allured by Hades' charm, Persephone ate six pomegranate seeds. The eating of the seeds is symbolic of her entry into womanhood. This, of course, permanently changed her relationship to her mother, which is part of Demeter's grief. This transition to womanhood and all its ensuing consequences is part of the developmental crisis of the feminine and becomes the essence of the Eleusinian Mysteries. Here the presence of Hecate, the crone, is essential. As wise woman, she completes the trinity in the life cycle of a woman that emphasized that change, like death, was not to be feared, but to be embraced. Thus the Eleusinian Mysteries provided a template for the initiates to revere, understand, and to ritualize the natural life cycles of the feminine, thereby accepting and facilitating the inevitable transitions.

The Great Goddess was seen to have three aspects, representing the three stages of life that all women contain: the maiden, the mother, and the crone. Demeter represented the life-giving, nurturing *mother* aspect of the feminine. Her daughter, Persephone, represented the *virgin,* or maiden. Hecate, was the *crone*, or old wise woman. Her grandmother was Gaia, the Earth Goddess, whose "shadowy presence is always in the background, lending magnitude and grandeur to her (Demeter's) mysteries."[17]

Demeter is sometimes referred to as the goddess of grain and is said to have symbolically given birth to grain. Worldly wealth and pleasure are made manifest as well as the treasure of everlasting life.

In hunter-gatherer cultures when famine was ever-imminent, women gave birth approximately every fifth year, and the procreation of the species was seen as a mysterious gift from the goddess unrelated to the scientific realities of conception through the fertilization of an ovum by a sperm. Horticulture, or the transplantation of herbs and grain, gave way to agriculture, or the systematic planting of grain for storage. The depiction of the Great Mother as large and fleshy was in keeping with the biological imperatives necessary for the miracle of birth to occur. The honoring of this mystery was reflected in primitive art equating female beauty with largeness. Biologically, this had to do with the health of the female and the fat content of her body that would ensure the nourishment of the offspring.

As an evolutionary step, the hunter-gatherers found large caves suitable to establish homes for more than one season. They continued to hunt and to gather food and firewood from the countryside and entourage. The next progressive stage was the birth of horticulture. It is speculated that the women gathering herbs, berries, and grain realized that if the plants could grow far from the home site, they may be able to grow at closer range. Transplantation began. As the seasons progressed, the perennials spawned new growth.

As the parent plants became more established, the harvest became more prolific. Grain and greens were then planted in rows. This evolutionary stage gave way to agriculture. This was a significant transition for primitive humans in that the bounty of the harvest provided ample food supplies and reserves for trading. What is more important, the people, young and old, were well nourished and the tribe flourished.

As a consequence, women began to procreate each year. It is speculated that the connection was then made that intercourse and the male seed may have something to do with impregnation. This realization had a dramatic effect on culture. Before this leap in consciousness, the male was the protector-consort in awe of the female's creative capacity to give life. When it was established that birth occurred approximately nine moons after sexual activity, the male contribution was confirmed.

Though it may be argued that this idea is unnecessarily simplistic, it does explain on both biological and psychological levels how the seeds of patriarchy were planted and how the worship of the Great Cosmic Mother gave way to male ascendancy.

Thus, gradual evolutionary progression eroded the status of mothering and erased from the collective unconscious the veneration of the Great Mother of

All. As a consequence, the existential need to connect with the archetypal Mother has been transferred to individual mothers and to individual women. The connection to the mother is the most fundamental connection on the earth plane. Most of us have not given the following statement much thought, yet it is a quintessential truth: *Everyone* has a mother.

According to a Homeric myth, Demeter is said to have given birth to a son, the personification of wealth and abundance, who was to be the one to introduce grain to the world and promote her rites. Interestingly, the change in identity from female to male comes at an important transition between matriarchal and patriarchal cultures. The question is raised: Did this have something to do with the male biological identification with procreation? This highly significant revelation occurred at a time when the populace was well nourished and when women began to give birth every year. In other words, it was understood that the male provided the seed for human birth. Hence:

> The changing identity of Demeter's son suggests a shift in spiritual values in keeping with the changing role of the Goddess and her Divine Child in the mysteries of the Hellenistic Age. That is Demeter's son, not daughter, who passes on her mysteries, reflects an even more fundamental change from a woman-centered world to a patriarchal one.[18]

Nurtured in and born from the very body of our mothers, we depend on her for primary connection, and in infancy, for our very survival. This is highly significant in that it amplifies the power of the maternal in the collective. Because the culture denigrates the very energy that is primal in the psyche, the depth of the maternal matrix can only live in the shadow of the collective. Because this fact is denied, it has been driven into the unconscious.

DEMETER WOMAN

The Demeter woman is emotionally tenacious. She is maternal, sympathetic, and genuinely concerned for the welfare of others. After all, as an ancient Greek proverb states: "The mother is the soul of the house."[19]

The Demeter archetype is primarily focused on others. She secures a loving and nurturing home. She strives to maintain stability, manage the family, and serve in the community. The Demeter woman values feminine energy, the precious, nurturing of the mother goddess. It is important for her to find a source of nurturing for the Self that is as loving and complete as she offers others.

To be in service to her children, the Demeter woman must drop her ego and postpone her own agenda. Her life becomes about the personal development of her children, and her own needs often get put aside. Unless a woman has a number of other archetypes functioning simultaneously, she will sacrifice her own advancement to serve the needs of others.

THE ANGEL OF STRENGTH AND NURTURING

The Angel of Strength and Nurturing provides the fortitude to persevere on the Red Road to the Realm of Cosmic Consciousness. The Red Road, according to native Indian elders, is the challenging road that keeps offering the spiritual warrior new opportunities.

Along the path, we are initiated in the Realm of the Underworld, fortified in the Realm of Roles, provoked in the Realm of Renunciation, before being released into the Realm of Cosmic Consciousness.

The Angel of Strength and Nurturing offers us comfort and an environment of clarity and warmth to give us vigor for the last leg of the journey. We are granted courage to help us face adversity and to confront opposition, interference, or temptation. We can then continue with confidence into the next stage of growth.

Nuit

Tree at the Violet Hour

Nuit

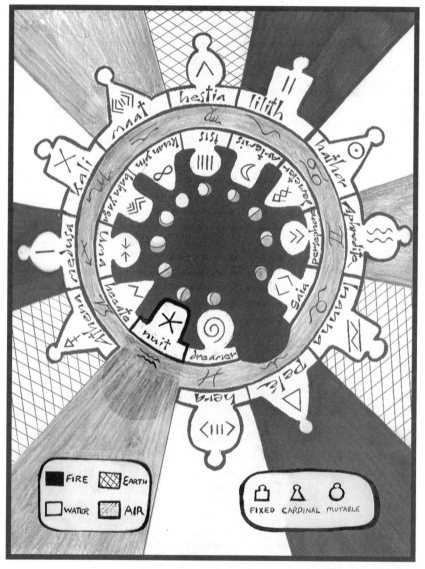

Moon and Sun in Aquarius – Open House
Fixed–Air

Chapter XXI

Nuit

17

Nuit is the archetypal Cosmic Gate. Her body is the galaxy, and the stars shine inside her being. In typical ancient Egyptian art, she is the sky arching over a scene, her hands and feet connecting to the earth. Aleister Crowley calls Nuit "Our Lady of Infinite Space."[1] Nuit, translated from French, means "night." Known as the Egyptian Sky Mother,[2] Nuit's energy enters the atmosphere at the violet hour, the time when day gives way to the enchantment of the night and the sky glows indigo. Our own spiral galaxy, the Milky Way, is named after the milk that poured forth from the breasts of Nuit.

Nuit is represented by the number seventeen. Seventeen is a prime number and is divisible only by one. The combination of one and seven is a fortunate one, for it is the individual (1) and the spirit (7) that inspires a heightened feeling for all things in heaven and the cosmos. This connects Nuit to the pure and conscious energy of Kuan Yin (17 is 1+7=8).

In the Tarot, Nuit is symbolized by the Star that promises universal understanding, hope, faith, and beauty.

> Aspects of the psyche, formerly imprisoned within stone walls and now freed, will come down to earth where they can begin to operate in a more realistic way. In the Star, a nature priestess initiates the task of discovering in the events of terrestrial existence a pattern corresponding to heavenly design.[3]

Nuit is positioned in an open house. As the archetypal Cosmic Gate, she allows Cosmic energy to enter the Earth Plane. As seen earlier in the evolutionary journey, Pele is the terrestrial portal exploding energy from the core of the Earth into the Cosmos. Both offer an essential energetic exchange.

Nuit simultaneously contains the introverted energy of the Moon in Aquarius and the extroverted energy of the Sun in Aquarius. A fixed air sign, it focuses on the intuitive, the occult, and the Cosmic and sustains energy that has been released.

MYTHOLOGY

In Egyptian mythology, Nuit swallows the sun at dusk and gives birth to it again at dawn. Nuit represents:

> The one life and intelligence, the one love and guiding power, that is working for the eternal progress and the good of the race—the Mother-God, the Holy Spirit, the Over-soul, that is always brooding over the earth and the human race bringing about the fulfilling of the natural processes and lifting all to spiritual understanding, consciousness, and expression.[4]

The human mind cannot conceive the wonders and immensity of the universe of stars in the heavens. The same light that radiates from the stars glows from Nuit. In ancient Egyptian mythology, stars represent psychic thoughts[5] and are the eyes of heaven. As above, so below; as within, so without. She is self-reflective, super-conscious, and self-realized. She has synthesized the spiritual teachings of the zodiac and integrated them into the whole of her indivisible Self. Nuit invites us to enter the crown where the soul lives.[6] She is graceful, ecstatic, beautifully naked, and psychically sensitive. At this stage, nothing is left in the unconscious. From this synergy, Nuit opens to the Universal force of love and gives birth to the divine human prototype, winged goddess Isis, Queen of the Night.

Stars are connected with the idea of immortality. Not surprisingly, one of Nuit's roles was to welcome the dead to *Amenti*, or the Afterworld. She lives in the timeless world of the stars and planets that have existed since the creation of the Universe. Her picture was painted with outstretched arms on the inside cover of coffins, or sarcophagi, to welcome the souls of the dead.

In ancient Egypt, Nuit was personified as a tree, embodying the intercon-nection and interdependence inherent in all nature. She was said to lean forward from the tree and to give food and drink to the deceased. Trees are rooted deep in the earth and tower high in the sky. They are a connecting link between heaven and earth, between body and mind, between the formless and the formed. As a personification of a tree, Nuit brings in energy from the Cosmos and grounds it on earth. The ancient Egyptians considered trees to be vital conduits between heaven and earth, as did many native peoples around the globe.

> Trees draw into themselves all four elements, synthesizing and transforming them into vital new growth. Hence trees are symbolic of the transpersonal, universal self. Yet the shape and pattern of each individual tree differs from all others. So trees can represent the unique way the transpersonal self is made manifest in each individual.[7]

There are ancient Mesopotamian seals showing the serpent, male and female forms holding cups, in attendance to a water-carrier, or Aquarius, in the presence of a world tree. There is no sign of danger, divine wrath, or guilt connected with the Tree of Knowledge. This is the symbol of the world axis from which flows life, enlightenment, and wisdom.[8] Archetypally, to know Nuit is *to know.* When a Truth resonates deep in our hearts, we *know.* We exclaim: "I knew it!" This can also be written: "I *Nu-it*!"

Through Nuit's cosmic dimensional portal, the Dreamer has now fully integrated the knowledge of Self and is fully individuated. This level of initiation allows for co-creativity with the divine. After a great spiritual illumination, with a clear mind and a compassionate heart, we have a new lease on life. Nuit represents the inexhaustible possibilities of existence and the spiral force of cosmic energy.

> Nuit is an initiation into the eternal present, the place of infinite time where every dimension is a possible reality.[9]

The Egyptians began training programs at middle age to prepare their souls for the journey to the other side into the light. They knew Nuit would be waiting to welcome them into her arms. Tales of the seven bardos, or transitional phases, were depicted on graves. The mystery schools explained the passage of a soul from third-dimensional reality to the multidimensional world.

THE NUIT WOMAN

The Nuit woman maintains a great desire for spiritual enlightenment. She synthesizes spirituality, humanitarianism, and the occult. All these were well connected for the ancients. The mind and the emotions reacted together. Astrology, Tarot, channeled information, messages from off planet, and intuition all fit together with the ingenuity and inventiveness in the Nuit woman. There is much creative energy represented here, and her fertile imagination lends itself to much originality. She is idealistic, broadminded, and ahead of her time.

The Nuit woman has stars in her eyes. She is highly individualistic, unconventional, and independent. She can be somewhat unpredictable, like life itself. She loves to learn, and she expresses useful knowledge.

The Nuit woman is a star. She is a leader and has influence because she has the capacity to inspire others. She feels comfortable on stage. She functions individually and has few peers and role models.

Her views will be unprejudiced, and she will be able to be detached and objective in her dealings with others. She is in touch with the needs of larger society, and she wishes to make a contribution to society as a whole.

THE ANGEL OF THE GALACTIC BEAM

The Angel of the Galactic Beam stimulates an outpouring of Love for all humanity laced with devotion and idealism. This Angel welcomes us into the Realm of Cosmic Consciousness where the long journey along the Red Road culminates in ecstatic bliss and in connection to the Source. Assisted by the Angels that

guide her and keep track of her mission, Nuit is the arched gateway to the Realm of Cosmic Consciousness, opening the Dreamer to the remaining initiations on the journey to collective enlightenment. Four remaining Angels are ushered through the doorway: the Angel of the Lunation Cycle, the Angel of Multidimensionality, the Angel of Cosmic Consciousness, and the Angel of the One Heart.

In its essence, it exemplifies the true meaning of harmlessness, inclusiveness, and a bonding with the planetary family. All sense of separateness and segregation dissolves and gives way to a feeling of oneness. As barriers are removed, we begin to see the world as an indivisible whole. A similar reaction takes place within, and we begin to experience ourselves as indivisible wholes.

> Accordingly, as the Initiate realized that boundaries and distinctions cannot exist in a cosmic sense, that all is of one omnipresent essence, a new dawning began on the inner plane, leading to the mystical marriage and the consummation of the Greatest Work. Through a consciousness of service, the personality and Self meet and become one, and through the marriage there is conscious union with God.[10]

This Angel draws upon the Aquarian energy, and as it is poured upon us, we awaken inspired. We become more altruistic, more inclusive in our thoughts, more democratic in our actions. We synthesize all that we have learned and value that which supports humanity as a whole. Each person carries a piece of the puzzle. When they participate fully in the "group mind," a synthesis into a grander design is made possible. In other words, the whole is greater than the sum of the parts.

> Remember that energy is all there is; there is nothing else. Everything seen and unseen, visible and invisible, matter and substance, is all pure energy and is the nature of all form. Move in consciousness into this real world of pure energy and see with the inner eye that vast energy field enveloping you and pressing upon your consciousness to manifest through you. You live and move and have your being in an ocean of God energy, or spiritual energy, and you should consciously channel that energy—which is your faith—in your meditations. This will open the way to see the plan, firm up your ideals, and move you forward to serve with Love and inspiration.[11]

The Angel of the Galactic Beam enables us to live an empowered life with absolute confidence. Through her we are aware that the Earth is being pulsed with galactic beams of energy. This is creating a new spiritual context on Earth and assisting us in our collective evolution. Through her we are able to see that we are in conscious control of our destiny.

Artemis

Primitive Village

Artemis

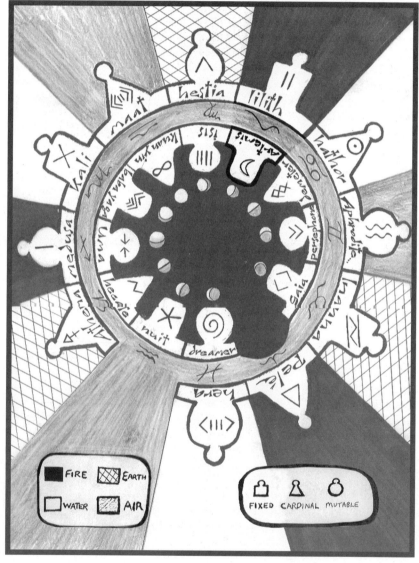

FIRE EARTH
WATER AIR

FIXED CARDINAL MUTABLE

Moon in Leo
Fixed–Fire

Chapter XXII

Artemis

Artemis is the archetypal Wild Woman. She is the prototype of earthy, natural humanness who is a personification of the power of nature and the nourishing force that tends to all sentient life. Artemis represents the soul qualities of vitality and creativity. In many North American Native traditions, humans were said to be the caretakers of life on the planet. They referred to trees as Standing Persons and to rocks as Stone Persons. Being the most evolved species on the planet, humans were given the responsibility by the Great Spirit to preserve the environment and the natural balance on the planet. Artemis represents the mature feminine that understands how to caretake, yet maintain balance within herself. Even though she is not herself a mother, she is alive with procreative potential.

Artemis is connected to the number eighteen. Numerologically, this is the embodiment of wholeness and of completion, represented in the number nine. This associates Artemis (18) with Hestia (9). Both share the joys of solitude and are *virgins*, or women who belong to themselves.

Artemis is kin to Tarot Moon. The diffuse light of *Luna* reveals many aspects of reality not visible in the blinding direct fire of the sun. Tarot moon magic reflects the ascent of human karma and the activation of genetic memory. The phase of reflected light in the lunation cycle is linked to our biological rhythms and to our emotions. Through this reflective cycle, we explore our true natures. At this stage of the journey, the energy of the dark moon is made conscious and the wild, natural, earthy humanness is embraced. The crescent moon, the first phase after the new moon, is Artemis' most potent phase. The regenerative new moon has initiated a crescent of light. The light returns after the new moon has initiated a new potential. In Whitmont's words:

> The moon crescent and the sickle-shaped sword occur repeatedly in mythological imagery. They refer to the rising power of the feminine.

> The crescent moon is symbolic of Artemis ... as yet *unrevealed,*
> *mystery of emotion, of love, generativeness, renewal, and change.*
> Symbolically, the moon weapon points to the fact that *the force of*
> *the moon,* the force of the psychic tides of life, of emotion rather
> than rational functioning, *represents an energy not to be dis-*
> *regarded.*[1] [emphasis mine]

Anchored in the energy of the Moon in Leo, the Artemis archetype is emotionally sensitive. As a fixed fire sign, the conscious will is the motivating force that holds on course that which is already established. She is therefore creative, self-sufficient, and self-reliant. The archetypal energy is straightforward and honest and has a sunny, self-confident disposition. She is highly principled and can be counted on not to compromise her values.

MYTHOLOGY

One of the seven wonders of the ancient world is a temple built in honor of Artemis at Ephesus in present-day Turkey, which was at one time a powerful center of learning and of commerce. To view Ephesus in its vastness conjures memories of an ancient culture that flourished in its honoring of the feminine. Most impressive is the library with four life-size statues of priestesses proudly honoring the virtues of love, wisdom, grace, and truth. Herein lies the power of the archetypal Artemis, she who can manifest in the material world while honoring and preserving the nourishing power of the feminine and of the earth.

Gifts from Artemis were called *Artemas,* meaning the gift of wholeness, or the gift of perfection.[2] Two such *Artemas* are the moon and the stars, which represent truth, light, and fulfillment.[3] In Greek legends, the seven stars of the Pleiades were said to be the companions of Artemis. They appear in the shoulder of the constellation Taurus that comes into view at the beginning of spring and disappears late in autumn. The "sweet influence" of these seven stars brought warm weather for growth and vegetation and were used for navigation. They were also referred to as the "seven daughters" and brought abundance, increase, and perfection to earth.[4]

Artemis has a wild, primitive side as a huntress and protectress of that which is untamed. Artemis is comfortable in the wilderness, and she is thus comfortable with her own wildness. We are indebted to Clarissa Pinkola Estes, who captivated the literary world with her bestseller *Women Who Run with the*

Wolves: Myths and Stories about the Wild Woman Archetype.[5] She nourished our collective hunger for material on the natural wild woman. She normalized and legitimized the place in us that longs to dig in the earth and to ground ourselves in our wildness. Artemis represents the Virgin aspect of *La Loba,* or the *Wild Woman.*

> In mythos and by whatever name, La Loba knows the personal past and the ancient past for she has survived generation after generation, and is old beyond time. *She is an archivist of feminine intention.* She reserves female tradition *Her whiskers sense the future;* she has the far-seeing milky eye of the old crone; *she lives backward and forward in time simultaneously,* correcting for one side by *dancing* with the other.[6] [emphasis mine]

Instead of seeing the huntress as animistic, we can see her as *anima*-istic.[7] Again, the anima is the aspect of self that is ultimately feminine and is said to give events the dimension of the soul. Her life work is in soul retrieval.

Artemis enlivens the connection between soul and solitude. Fear of Artemis could be fear of self-confrontation. When we become accustomed to retrieving ourselves and thriving within our own soul space, we heal and we become internally strong. Artemis promotes a powerful archetypal way of being.

> Soul making is not confined to the making of our own soul but to the recreation (or rediscovery) of the world within which we live as a realm of souls, of living, meaning-full-in-themselves, beings.[8]

From a planetary standpoint, the spiral dance between the earth and her moon is reflective and poetic. Artemis is connected to the lunation cycle, and her etheric field encompasses the moon. By intuiting the mysteries of the moon, Artemis lives a grounded life on the planet, and is creative as an expression of personal power.

> Like the moon, this gestating affirmation reflects; it has a mirroring and gently revealing affect.[9]

If the lunation cycle is applied to the calendar year, the first crescent represents *Candlemas,* celebrated February 2, halfway between the longest night of Winter Solstice and Spring Equinox. Here the masculine and feminine energies are in perfect balance. They create a *hieros gamos,* or a marriage within. By tuning into this energy, we can break karmic patterns in relationship and establish more conscious ways of relating.

Artemis is the prototype of the exalted self-sufficient feminine. She carves out an independent life, in tune with her moon, and embracing the reflective cycles. The stages on the journey toward consciousness that precede this archetype prepare the ground, open the channel, and are the rites of passage that births Artemis, the virgin moon goddess.

> Artemis is a tender nurse of all that is young and vulnerable, be it human or animal; but she has no patience with those who remain childish, who stay dependent and needy, as adult women.[10]

THE ARTEMIS WOMAN

The Artemis woman is a woman who belongs to herself. She is a manifestation of the secure feminine. She relies on her own values and is not easily swayed. She is able to quickly evaluate people and their motives, and because her motivations are clearly oriented, she quickly knows who is kindred to her and who is not. She loves music, art, luxury, and children. She has powerful emotions and her affections are given generously.

The Artemis woman is the woman who has "invented" herself. She creates her work by devising a need for what she wants to do, whether she starts her own business or works for hire. This is the mastery of the Artemis businesswoman. She has not sold her soul to the patriarchy, like her sister Athena. Artemis has an awakened feminine consciousness in balance with masculine consciousness. Her business success depends on her acumen, her ability to bring forth the treasures of the feminine in the business world. This is Artemis' forte.

The Artemis energy asks us to be congruent and uncompromising. She asks us to consider the values that reflect our actions. She is astute, conscientious, and honorable.

The Artemis woman is extremely practical. She learns quickly and is educated, sincere, and well researched. Her values are well established. They are the values of the humanist who honors our jewel planet, all sentient life, the Great Cosmic Mother, and the magnificent beauty on the Earth Plane. Preservation and evolution are paramount concerns to the Artemis woman. She has grown quite comfortable engaging in service that promotes organized responses to that which threatens our delicate ecosystem. Though she is often shy and reserved in a social or professional setting, the Artemis woman, if need be, will speak up and challenge anyone who makes assumptions about supremacy and domination. Any statement that denigrates the feminine or the principle of procreation, or any show of disrespect, will be plainly unacceptable to her.

The huntress aspect of Artemis can be distressing if it is not fully understood. Meat-eaters often take for granted the meat in the grocery coolers, not giving much thought to how it appears in our local supermarket. It is challenging to stay conscious of the hormonal additives, the antibiotics given commercially raised animals, and the fear instilled in cattle during slaughtering. Being a responsible meat-eater, even if we only eat it occasionally, involves consideration of how the meat arrived on our table. North American Native tradition teaches about honoring the life of the animal given up for us to have leather footwear, protein on our platters, and warm winter clothing. All this is considered part of the natural cycle of birth and death within our ecosystem. In more direct terms, if we as modern women want to wear leather jackets and shoes, and enjoy the occasional burger, we must incorporate the aspect of Artemis that is willing to carry the consciousness of the four-leggeds.

The matter-of-fact ambiance concerning this challenge is a trademark of the Artemis woman who quite simply refuses to be invalidated. This disposition is invariably hard-won by the Artemis woman, whose independent actions over the decades have caused definite reactions in the circles she moves in. Like the Lillith woman, the Artemis woman eventually learns there is a certain measure of ostracism experienced when a woman speaks out expecting equality with men.

A story comes to mind of the feminist who visited Russia in its newly liberated political climate, with her husband who was on business. This woman had a political life in North America. She was an avid feminist, solid, well educated, well spoken, well informed, fully present in the reality of scene. At a formal dinner, the conversation warmed the atmosphere, how novel the differing customs were, yet how all were part of the human family.

The men stood up to make a toast, and she stood too. Everyone stopped and stared at her. She then noticed all the women were sitting. She went to speak: "In our country, the women..."

She was stared down by full agreement. Even the men from her own country, even her husband, entered the conspiracy of silence. This conspiracy instructed her to be mute. It instructed her to sit while the men stood.

For the high-functioning Artemis woman, an experience like this would be disturbing. Perhaps when her mortification surfaces and she and her husband are in their private quarters, a conversation could appease her suppression, she thinks. The humiliation experienced in such a situation when a woman assumes equality is nothing short of devastating. When she realizes that her husband, even in the privacy of their relationship, largely agrees with the consensus, her eyes widen. Like Hera, she is astonished at the insensitivity and bastardization of power. These experiences exemplify the reaction women of conviction endure in a culture that has disempowered us in the name of progress and supremacy.

Where Lillith would be indignant and Medusa would be planning the International Foundation for Gender-Equitable Etiquette, Artemis would simply be astounded. Suffice it to say that if these archetypal women got together, they would roar the great lion's roar, strengthen their sisterhood, and declare their right and their might.

The Artemis woman, then, compels deep respect. This makes it easier for the next woman to protest because the path is cleared to the front of the room. In wishing we could be more like her, we are imagining ourselves in her shoes, which is the first step in becoming more like her. Thus she represents the divine prototype of modern woman. She is what we aspire to when we achieve new levels of personal integrity and self-understanding.

THE ANGEL OF THE LUNATION CYCLE

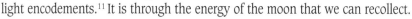

The energy of the moon returns indirect solar energy to us. It is as though our external reality is reflected in the holy lunar mirror. The Angel of the Lunation Cycle is the soul of the moon. She emanates the opalescent, tranquil, refined, peaceful, silvery vibration of *Luna.*

This Angel is, all at once, the reflection of the planetary mind and personal emotions. She teaches us that personal mastery is based on how we deal with our emotions. It is *Luna* that holds the soul of our matriarchal experiences in our multiple incarnations through reflective light encodements.[11] It is through the energy of the moon that we can recollect.

> The moon wisdom of biding one's time, of accepting and ripening, absorbs everything into its totality and transforms what has been taken in and itself as well. It is always concerned with wholeness, with giving form and actualizing—that is, with creating—and let it never be forgotten that by its very nature creating is bound to matriarchal consciousness, not because consciousness is creative but rather because the unconscious is, and because every creative accomplishment presupposes all the attitudes of pregnancy and relatedness that we have recognized as characteristic of matriarchal consciousness.[12]

Humans, animals and other life forms magnetically draw energy from the moon. These energies are subtle and spiritual, and they diffuse rather than polarize. Through intuitive transmissions and through cellular mutation, we are beginning to be able to access our subconscious memory banks. Exposure to the refined energy of the moon activates us. As we integrate these memories, we are illumined, made wiser, and validated.

The moon transduces energies from galactic beams into encodements that are accessed by our etheric bodies and integrated by our emotional bodies. The Angel of the Lunation Cycle assists us in releasing our mental bodies and the ensuing internal chatter and allows us to become responsive to these energies.

At new moon, the earth shields the surface of the moon for a precious few minutes. In that darkness, the moon imprints an emotional field of new potential. This is the time in the lunation cycle to plant new seeds for a psychic harvest at full moon. Through visualization, we can bring our dreams to manifestation.

The ancient mystery schools taught the art of visualization. Initiates practiced holding abstract colors, shapes, symbols, and the motion of energy in their mind's eye. The art of conscious visualization and intuitive perception were practiced by initiates. Initiates developed an inner pictorial sensitivity that was used to grasp past soul lessons and to create future realities.

Through the clarification of consciousness, the power of our thoughts also increases. The Angel of the Lunation Cycle helps us access what will put us *over the moon*. This is the secret to creating an impassioned life of lunar rapture.

Hathor

The Giza Plateau

Hathor

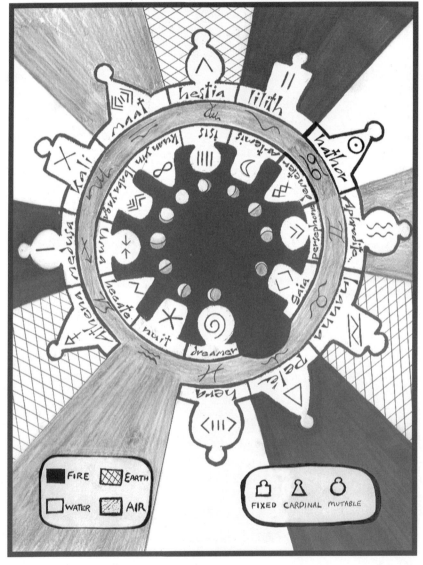

Sun in Cancer
Cardinal–Water

ᴎathor

ᴎathor is the archetypal Shapeshifter. She was revered as the ancient Egyptian Queen of Heaven and the mother of all the gods and goddesses. Hathor is reputed to be the mother of the gypsies and patron of dancers. Hathor's name translates as the "House Above" or the "Womb Above." Hathor derives her name from a benevolent race of light beings who have tremendous love for the earth and for humanity. The Hathors are a race of fourteen-foot-tall beings whose original home is the star, Sirius. The origins of Hathor are part of an ancient mys-

tery. As we emerge from an age of darkness and seek to understand the origins of the human family, our belief system becomes directly challenged. Yet, if we open our minds and don the cloak of courage, we may open to a world of awe, wonder, and magic.

Hathor resonates with the energy of the number nineteen. Nineteen is a powerful number because it begins with one and ends with nine, the complete spectrum of root numbers. It contains the number of the individual (1) and the number of humanity (9) and together they find a spiritual rebirth.[1]

Classic descriptions claim that the most ancient lore on the Wheel of Tarot was an expression of the law of Hathor. The connection between the words Tarot, Hathor, and Wheel (rotate) can be made by analyzing the following four-letter combinations: "rota, taro, orat, tora, *ator.*" Hathor specifically reflects the energy of Tarot Sun. The sun is the center of our planetary system and a generator of light and radiant power. According to Manly Hall, the gods of antiquity resolved themselves into the solar fire.[2] In the Sun card, we see energized figures sunny of heart, joyously celebrating the new dawn and the dance of life. With the illumination of the central Self, full mental understanding bursts forth, and in the bliss there is expansiveness, holistic awareness, and conscious transformation. Various cultures around the world, including Australian aborigines,

American Indians, the Aztecs, the ancient Egyptians, and modern Germans, mythologically and linguistically consider the sun to be feminine, symbolic of its nurturing qualities.[3]

Hathor anchors the astrological energy of Sun in Cancer. A cardinal water sign, it initiates and protects, functioning through emotions. In this position, we find a compassionate, receptive archetype with a genuine maternal concern for humanity. The energy lends itself to an interest in understanding the spiritual truths of the people who came before her.

MYTHOLOGY

Hathor's primary connection was not to the earth but to the sky. She was a mighty goddess with creative force and appeared in many guises. She was beloved to both the living and the dead, and she remained faithful to the cosmic order of the Universe.[4]

According to Drunvalo Melchizedek, the Hathors are a race of fourteen-foot beings from the fourth dimension of Venus.[5] In the third dimension, Venus appears uninhabited and unable to sustain life. In the fourth dimension, it is very alive and beautiful. Considered to be the most advanced planet in our solar system, Venus is the planetary representative of the Sirian energy.[6] The Hathors are a loving race of light beings who have a tremendous commitment to the evolution of the earth. The Hathors exist in the exalted state of Christ consciousness.

> The ancient Egyptian goddesses have a quite different nature in two respects: first, each originally possessed her own separate character that was maintained over the course of centuries so that the goddesses were not configurations of one and the same type; second, *they were not intrinsically related to the earth, conceived as divine*, motherly beings.[7] (emphasis mine)

Symbols of Hathor are prolific in ancient Egypt. It is highly significant that Hathor is depicted from a front view, not in profile, as are all the other gods and goddesses in ancient Egyptian art. This indicates that Hathor had a type of prominence amongst the gods and goddesses and is a symbol of dimensionality. In other words, human figures anchored in third-dimensional reality are depicted in profile or two dimensions, while Hathor a fourth-dimensional being, is depicted in three dimensions.

Hathor carries the energy of the winged Lioness, symbolizing courage, initiative, and fearlessness. Hathor manifests as the powerful spiritualized force of the Sphinx whose mysteries are yet to be fully revealed.[8] The Sphinx is a dimensional portal that demonstrates the laws of inter-dimensional existence. Originally, it was thought that the Sphinx was constructed at the same time as the pyramids at Giza. Recent information based on rain and water erosion has shown that the Sphinx is far more ancient than most Egyptologists ever speculated.

The Sphinx was built by feline gods from Sirius in 17,800 BC to hold open sacred geometric portals to the stars. This allowed the Hathors multidimensional access to the electromagnetic, or telluric, fields around the earth. The Sphinx is built over a network of tunnels and chambers that house the main transducer for the planet.[9] Galactic Knowledge is stored beneath the Sphinx in what is known as the Halls of Amenti, or the Hall of Records.

There is still great controversy among scholars, mystics, archaeologists, and Egyptologists regarding the dates that the Sphinx and the Great Pyramid were built. Schul and Petit report that an Arab writer, Abu Zeyd el Balkhy, found an ancient inscription suggesting that the Great Pyramid was actually constructed about 73,000 years ago. This corresponds to a carbon-14 reading on the structure dating it to 71,000 BC.[10] Wilks states:

> The strange thing about the history of the Great Pyramid is the almost total lack of it. Very little hard knowledge exists about the who, why, and when of its construction.[11]

The Pleiadians report that the Great Pyramid was built during the Age of Leo, which was the last Age of Light, approximately 12,500 years ago, or 10,800 BC. During this time, the earth was traveling through the Photon Band, a powerful band of light the entire solar system passes through each 12,500 years. The Great Pyramid had significance as an instrument during the high frequency and high magnetism that the earth experienced during that time. The earth will enter the fringes of the photon band for a few weeks per year beginning in 1996. The ancient encodements of the Great Pyramid are significant as we enter the Age of Light.

In 2450 BC, which most historians erroneously attribute as its date of construction, the entire surface of the Great Pyramid was covered with smooth white limestone that reflected solar rays into space. At the golden apex was a crystal that distilled the solar spark, the fire of which fertilized the essence of terrestial life.[12]

> At the Pyramid, the marriage of heaven and earth was performed, a union between the terrestial current accumulated within its enormous

bulk and the divine spark of the celestial fire distilled from the ether at the point of the crystal and the gold apex. From this union was born the spirit of God [Goddess] in men [women].[13]

For this reason, Hathor's environmental archetype is the Giza plateau, which contains the mysteries of the ancients. Here, matter and spirit merge indivisibly, a circle squared. In a balanced cosmology, the Egyptians practiced and embodied this principle, exhibiting great reverence for humanity's place in the Universe and the divine purpose for life on earth. Concerning the Great Pyramid, Michel states:

Certainly the whole edifice was built by men who knew something of the laws which govern the intergalactic flow of living energy and of their application to the development of life on earth by acute observation of nature, leading to the detection of certain numerical knowledge of the universal system, verifiable both by reason and directly by the senses.[14]

Close examination reveals that the patterns of life, the structure of the cell, and the mechanics of the Universe were contained within perfect geometric sequences spaced by cosmic intervals, ratios, and numbers. These were crystalline structures, and prior to the spread of superstition and confusion, they were understood by initiates and mystics.[15]

The Cult of Hathor

Secret teachings of the cult of Hathor involved elaborate preparation for movement into the seven spiritual, or heavenly, spheres. The Egyptian Book of the Dead, whose correct title is *The Book of Coming Forth into Day*, is the guidebook to travel between the dimensions. The consciousness, or *ka*, remains intact, even though the physical vehicle has been dropped. The journey into the seven spheres begins at the Gateway to the first Bardo. Hathor is said to have nourished the dead and to have brought joy to souls after their passage through the Hall of Judgment.[16] The message is simple: "You are dead." Perhaps this is what is being referred to in the Gospel of Saint John (3:1-21), when Jesus states: "Truly, truly, I say unto you, unless one is born again, (s)he cannot see the Kingdom of God."[17]

Initiates in the temples understood the cycle of incarnations, the starry origins of their souls, and the immense opportunity for soul development on the Earth Plane. They were clear that the soul inhabited the physical body temporarily and that ascension was the release of the soul back to source. Preparations for ascension involved many disciplined years, meditation, biochemical precision within the physical body, and firm commitment.

The archetype of Hathor is an embodiment of the sophistication of this mythology. Hathor is the personification of the state of spiritual realization. Queenship was based on the successive incarnation of her spirit. According to Bleeker, Hathor was surnamed "The Golden One" and was seen to defy transience.

Three centers of the ancient cult of Hathor were Memphis, Thebes, and Sinai. Daily practice in the cult of Hathor involved the bringing of water, the purification of the offering, and concentration on the offering. Joy, optimism, and enthusiasm were manifest at the festivals of Hathor. There were four specific festive rituals outlined by C.J. Bleeker.[18]

The *first* was the rustling of papyrus. Papyrus, a sacred and valued commodity, was an elegant form of paper on which scribes would note temple activities and the great mysteries embedded in the sacred teachings. The information was then taken to the port of Isis at Alexandria, where the great library stored the invaluable information.

A *second* ritual, on the 20th day of the month of Thoth, was the festival of inebriety. Hathor was said to have become wrathful at times, needing the pacification with inebriants.

A *third* ritual involved a voyage on a boat and was symbolic of an overcoming. Hathor was said to face fears and overcome chaos and death by battling the elements of the sea. This symbolically represented the victory of the goddess over destructive forces.

The *fourth* ritual was a visitation to Edfu, a sacred temple along the Nile. Here the male and female energies came together to birth the Divine Self.[20]

At the temple of Dendera, also dedicated to Hathor, there is an engraved astrological wheel embossed on the ceiling, which is reputed to be the oldest known astrological sky chart in the world. The astrological signs are surrounded by and supported by figures of Hathor and of Horus. Eleven of the twelve zodiacal signs are animals, all except Aquarius. Surrounding the astrological constellations are the animal-headed Netters, or archetypal principles, also referred to as the Gods and Goddesses. These represent the chromosomes of the genetic code, each animal a "totem" for an aspect of humanness.

The Heart of Hathor

Like Inanna, Hathor was a mistress of love, and she reigned over the domain of fertility. Hathor was said to stimulate sexuality. Again, we see the exaltation of the feminine in ancient mysteries being intricately linked to the divine magic of sexuality, or serpent energy. In the temples, sacred sexual rites were a form of veneration of the goddess.

> Man's redemption is found in the Serpent, but we should be on guard against the *astuteness of the Serpent.* We must contemplate the forbidden fruit and inhale its aroma, but remember what Lord Jehovah

said: "If thou eatest of this fruit, thou shall die" [Genesis 2:17]. We must *enjoy love's bliss and adore the woman.* A good painting enraptures us; a beautiful piece of music brings us to a state of ecstasy, but an adorable beautiful woman makes us want to possess her in the act. *She is the living representation of the Mother God.* The sexual act with one's beloved has its indisputable delights.[21] (emphasis mine)

All ancient Egyptian female royals were given a Hathor name, to assure *matrilineal accession.* Metaphysically, the name Hathor refers to:

A much exalted state of thought in man...the ruling power of intellectual vitality which has become the executive power of the divine law to the highest religious and spiritual thoughts of the individual. The directive quality of the higher consciousness of divine law into which the individual is entering.[22]

Hatshepsut and Nefertiti were also personifications of the divinity of the feminine that Hathor represented. At the exquisite temple of Queen Hatshepsut, a female Pharaoh, faces of Hathor abound, signaling Hatshepsut's royal ancestry and her connection to the Hathors.

The following *Hymn to Hathor* depicts her grandeur and power as well as her connection to the Uraeus, or serpent energy.

All hail, jubilation to you, O Golden One, Sole ruler, Uraeus of the Supreme Lord himself. *Mysterious one who gives birth to the divine entities,* forms the animals, models them as she pleases, fashions men...O Mother...Luminous One who thrusts back the darkness, who illuminates every human creature with her rays. Hail Great One of many names...It is the Golden One...the lady of drunkenness, of music, of dance, of frankincense, of the crown, of young women, whom men acclaim because they love her. It is the Gold of the divine entities, who comes forth at her season, in the month of Epiphi, the day of the new moon, at the festival of 'She is Delivered'...Heaven makes merry, the earth is full of gladness, the Castle of Horus rejoices."[23] (emphasis mine)

Hathor is portrayed full-faced crowned by the full moon, with horns, also representing fallopian tubes, surrounding the disk. In some images, she is depicted holding "soul doves" in each hand. Hathor, the archetypal Shapeshifter, often appears as a cow whose horns resemble the crescent moon lying on its back.[24] To the Egyptians, cows were magnificent and mysterious creatures who were sent to Earth by the Hathors. Cows were symbols of prosperity, vitality, and immortal life.[25] They selflessly gave their milk and their flesh as a gift of strength to humanity.

The Story of Hathor and Ra

The Egyptians believed that Nuit gave birth to Ra, the Sun God, each day at dawn and that she swallowed him at dusk. Ra would wander through the Underworld at night and travel in the Upperworld during the day.[26] Hathor herself was the eye of the sun. In one ancient myth, Hathor with her sun-eye was sent out to chastise some rebels who were defying Ra. She was so thorough in her retaliation that Ra, observing the flow of blood, began to fear that she would exterminate mankind. He ordered that a red dye be added to a thousand gallons of beer. Waking to observe the abundance of beer, Hathor is said to have drunk profusely and to have forgotten her instructions. Like Kali, Hathor sometimes exposed a fiery, independent temperament. She is referred to as the mistress of inebriety[27] and the mistress of song, dance, and music. Bleeker states that Hathor "was too independent to be fettered by conjugal obligations. One might say that she was a true feminist in the divine world."[28]

THE HATHOR WOMAN

The Hathor woman is a sensuous woman. She is a supreme nurturer and a spiritual warrior. She is compassionate, deep, sensitive, self-sufficient, and secure. She listens with her heart and follows the guidance she receives. She is the quintessential feminine and her emotions are finely tuned. Her environment reflects the conscious feminine and reflects her love for the goddess.

The Hathor woman is highly evolved spiritually. She has put herself through painstaking self-examination and much personal growth. She has been on the Red Road for decades and has had multidimensional experiences. She sometimes has a sense of being in two places at once and she is repeatedly delighted by strange cooincidences. She has explored most psychological concepts, metaphysical theories, healing techniques, and ancient oracles. She has likely traveled to sacred sites, met with spiritual gurus and masters, swam with the whales and dolphins, done a fire-walk, and experienced parlor sittings from numerous channels and psychics.

The Hathor woman is determined to decipher the mysteries of the Universe. She likely had an avid interest in the Pyramids, Stonehenge, Easter Island, Machu Picchu, and other encoded sacred sites. She is interested in sacred geometry, extraterrestrials, and off-planet colonies. She has developed her ability to integrate past experiences and is ready to give concrete expression to her knowledge.

The Hathor woman will love to express herself through sensuous movements and exotic dance. It is as though she is remembering the temple dances of the priestesses of ancient Egypt. Guided by Hathor, she may find herself in sensuous gyrations, making spiral waves with her hands and figure eights with her hips. Suspended in a trance, she rides on spiral waves and spins herself into new dimensions. Watching her, it seems she is being *moved* by a mysterious force. Uplifted by spirit, it is as though her feet hardly touch the ground. We begin to wonder if she can fly.

THE ANGEL OF MULTIDIMENSIONALITY

The Angel of Multidimensionality emphasizes that full access to other dimensions and to the Realm of Cosmic Consciousness is attained through personal evolution and cellular mutation. This initiates a chain reaction throughout our individual energy field, which reverberates with the force field of the crystal grid around the planet. We cannot comprehend the true meaning of our evolution if we only rely on our human perspective.

The Angel of Multidimensionality teaches us how to tune into the subtle vibrations that are transmitted through our glandular system. When we resonate within a higher frequency range, intense emotions are stirred that activate dormant evolutionary codes. As we access these codes, we literally begin to mutate and to dissolve into higher dimensions.

Our thymus gland, our pituitary gland, and our pineal gland are connected to the higher energy centers, or chakras, in the body. The thymus chakra functions as a psychic regulatory center and emanates four protective concentric rings of energy around the heart and the higher heart. These rings transmute electrostatic energy into electromagnetic energy. The thymus is connected to the higher heart on the front of our bodies and to the *wing point* on our backs. This is the point where our etheric wings extend into our light body, or auric field.

The pituitary gland is connected to the third eye, or intuitive center. When we close our eyes, the distractions of the outer world are temporarily out of sight. Our ego is no longer dominant. Our inner sight is thus activated and much information is available from our Higher Self.

The pineal gland is connected to the crown chakra located at the top of the head. The pineal gland functions as a light transmitter and is physiologically similar to a human eye. In Hopi legends, people were encouraged to keep their *door* open, meaning the pineal gland. This was known as source of cosmic intelligence, transmitting light encodements from the Cosmos.[29] In the modern world, overhead fluorescent lights directly interfere with these more subtle light transmissions. For those whose crown chakras are closed, there is little sensitivity. For those light warriors who have evolved, overhead lights are uncomfortable and jarring and can scramble incoming encodements.

The Angel of Multidimensionality offers an infusion of Galactic energy to descend into our light bodies. It is an acknowledgment of the balancing and strengthening of our twelve chakras and the physicalization of twelve strands of DNA. The ensuing brilliance, the mental freedom, and the propensity for mysterious synchronicity are tributes to this evolutionary mutation.

It is imperative to interact with other dimensions to understand the scope of the global shift in consciousness that is currently occuring. When we embrace the Angel of Multidimensionality, we open ourselves to a corridor of potentiality. A huge canopy of holographic information opens and we are rebirthed as a galactic star-child of Gaia while we are simultaneously anchored in the magnetic crystalline mantle of the Earth. As we continue our journey along the Red Road, the Angel of Cosmic Consciousness and the Angel of the One Heart are primed and ready to reveal more dimensional secrets.

Maat

Step Pyramid

Maat

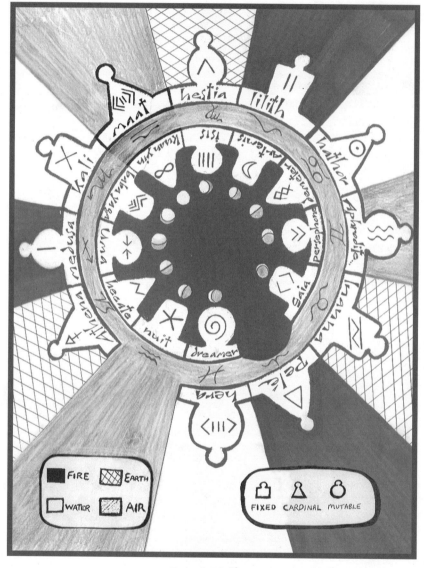

Sun in Libra
Cardinal–Air

Chapter XXIV

ᛗaat

|20|

ᛗaat is the personification of Cosmic Consciousness. Maat is part of a great family of deities from predynastic Egypt whose mythic system is already well established by the time history begins. As archetypal Seeker of Truth, she is the embodiment of accuracy, honesty, fairness, faithfulness, authenticity, legitimacy, integrity, and justice.[1] She represents the soul qualities of equilibrium and poise, the essence of the rhythm and order of the Universe.[2] She is a reflection of heaven and represents the perfection of the divine order of the Universe that has reigned since the beginning.

Maat is rooted in the number twenty, numerologically linking her to Isis. Whereas Isis' energy is veiled, Maat's is direct. She supports a clear global vision and takes full responsibility for her perspective on reality. As a divine healer, she is a transcendent channel for the highest Cosmic energies.

Maat is the embodiment of Tarot Judgment symbolized by an Angel at the gateway to a new world. Lord Archangel Michael calls us to a heavenly life, lived in accordance with master principles. She implies a "female-oriented, cyclic cosmology" where Judgment is "not the judgment of men by god, but the judgment of the gods by the Mother."[3] Cosmic Law, which is symbolically administered by Maat, is therefore the fulfillment of the destiny of the Dreamer's journey. The Dreamer has one more station on the Red Road, the expression of humanitarian ideals through Gaia. Yet, it is Maat who declares the Dreamer's journey a success and motivates the spiraling revolution of the next archetypal Great Round.

Maat's energy is astrologically rooted in the Sun in Libra. A cardinal air sign, it relies on intuition and leads primarily through influencing others. The energy of this sign is diplomatic and charming, embracing peace and harmony. It loves beauty, refinement, and social graciousness. In this position, there is a search for balance. It exemplifies divine will.

MYTHOLOGY

Maat is the motivating force to become consciousness. In its essence the Universe is nothing but consciousness, and in its perfection it reveals the inevitability of the evolution of consciousness. The ancient Egyptians had a notion of the "double Maat" that referred to the ultimate treasure of individual consciousness merged with Cosmic Consciousness. This signifies a new interaction between the lower self and the Higher Self, representing unconscious and conscious processes. The communion with the divine is depicted in ancient Egyptian frescos, showing a small figure of Maat holding her double who is much larger. The lower self, or individual consciousness, is the anchor for the Higher Self, or Cosmic Consciousness.

> Maat is Cosmic Consciousness, the ultimate goal of creation and of every creature, the immortal fruit of constant acquisition. Maat is the greatest treasure that a being might wish for.[4]

The Ceremony of the Weighing of the Heart

A famous ancient Egyptian papyrus scroll depicts an elaborate Ceremony of the Weighing of the Heart. The setting is the Gateway to the Hall of Judgment, where souls arrive after death. Maat is presiding over the ceremony. Thoth, the record keeper, is gazing over the records of the deceased's life. The jackal-headed Anubis, the *Opener of the Ways,* and Maat's 42 assessors are present.

The assessors stand 21 on either side, while a deposition presents the entire scope of the deceased's life. Anubis guards the door at the end of the Hall of Judgment. He is a preserver of life who protects the soul between incarnations. He has a direct relationship to Sirius, known to the Egyptians as the Dog Star. Sirius governs alchemical processes, and Anubis is responsible for the transmutation of the soul between incarnations.

The 42 assessors judge the soul's spiritual development while on the Earth Plane. The heart of the deceased is weighed against Maat's feather of Truth that she removes from her headdress and places on the scales. If the heart is heavy due to immoral living or lack of integrity, it tips the balance. It is only those who are light of heart, who have lived well and who have honored Spirit, that can make the transition through the seven bardos to the Netherworld. The cosmology of ancient Egypt encouraged the populace to listen with their hearts and to speak the language of the heart.

> When they seek light concerning the judgment it is given, and they
> learn that the judgment is all a matter of divine law. They find that
> for every departure from this law they must suffer, not in some future
> time of great tribulation.[5]

The Christian Church has emphasized the idea that the Last Judgment is an external evaluation. God was presented as judgmental, vindictive, and punitive. Being good enough seemed impossible, and fear of hell was instilled. In the Ceremony of the Weighing of the Heart, the assessors are projections of the deceased. The ancient Egyptians knew that the soul actually judged itself.

> The Kingdom of heaven is attained, first, by one's establishing in
> one's mind the consciousness of the truth of Being; second, by one's
> adjusting one's outer life to Truth.[6]

Maat and the Control of the Mind

Maat represents the ability to manifest co-creatively with the Divine to fulfill one's true destiny. She transcends ego and allows for participation with the greater whole. This implies psychological wholeness and the ability to manifest through the principles of intent and creative visualization. We are also engendering Maat when we seek to live beyond judgment of the self and of others. When we see ourselves and others with complete clarity and acceptance, we are lifted to a most holy place, fully progressed in our understanding of the human condition.

In ancient Egypt, the staff was a symbol of the control of the mind. The idea that *thought is creative* was part of the discipline in the temple teachings. It was thought that "the Divine Mind creates by thought, through ideas."[7] The word is creative and law giving, revealing the activity of God.[8] The Kingdom of heaven is the orderly adjustment of divine ideas in man's mind and body.[9] The idea was that initiates would have a consciousness of love and would be self-regulating in their behavior. After all, Maat's eyes of Truth were always watching.

> Thought is the process in mind by which substance is acted on by
> energy, directed by intelligence. Thought is the movement of ideas
> in the mind.[10]

This is symbolically represented in the step pyramid. After each integration, initiates must contend with the next challenge. In the ancient mystery schools, entombment and resurrection were enacted symbolically while the initiate remained in a trance. After three days, the temple priestesses would rouse the initiate, who would awaken to a new order.

THE MAAT WOMAN

The Maat woman is pure of heart and whole. She pulses with the moment. She senses others. She knows. She is evolved, transparent, and candid. She dreams, and drifts.

The Maat woman is fair, capable, generous, balanced, strong, wise, soft, and aware. She lives in a world of synchronicity. She is finely tuned to the moon and experiences life through her heart. She witnesses the miracle of heaven on Earth. Her Higher Self is integrated within her physical being. She is the personification of evolution.

The Maat woman is open. She has cleansed and energized her physical body, done her emotional work, and consistently meditated to quiet her mind. She has consciously participated in earth-healing work and has been a conduit for the cosmic energies that are being pulsed onto the planet.

The Maat woman seeks the ultimate Truth. She longs to go beyond duality and refuses to see things in terms of right and wrong, or good and bad. She perceives beyond space and time. She knows her purpose. She is conscious.

If you meet the Maat woman, she may reveal information about star systems and the Orion nebula. She may have vivid past-life memories of being a spaceship commander. Deep in a trance, if you ask her where she is from, she will list her planetary incarnations and her cosmic mission on Earth.

Expect to learn from the Maat woman. She has a deep understanding of the cosmic scheme of things. She enhances our sense of the perfection of the Universe. She rides on the purity of Truth.

THE ANGEL OF COSMIC CONSCIOUSNESS

The Angel of Cosmic Consciousness has full access to all realms in the Universe and the twelve dimensions of consciousness. With the assistance of the Angels at the preceding cosmic stations, our vibrational frequency is fine-tuned, our DNA has mutated to activate twelve strands of DNA, and we have access to the full range of dimensional energies harmonically accessed through the twelve chakras. Eight chakras exist within the human body and connect to the dimensional energies 1D through 8D. Four exist in the light body that encompasses the ninth, tenth, eleventh, and twelfth dimensions extending to the edge of the Universe.

The first dimension exists in caves in the mantle of inner Earth. The storytellers of Gaia, the soul of Mother Earth, whisper tales of liquid light from the molten core of planetary consciousness. In the second dimension, or 2D, crystalline essences fuel elemental powers that generate *kundalini waves.** Metallic, radioactive, and chemical, the second dimension is connected to our deepest instincts and to our reptilian brain. Second-dimensional metallic elementals register subtle emanations from the cosmos at the new moon.

The third dimension is densified, polarized, and anchored within the physical body. It is locked into linear space and time. It is governed by the wheel of karma. The third dimension is limited to a narrow frequency band and a slowed creative force. Experience is viewed through mirroring and projection.

The fourth dimension is a non-physical realm that exists beyond duality and is ruled by the emotional body. In 4D, we take responsibility for our karma. Here, energy flows smoothly while archetypal energies constellate in clusters. These archetypal clusters form the collective unconscious. Angelic messengers can densify and manifest in the fourth dimension. They bring starry energies and information from the higher dimensions.

The fifth dimension emanates love and creativity and is linked to the mental body. Kundalini waves catapult us through a cosmic corridor. We experience simultaneous realities in multiple dimensions. We no longer act out karmic patterns, and participate in the mighty essence of human evolution.

The sixth dimension links us to morphogenetic fields, or a circuitry system of divine, sacred geometric currents. It is connected to the spiritual body and to Sirian consciousness. In the sixth dimension, we have direct access to the bliss of oneness with the Ascended Masters. The sixth dimension is the source of synchronicities that form a geometric matrix to create what we hold in our minds. Through thought, we magnetically imprint energies from the sixth dimension that manifest as uncanny coincidences in 4D and 5D.

In the seventh dimension, we pass through a key doorway. In dimensions one through six, we deal with Earth experiences. In the seventh to the twelfth dimensions, we access Galactic levels of consciousness. The seventh dimension is connected to the crown chakra. It is the vortex through which we reframe dimensional structures. Coined *experiential objectivity*[11] it is the pivot between inner and outer experiences. The seventh dimension operates on photonic light.

---

*Kundalini Waves are strong currents of terrestrial energy that are generated within the Earth. If one is aware and avails themselves to these energies, they can pass through the human body and be directed for healing.

Photonic information highways are dimensional communication linkage systems that transmit pure thought. As we enter the Photon Band, we have greater access to this 7D light energy. The Earth spends approximately 2000 years in the Photon Band every 12,500 years. The Solar System is on the fringes of the Photon Band at the time of writing. Each year, the Earth slowly penetrates farther into the Photon Band until the Sun is fully immersed in the year 2012. This is the magnificent importance of the end of the 5000-year Mayan calendar on December 21, 2011.

All potentialities exist in the eighth dimension. It is as though there is one set of rules for 1D through 7D and a different set of rules beyond the eighth dimension. It is an experimental zone where energies are transmuted from the outer dimensions and are pulsated into dimensions one through seven.

The ninth dimension is the last stage before leaving the cosmic physical. From this expanded perspective, we grasp the notion of immortality. Christ was a model of the ninth-dimensional human. This is the dimension of eternal *Samadhi*, or divine bliss. From here, cosmic orgasms of light are pulsed into the Galaxy. This is the administrative level for all dimensions.[12] The experiences of all twelve realms are contained within the ninth.

In the tenth dimension, we meet the Great Cosmic Mother, who is pure procreative feminine consciousness. We are all born of a mother and in the end return to the Great Mother. Here, the initiate leaves the physical solar system and is merged with the nurturing, symbolic aspect of the Galactic Core.

The eleventh dimension is a portal gateway to the realm beyond realms. Here, simultaneous realities exist in no time and no space. Here we operate in more than one dimension at a time and we have the reflective consciousness to perceive it. It is possible to jump from the fifth dimension to the eleventh dimension through astral projection, in dreamtime, through a peak experience, or a shamanic initiation. These experiences can be disorienting if we digitally skip through several dimensional realms. It is only when we have evolved *through* the dimensions with all twelve strands of DNA operational that we have full footing in the eleventh dimension.

In the twelfth dimension, our consciousness extends to the edge of the Universe. When we travel there, we stay connected to our physical selves by a gold cord that extends from our crown chakra. We must be met by an Ascended Master to access the twelfth dimension. On the etheric level, the Master explains the secrets of this dimension. If we gain access unattended, we can become overcharged because we are accessing information that is beyond our capacity to comprehend and integrate. In the twelfth dimension, we become cognizant of new realms and gaze through a window into the next Universe.

Gaia

The Earth from Space

Gaia

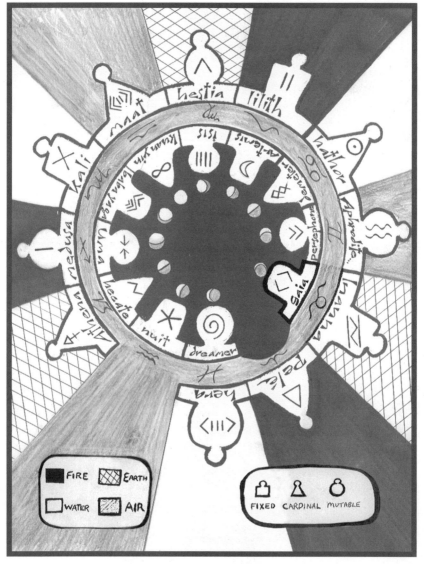

Moon in Taurus
Fixed-Earth

Chapter XXV

Gaia

$\mathbf{A}$s the personification of the planet, Gaia is the living presence of the Earth. She is rebellious, alive, tolerant, self-healing, and eruptive. She represents the soul qualities of faithfulness and sentimentality. She symbolizes all that cannot be brought under control, the life force itself. Gaia represents the archetypal Humanitarian.

Gaia is represented by the number twenty-one, a number of completion and of creation. Numerologically, it is the manifestation of the sacred trinity, two souls creating one that equals three. Gaia is numerologically connected to Hera; they embody the ideas of joy, harmony, and self-integration. They are expert at manifestation and are embodiments of abundance.

Gaia's energy is linked to Tarot World. The evolutionary journey is complete and the Dreamer has gained an understanding of the workings of the Universe. She is less attached to the material world, and she measures success in terms of spiritual connection instead of material accumulation. There is an invitation to walk the Red Road again, bidding the Dreamer to dream anew. As the planet spins round the sun, so does the Dreamer cycle the Great Round again. Every cycle spirals the Dreamer toward ascension, and each time she has more clarity and is more conscious of how the archetypal energies function in her life.

Gaia is anchored in the astrological energy of the Moon in Taurus. A fixed earth sign, the tendency is to maintain energies in a grounded, centered way. The sign exemplifies sound judgment, strong intuition, and an accurate memory. The energy is steadfast, solid, and melodic. It is reflective of humanitarian values and the conscious use of resources.

MYTHOLOGY

According to Greek mythology, Gaia is the grandmother of Demeter, Hera, and Hestia, and is the great-grandmother of Athena and Artemis. Born of the severed genitals of Gaia's son-lover, Ouranos, Aphrodite is also genetically related to Gaia.[1]

Gaia is perhaps much older, for some say she is the Primal Mother who came into being at the very beginning. According to Downing, all humans have their source in Gaia. For this reason, Gaia is never wholly personal; she is Mother Earth, both animate and divine, yet not humanized.[2] Gaia is the ground from which the aforementioned goddesses emerge. The umbilical cords of the goddesses connect to the very navel of the Earth Mother, to Gaia herself, both figuratively and psychically.

> Her prophecies come not from being able to read the stars or the entrails of birds or beasts, but from her deep knowledge of what is really (and inevitably) going on. One cannot understand Gaia simply in human or psychological terms. Nevertheless, she is nature moving toward emergence in personal form. The most usual artistic representation of Gaia expresses this beautifully. She is shown as a human woman emerging breast-high from the earth itself.[3]

Delphi was the oracular sacred site where the human met the divine and the Earth met heaven. Long before the oracle at Delphi was attributed to Apollo, it was Gaia's.[4] Delphi was a major spiritual center in ancient Greece where many sacred rituals transpired. Delphi is a powerful metaphor for the sacred feminine. The main message of the Delphic oracle was: "Know Thyself."[5]

The Greeks thought of Delphi as the navel of the Earth. Delphi is knowingly built across two major ley lines, 22 degrees longitude East of Greenwich and 38 degrees latitude North of the equator. The navel stone, representing the "navel" of the planet, was found around 500 BC.[6] In humans, the umbilical cord connects an embryo to maternal sustenance and to life itself. Metaphorically, the navel stone at Delphi connected the populace to the eternal sustenance of Gaia. The original stone is on permanent exhibit in the museum at Delphi although a facsimile has been placed at the temple site.

> Delphi seems to exert a powerful, downward current that the body must add to the weight of its stores, its brooding eastern precipice,

its vertiginous, or seemingly vertiginous, mountain air ledge, and beside it, the dark awesome ravine that rising wide sea coast narrows into a dark isosceles triangle before plunging upwards into the mountain's foundation. From that dark core the Castilian waterfall tumbles into the Oracle's purifying Castilian Spring, cool water from a chasm.[7]

As a goddess of the Underworld, Gaia was often worshipped in association with the dead. On All Souls' Day, the day after All Hallow's Eve, the sheath between the spirit realm and the human realm was the thinnest. Gifts were brought to the graves of the dead in honor of Gaia.[8]

Gaia is the earth made invisible, earth become a metaphor, earth as the realm of soul. She is never just vegetal fertility nor even the physical globe at its most volatile and destructive ... The Greeks understood that the soul inhabits the earth, not the sky.[9]

At this stage of the journey, the old world is complete and a new one has taken shape. Our personal development is evident. There is a tantric dance with all life, and life and death are on a continuum of renewal. Matter is spiritualized and spirit is materialized. Kundalini energy has risen to the higher centers in the body and is not locked into the survival functions of the lower chakras. We are blissful and empowered.

New paradigms are in place. We are transformed. We are connected to Gaia, to the planetary consciousness, to Mother Earth herself. We honor her sacred seasons, the solar cycles, and the lunar cycles.

The return of the Goddess implies a return of her many priestesses— the powerful female transmitters of the energy of the *feminine ray*.[10] (emphasis mine)

The birth of Gaia consciousness into the collective was emphasized that incredible moment when astronauts first landed on the moon in 1969.[11] The transmission of pictures of the Earth from space brought to consciousness the notion of Earth as a single living organism. From this vantage point, no national boundaries were visible, only one unified Earth that we share equally.

When the evolutionary journey is complete, the querant will find herself manifesting jubilation and fulfillment. Success is the release from karmic ties as a surge of creative energies that are sustainable and productive. This is the essence of soul. "To return to the beginning, to Gaia, is not to finish but precisely to begin."[12]

Because the wheel of karma continues to turn, the Gaia energy is the culmination of the cycle and a return to a new journey around the wheel. We are entirely supported by the Universe and we are now confident in this fact. The values of preservation on the planet and evolution for all of humanity have been achieved.

Gaia is seen to be the source of dreams.[13] In Downing's words:

> She is a mother whom we come to know only as we begin to long for a mother from whom we are not separated, as in time, in consciousness, we find ourselves to be separated from the mother of the present. She [Gaia] is a fantasy creature behind the personal mother, construed of memory and longing, who exists only in the imagination, in myth, archetypally—who is never identical with the personal mother. Although she is there from the beginning, our discovery of her is always a return, a re-cognition.[14]

There is a safe asylum for the newly emerging self. This state of awareness can be pictured as a dance. As we dance, we allow the spirit to move us, and our bodies become the resonance chambers for the music and the energies. Through rhythmic dance, we bridge the gap between mortal time and transcendental time. Through ritual dance, the dancer becomes the dance and the self is one with the movements. We tune into the pulsations of the Universe, we restore internal and external equilibrium and open to healing energies.

THE GAIA WOMAN

The Gaia woman is the ultimate humanitarian. She recycles with a passion and may be involved in establishing recycling programs in the community and global conservation initiatives.

The Gaia woman has genuine concern for Mother Earth. She feels the impact of earthquakes and natural disasters from the perspective of the people and animals they affect. She is also connected to Gaia as a living organism with feelings, frustrations, tensions, and passions.

The Gaia woman is concerned for disadvantaged children, refugees, and victims of war and violence, those that live in her community and in third-world countries. She opens her heart to humanity. She knows that we are one humanity, one global family. She knows that she will not be completely free until the world is totally at peace.

The Gaia woman will participate in Earth healing ceremonies as well as solstice and equinox celebrations. She thinks holistically. She has an extended family and a chosen family.

THE ANGEL OF THE ONE HEART

The Angel of the One Heart rests within the pink and gold auric field of each individual. She is ready to inspire us with divine love. Spiritual success is the ultimate merging of the soul with the Higher Self. Through the Angel of the One Heart we understand that the personality is a channel through which Spirit breathes. It radiates from the inner chamber of the heart.

The heart is the entry point of the soul within the body.[15]

> Negative emotions such as frustration, unhappiness, anger, hatred, jealousy and the like generate chaotic, weak, high frequency heartwave graphs. Positive emotions, on the other hand, such as love, appreciation and gratitude generate very orderly, low frequency, but very powerful waves on the graph.[16]

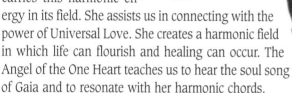

When the heart is loving and coherent, harmonic energy is generated. The Angel of the One Heart carries this harmonic energy in its field. She assists us in connecting with the power of Universal Love. She creates a harmonic field in which life can flourish and healing can occur. The Angel of the One Heart teaches us to hear the soul song of Gaia and to resonate with her harmonic chords.

Applications
Activating the Angels and the Archetypes

Working with the Angels and Archetypes system can be a highly creative process. You can form a study group and explore a different Archetype and Angel each week. Working with archetypal energy naturally stimulates creative expression. You can get together and make drawings, power objects, sculptures, or masks pertaining to the Archetypes or the Angels of your choice. You could make costumes and come dressed as a different Archetype each week. The possibilities are endless.

Many people on the spiritual path create altars in their homes where they place power objects and special rocks, crystals, or images that brings meaning to their lives. These sacred objects carry elemental energy and the intelligence of the Earth. We can access different Archetypal and Angelic energies through symbols, stories, and objects. Healing can occur when we focus and seek guidance. Candles, incense, aromatherapy oils, and a variety of symbols and natural objects help us access the elements of earth, air, fire and water, and the power of Spirit.

MAKING ANGELS AND ARCHETYPES RUNES

If you wish to make your own Angels and Archetype Runes, you will need to collect 22 similar sized rocks and follow the instructions below. Alternatively, you can use strong flat shells, bits of wood, or bone. As you acquire these, ask if they would like to carry the energy of a particular goddess and her Angel. When you are ready to create a set of Runes, you will need white, red, and black enamel paint and three sizes of brushes. You may wish to shellac the Runes upon completion to protect the paint from scratching over time.

You will also need a silk, cotton, or leather bag with a drawstring to store the Runes. It is important that they be kept in a natural fiber and that they are painted on something natural so they can transmit the energies of the Angels and the Archetypes. Runes can also be bundled in a special scarf or cloth and tied with a ribbon or leather thong.

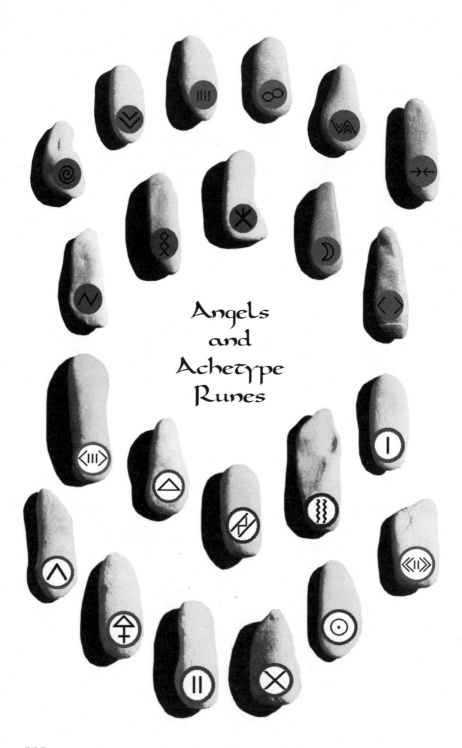

Angels
and
Achetype
Runes

Light a candle.
Take a deep breath and get centered.

Divide the 22 rocks into two sets of 11 by size. Assign the smaller, or more "yin" set, to the Lunar goddesses and their Angels, and the larger, or more "yang" set, to the Solar goddesses and their Angels.

Using a flat wide stiff-bristled paintbrush, paint white circles on the bellies of the 11 yang rocks. Clean the brush and then paint red circles on the bellies of the 11 yin rocks. After the yang set has dried, take the medium sized narrow-tipped brush and paint a thin red outline on the edge of the white circle. Dance a little while you let all 22 rocks dry.

Settle in again and decide whether you will begin with the red-bellied Lunar goddesses and Angels or with the white-bellied Solar goddesses and their Angels. Spread the set of 11 in front of you and center yourself.

Scan the set of 11 yin rocks and ask which among them would agree to carry the energy of the Dreamer, Persephone, Isis, Kuan Yin, Baba Yaga, Uma, Hecate, Demeter, Nuit, Artemis, and Gaia. Ask for a steady hand as you paint each Rune. With the thinnest paintbrush, anoint each Rune with a glyph, or energetic symbol, of each Lunar goddess. Feel the energy of the Archetype and her Angel enter the molecules of the rock and welcome her into your world.

Repeat the process with the 11 yang rocks, anointing each with the energy of a Solar goddess and her accompanying Angel.

You may wish to shellac the Runes after they are dry to protect them.

Before you put them away, do a meditation to program each Rune. You may wish to take a few sittings to accomplish this. Hold one Rune at a time, red-bellied Lunar Angel and Archetype Runes in your left hand, and white-bellied Solar Angels and Archetype Runes in your right hand. For each, feel the shape of the glyph, or symbol, like a pattern of light sitting within your energy field. Meditate on the goddess and her Angel. Take a deep breath and make a sound or low hum as you let out your breath. Breathe in the Archetype and the Angel. Offer gratitude and move on to activating the next Rune.

You make wish to include a "guardian stone" or a crystal to your bag of Angels and Archetype Runes. Program the guardian stone to keep the energy of the Runes clear and future readings accurate.

Celebrate, dance, sing. Go out in nature. Wait a day and a night before using the Runes and allow the Angels and the Archetypes to settle and brew their charm.

HOW TO DO A READING

There are an infinite number of ways to work with Angels and Archetypes Runes. Remember, ultimately, it is the Rune that picks you. The energy of the Rune will magnetize to your fingers. As you dig in the bag, let your hand rest. Feel which Rune is vibrating against your skin as you ask your question. Pull it out and see which goddess has a message for you.

The most common way to use the Runes is to ask for the guidance of one Archetype and her Angel per day. You may wish to do a meditation absorbing the energy of the glyph. It is also fun to carry the Rune with you all day or wear it in a small leather pouch like a necklace. You can also sleep with the Rune under your pillow. You may wish to make a dream pillow with a pouch sewn on it so the Rune does not get lost.

Another way to access the Angels and Archetypes is to ask specific questions and to draw more than one Rune. Hold the bag of Runes and formulate a question. Ask for either an Angel, if the nature of the question is spiritual, or an Archetype, if the nature of the question is worldly. For example, ask: "Which Angel is guiding me in my healing?" Or, "Which Archetype has a message for me regarding my new job?"

A third way to work with the Runes is to pull 11 and to make an Angels and Archetypes Sculptogram. The first thing to notice about the Runes you draw is how many are red-bellied and how many are white-bellied. If you have more red Lunar Runes, your energy is more introverted. If you have more white Solar Runes, your energy is more extroverted.

Arrange the Runes in a pattern according to which energy you feel connected to and which feels foreign. Place the "connected" ones close to the center and the "foreign" ones in the periphery. Move the Runes around until the Sculptogram "feels" right. Do this intuitively. You do not need to know a lot about the Runes before you begin. You can read about the Runes after you place them. If you let yourself play, you may be surprised what you learn about yourself and your guides.

After you examine the spread, you may wish to invite the Archetypes you placed peripherally to come in closer. On the other hand, if you are finished rampaging, you may want Pele or Kali to take a back seat and further away from the "center" of your process.

Divinatory Meaning of the Archetypes in a Reading

0 - THE DREAMER IN A READING

If you draw The Dreamer in a reading, you may wish to pay attention to a dream you had recently. You can also ask to have a dream that will shed light on a particular issue. What symbols are active in your dream language? Where does The Dreamer take you at night? Which dreams do you indulge in by day? Remember to be attentive to which daydreams you hold, because dreams often come true.

1 - PERSEPHONE IN A READING

If you draw Persephone in a reading, you may wish to ask yourself: How am I being overpowered? In what ways do I feel victimized today? What did I do today that was compulsive? What was I avoiding feeling by indulging in compulsive behavior? Ask Persephone to assist you in increasing your emotional capacity and to help you face the real issues. Perhaps Persephone can assist you in being more perceptive of the behavior of others around you and give you the strength to no longer buy into their manipulations.

2 - ISIS IN A READING

If you draw Isis in a reading, notice how you are being initiated in your life. As you deal with the challenges that life offers, you evolve. The gifts that Isis offers are often subtle and her initiations come in mysterious forms. What "tests" have you passed recently? What have you re-membered? Are past-life fragments being activated in your relationships? To whom have you been loyal?

3 - HERA IN A READING

The Hera archetype in a reading represents the ultimate feminine energy, which is receptive, vulnerable, nurturing, beautiful, and generous. It is in tune with the goddess within and honors the intuitive aspects of self. If your energy is lurking in the shadow of the Hera archetype, it could mean that you are caught in the grips of insecurity, envy, jealousy, or family discord. It could be that you have been giving too much and containing others' emotions instead of giving to yourself. Take heart, Hera knows about infinite tolerance and resilience. Get in touch with the beauty that you are. Take pride in your courage. Reach out to supportive friends. Love yourself.

4 - PELE IN A READING

When Pele visits you in a spread, you can be sure there is some outrage to confront or some unspoken words that need communicating. Where have you silenced your truth? When values that support life and freedom for all are infringed upon, or when someone feels they have the right to be controlling, Pele will help you speak up and say "NO!" Go ahead, rock the boat, and Pele will smile upon you and assist you to express yourself. Be prepared for the energetic release that will follow.

5 - INANNA IN A READING

When Inanna visits in a reading, perhaps you can shudder a little. Inanna is a tough task-master. She requires that the entire inventory of your psyche be available for examination. In what ways has life "stripped you bare?" Have you been sent to the depths of the Underworld to face yourself and your dark sister? Are you emerging from this descent? Ask Inanna to guide you on your way and to ensure that you harvest the benefits from this important journey.

6 - APHRODITE IN A READING

If you draw Aphrodite in a reading, relax in the soft glow. Love is in the air. It could be you are about to attract a relationship. It could be someone will admire you at a distance. Whatever the case, you can wear your beauty with ease. Allow Aphrodite to grace you with confidence and loving splendor.

7 - MEDUSA IN A READING

If you draw Medusa in a reading, it may be an opportunity to become focused. If there is a project that needs your attention, Medusa will drive you to complete it. Clear yourself and let her in. Medusa will keep you on track. Perhaps you are more perceptive of the behavior of others around you and no longer buy into their manipulations. Light the Sagittarian fire within and persevere. You can rest later.

8 - KUAN YIN IN A READING

If you get Kuan Yin in a reading, you can rest assured that quieting the mind will assist you. Whatever the question, whatever the upset, sit peacefully and make way for the equanimity of Ascended Master Kuan Yin to come to you. It has been said that prayer is talking to God/Goddess and that meditating is listening to the God/Goddess. As you meditate, simply ask for a message of the day, and await the wisdom and tranquillity that Kuan Yin will grace you with.

9 - HESTIA IN A READING

If you draw Hestia in a reading, prepare yourself to be at home. Give yourself the gift of sorting through possessions and clearing your personal environment. Even if you have resistance to this, invite the gentle yet sharp energy of Hestia in. She will help you honor your own space. There is no greater blessing than clarity. All else is a muddle of confusion and wasted energy. Invite Hestia to be precise and help you know what stays and what goes.

10 - ATHENA IN A READING

If you draw Athena in a reading, you may wish to settle down and study. Athena appeals to the studious mind. Are you trying to finish a book? Is there something you wish to learn? Are you looking to Master a skill or to develop a hobby? Invite Athena to show you the life-long value of such endeavors.

11 - LILLITH IN A READING

If you draw Lillith in spread, brace yourself. You may be getting ready to stomp off. Expect liberation and a burst of energy. Invite Lillith to help you delight in your independence. Do not let anyone stop you.

12 - BABA YAGA IN A READING

If you draw this rune, you are being put on notice to spend a day in bed, to regroup, and to withdraw temporarily from your busy schedule of outwardly motivated activities. Let your hair down. Confront your 'hang-ups'. Unplug the phone and let the world pass you by. Baba Yaga will greet you at the entry to the Underworld.

13 - KALI IN A READING

If you draw the Kali Rune, ask, what could be dying in my life? What repressed trauma is buried in my psyche, warded off by my various distractions? What could I be getting ready to let go of? What has died that I have not fully grieved? What new seeds can grow in the fertile soil of my recent lessons? What am I enraged about? Invite Kali to assist you in cutting the ties that bind. Let her move you to let go and move on. She will help you grieve the loss, assisting you in valuing what or who you are releasing. The process will be quickened but not avoided.

14 - UMA IN A READING

When you draw this Rune, you are being asked to be a conduit for energy. Turn on the music and dance wildly to energize your self and your goal. Breathe, open, and let yourself be a conduit for cosmic energy. Let the energy come up through your feet, pass through your body, and transmit to the heavens. Alternately, bring the energy down from the heavens, let it pass through your body, and ground it into the earth. Join Uma and bring down sufficient energy to manifest your creativity, as well as to balance yourself. She can transmute the electromagnetic energy generated by the activity into healing energy, productivity, regeneration of the body, and effective action. Identify with your animalistic passion.

15 - HECATE IN A READING

If you are visited by Hecate in a reading, rejoice! Allow Hecate's wisdom to bless you. You are becoming a crone unto yourself. Invite Hecate to ground you in your own "knowing." Connect with your core. What do you "know." What are you sure of?

16 - DEMETER IN A READING

If you draw Demeter in a spread, feel your strength. Allow Demeter to nurture you from within. If you are weary, invite Demeter to care for you, to offer the warmth of maternal love. Be gentle with yourself.

17 - NUIT IN A READING

If you draw Nuit, go to the stars. Feel the energy of the Cosmos and your place in the cosmic scheme of things. Feel your immense ability to be. Know that all is unfolding as it should. Allow Nuit to activate your trust in the divine plan.

18 - ARTEMIS IN A READING

Hail Luna! If you draw Artemis in a spread, feel the magnetism of the Moon. Allow the luminescent, silvery radiance to permeate every cell of your being. Honor the periodicity of your life. Is the moon waxing or waning today? Is it new moon, full moon, or some phase in between? Identify with your Lunation birthday, the exact phase of the Moon on the day you were born.

19 - HATHOR IN A READING

If Hathor's energy blesses you today, open your heart. Let her dance with you in fullness and grandeur. Listen carefully with your heart. Speak from your heart. Feel embraced by Hathor's compassion and pass it on to someone in your world.

20 - MAAT IN A READING

If you drew the Maat Rune, you have achieved some new level in your quest for consciousness. Pat yourself on the back. It is time to acknowledge the power of thought in creating your perceptions. Your habitual visualizations have as much to do with your reality as you experience. Now you are being asked to visualize some aspect of your future. The Angel of Cosmic Consciousness is on your side. As you focus on your goals, you begin to manifest them.

21 - GAIA IN A READING

If you draw this Rune, you have the humanitarian values that support the earth fully integrated into your psyche. It could be that you are still looking to integrate these new values into your career, but it is certain that you will not rest until you achieve your goal. Know that global consciousness in each of us is the most direct solution to world problems. Gaia asserts: "All for one and one for all."

PERSONALIZED GODDESS CHARTS

Following the Astrological Template, it is possible to make Personalized Goddess Charts for any individual. This will assist in ascertaining which Archetypes figure most prominently in someone's chart and which aspect of life, or house, the energy touches. The procedure is as follows:

Begin with an accurate astrological chart. These can be obtained from any astrologer, calculated using an astrology computer program, or obtained off the Internet.

Rotate the Goddess Chart Template to line-up with the astrological signs already on the chart. Draw a line across the horizon of the chart where the twelfth house meets the first house and where the sixth house meets the seventh house as per the diagram on page 232.

Assign Lunar Archetypes to the houses below the horizon (1-6), and Solar Archetypes to those above the horizon (7-12) according to astrological signs. For example, if the person's Sun is in the third house in Sagittarius, Uma would be assigned since she is the Lunar Archetype for Sagittarius, and the person's Sun was below the horizon at birth. If the person's Moon is in the eighth house in Taurus, for example, their Moon energy would be ruled by Inanna.

Examine the chart noticing the relationships between the goddesses and the planets. Notice the *key words* for the planets on the chart on page 232. Link the characteristics of the Archetype to the energy of the planet. For example, in the sample Personalized Goddess Chart on page 232, Pluto (transformation) is activated by Lillith. This means that this person will be strongly influenced by Lillith's sense of not being controlled. Her life will be focused on transforming her relationships to others so as not to feel controlled. If a person has many planets below the horizon, they will also have more Lunar Archetypes in their chart and hence tend to be more internally oriented. If the chart depicts more Solar Archetypes, or planets above the horizon, they will be generally more extroverted. Understanding Personalized Goddess Charts is a study in itself that is closely linked to understanding astrological charts.

SOUL PATH READING

It is possible to calculate which archetypal energy governs an individual's process. This dominant Archetype and her accompanying Angel is called the person's Soul Path. To find out an individual's Soul Path, make the following numerological calculation. Write the numbers of the month, day, and year of the person's birth. Add the numbers together until they reduce to a digit between 1 and 21. For example, December 8, 1954 translates to $12 + 8 + 1 + 9 + 5 + 4 = 39$. Thirty-nine reduces to $3 + 9 = 12$. Therefore, Baba Yaga, number 12 in the Angels and Archetypes system, governs this person's process. Further reduced, $1 + 2 = 3$. Hera, number 3, would also be an important ally to this person.

Signs		Keyword*
♈	Aries	Activity
♉	Taurus	Stability
♊	Gemini	Versatility
♋	Cancer	Devotion
♌	Leo	Magnetism
♍	Virgo	Practicality
♎	Libra	Harmony
♏	Scorpio	Intensity
♐	Sagittarius	Visualization
♑	Capricorn	Ambition
♒	Aquarius	Imagination
♓	Pisces	Understanding

* March and McEvers, 1976.

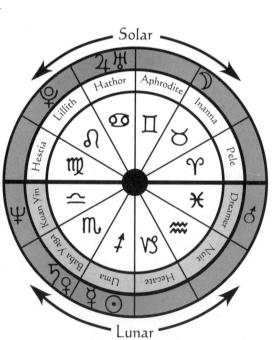

Rotate to line-up signs

Goddess Chart Template

Planets		Energy
☽	Moon	Emotions
☿	Mercury	Expression
♀	Venus	Affection
☉	Sun	Personality
♂	Mars	Action
♃	Jupiter	Expansion
♄	Saturn	Identity
♅	Uranus	Break Traditions
♆	Neptune	Ideals
♇	Pluto	Transformation

Example of Personalized Goddess Chart

Appendices
Summary Charts

The Twenty-two Archetypes

| | | | | | | | REALM OF THE UNDERWORLD |
Glyph	Number	Archetype	Tarot	Affirmation	Characteristics of The Archetype	Astrology	Environmental Archetype
	0	The Dreamer	THE FOOL	I am free	**Archetypal Seeker.** Responsive to the depths of human experience. Journey into the internal world. Romanticism, silent magnetism, Body, mind, and emotions are mutable and impermanent.	Moon in Pisces Mutable, Water	Spiraling Galaxy
	1	Persephone	THE MAGICIAN	I take risks	**The Archetypal Victim.** Consciously releases the burden of victimization. Learn the interaction between conscious and unconscious processes. Detachment from parents. Transcendence of the ego.	Moon in Gemini Mutable, Air	Entry to Underworld
	2	Isis	THE HIGH PRIESTESS	I come from myself	**The Archeypal Initiate.** Vessel for holiness and for divine expression. The essence of Spirit descended into matter. Quiet, shy, unpretentious and adaptable. Veiled yet we know that she knows.	Moon in Virgo Mutable, Earth	Ornate Pillars
	3	Hera	THE EMPRESS	I give of myself	**The Archetypal Wife.** The power of love is dearer than the love of power. Embodies material wealth, luxury, fertility, abundance, courage, gentleness, kindness, beauty, deep emotions, harmony.	Sun in Pisces Mutable, Water	Large Vessels
	4	Pele	THE EMPEROR	I confront facts	**The Archetypal Gate of Power.** Blasting terrestrial energy from the crystalline core of the Earth into the Cosmos. Breaks the conspiracy of silence. The Holy Fire of Spirit. Stable foundation.	Sun in Aries Moon in Aries Cardinal, Fire	Volcano
	5	Inanna	THE HIEROPHENT	I am in the world, but not of it	**The Archetypal Queen.** Sinks into the dark vortex of the Underworld. Mastered all the tests of life. Persistent, determined, cautious. Mature conviction, reconciliation, miracles.	Sun in Taurus Fixed, Earth	Stairway to Heaven
	6	Aphrodite	THE LOVERS	I am loved	**The Archetypal Beauty.** Internal marriage, true love, passionate affection, multidimensional learning, rapture. Merging of the physical and the light body. Sensual and sexual mysticism.	Sun in Gemini Mutable, Air	Entwined Lovers

Rune	#	Goddess	Card	Affirmation	Archetype	Astrology	Image	Realm
➊	7	Medusa	THE CHARIOT	I am focused	**The Archetypal Amazon.** Steadfastness, stability, independant action, tenacity, persistence, determination, victory, triumph over obstacles. Snake energy. Spiritual warrior. Fiery heroine.	Sun in Sagittarius, Mutable, Fire	Warrior Woman	Realm of Roles
⌀	8	Kuan Yin	JUSTICE	I am balanced	**The Archetypal Meditator.** Passion for peace and peace through passion. Spiritual devotion. Holy Mother of Compassion. Sensitive and aware. Serene, tranquil, warm, poised, inspired.	Moon in Libra, Cardinal, Air	Temple at Sunrise	Realm of Roles
ᐸ	9	Hestia	THE HERMIT	I keep the home fires burning	**The Archetypal Vestal Virgin.** Brings own light into the world. Forsight, chaity, exemplifies the joys of solitude. The essence of soulfullness. Light that dispels spiritual chaos.	Sun in Virgo, Mutable, Earth	The Hearth	Realm of Roles
⌘	10	Athena	THE WHEEL OF FORTUNE	I manifest	**The Archetypal Animus-Driven Woman.** Ambition, aspiration, expansion, opportunity. Impersonal love, altruism, creativity, scholarly wisdom, power to succeed. Father's daughter.	Sun in Capricorn, Cardinal, Earth	The Parthenon	Realm of Roles
‖	11	Lilith	STRENGTH	I stand firm on my convictions	**The Archetypal Unshakled Woman.** Self-determination, vitality, resolution, refuses to be controlled, quiet strength, bold, undaunted. Strength provides force to give power to the will.	Sun in Leo, Fixed, Fire	Restless Sea	Realm of Renunciation
ᛟ	12	Baba Yaga	THE HANGED MAN	I go deep within	**The Archetypal Hag.** Willingness to surrender everything. Break with dependencies, material temptations conquered, prophetic powers and vision. The marrow of the wild woman.	Moon in Scorpio, Fixed, Water	Mossy Forest	Realm of Renunciation
✕	13	Kali	DEATH	I let go	**The Archetypal Destroyer.** Release of ego energies. Dying daily. Superconscious. Transformation. Synthesizes information. Faith in invisible. Ultimate creatrix.	Sun in Scorpio, Fixed, Water	Woman Touching the Void	Realm of Renunciation
↓	14	Uma	TEMPERANCE	I ground cosmic energy	**The Archetypal Ecstatic Dancer.** Come to terms with shadow. Fierce loyalty, optimism, freedom. Spiritualizes collective. Trusts self. The cosmos and the Earth conjugate through her.	Moon in Sagittarius, Mutable, Fire	The Cave	Realm of Renunciation

Glyph	Number	Archetype	Tarot	Affirmation	Characteristics of The Archetype	Astrology	Environmental Archetype
	15	Hecate	THE DEVIL	I illuminate my shadow	**The Archetypal Crone.** Live with feet in heaven and head in heaven. Right livlihood without toiling. Know all things and know nothing. Fully alive. Wise woman.	Moon in Capricorn Cardinal, Earth	The Gateway
	16	Demeter	THE TOWER	I persevere	**The Archetypal Great Mother.** The harvest of the Self. Primary maternal preoccupation. mother-daughter bonding. Divine sustenance. Eleusinian Mystery Schools.	Moon in Cancer Cardinal, Water	Tall Tower
	17	Nuit	THE STAR	I radiate the oneness of all	**The Archetypal Cosmic Gate.** Divine fusion, transfiguration, individuation. Conscious control of our own destiny. Energy is all there is. Energy comes through at the violet hour.	Moon in Aquarius Sun in Aquarius Fixed, Water	Tree at the Violet Hour
	18	Artemis	THE MOON	I intuit the mysteries of the Moon	**The Archetypal Wild Woman.** Divine human prototype. Intuitive imagination. Holy mirror. Divine splendor. Psychic powers. Lunar consciousness. Procreative potential.	Moon in Leo Fixed, Fire	Primitive Village
	19	Hathor	THE SUN	I transcend	**The Archetypal Shapeshifter.** Compassion, unconditional love, beauty, sensuousness, multidimensionality. Alchemical mysteries. Mother of the gypsies, patron of dancers.	Sun in Cancer Cardinal, Water	The Giza Plateau
	20	Maat	JUDGEMENT	I am conscious	**The Archetypal Seeker of Truth.** Final blast of liberation. Cosmic order. Accuracy, honesty, fairness, authenticity, legitimacy, integrity, and justice. Soul qualities of equilibrium and poise.	Sun in Libra Cardinal, Air	Step Pyramid
	21	Gaia	THE WORLD	I am part of the divine plan	**The Archetypal Humanitarian.** Mastery over manifest world. Completion. Triumph in undertakings. The living presence of Mother Earth. Soul qualities of faithfulness and sentimentality.	Moon in Taurus Fixed, Earth	The Earth From Space

The Twenty-two Angels

#	Angel	Archetype	Purpose of the Angel	Result of Ego Projection	Root of Block
0	The Angel of Karmic Destiny	The Dreamer	Introduces the Realm of the Underworld. Beginning of the processing of unconscious material into consciousness. Feeling unconditional divine Love. Grasping that earth is a free-will zone.	Fear, guilt, feeling of repression, feeling judged.	Judging others + situations on appearance.
1	The Angel of Surrender	Persephone	Guardian of the Realm of the Underworld. Helps us break through illusions. Mediator between two worlds. Lifts veils of perception. Helps us understand the concept of projection.	Manipulative, compulsive, not knowing what is real.	Denial, tendency to worry; seeking distraction.
2	The Angel of Cosmic Intelligence	Isis	Allows for the wisdom through divination and channeled information; Invites us to be divine instruments of service. stimulates instincts and intuition. Helps us know that with wisdom we can have and be all things.	Instincts blocked spiritually disconnected, indecisive, confused.	Overly rational and cerebral, suspicious of channeling.
3	The Angel of Prosperity	Hera	Instills a deep trust in the Universe to provide all we need. The vortex through which material and spiritual prosperity passes. Manifestation of prosperity, luxury, rich experiences, and material desires.	Insecurity, envy, financial struggle, feeling of futility.	A belief in lack and insufficiency, unreceptive.
4	The Angel of Empowerment	Pele	Gives us a voice and the fortitude to speak out. Vitalizes assists us to take charge. Dam breaker. Helps us know the only true power is from deep within. Blasts energy from the Underworld into the Upperworld.	Arrogant, pretentious, vain, condescending, inappropriate raging.	Desire for power over, inability to surrender to Spirit.
5	The Angel of Descent	Inanna	Moves us to a deeper soul-place. Helps us grasp our purpose for incarnating into our present situation. Appreciates the meaning of our challenges in life in a deeper context. Makes sense of dark passages.	Depressed, stubborn, unyielding, hangs on, wallows in pain.	Not seeing descent as a profound tool for growth.
6	The Angel of Love	Aphrodite	First Angel in the Realm of Roles. Brings lessons through relationships. Engenders romance. Opens us to healthy vulnerability. Acts as the cosmic cupid. Arranges for divine timing in meeting partners.	Unrequited love, poor choices in partners sexual problems.	Fear of rejection, poor self-worth, dependence.

#	Angel	Archetype	Purpose of the Angel	Result of Ego Projection	Root of Block
7	The Angel of Focus	Medusa	Gives us the initiative to persist and fortitude when we falter. Offers us effortlessness in our work. Brings in divine grace that leads to immense productivity. Stimulates tenacity and determination to complete tasks.	Lack of motivation, wasted efforts, incomplete tasks.	Fear of failure, doing things for the wrong reasons.
8	The Angel of Peace	Kuan Yin	Radiates serenity and tranquility. Stands in full acceptance of what is. Recognizes disasters as disguised opportunities. Waits patiently for evidence of the perfection of the moment.	Creates disorder and chaos, restless, crisis maker.	Peace seen as boring and empty, distracted mentally.
9	The Angel of Discernment	Vestia	The inner sanctuary of the sacred feminine. Assists us in expressing our essential selves and in disentangling our identity from the mass of mankind. Evaluation with the heart. The tranquillity of the inner self.	Disorganized household, is agitated at home.	Fear of being alone, overidentification with the external cues.
10	The Angel of Magnetic Resonance	Athena	The ability to tune into the electromagnetic harmonics of the planetary field and to function as a human transmitter of divine currents of photonic light. Goes within to assimilate divine impressions.	Tolerates synthetics, surrounded with electrostatic noise.	Not enough fluid, not fluid enough. Vibrational portal.
11	The Angel of Courage + Conviction	Lilith	Gatekeeper to the Realm of Renunciation and Regeneration. Fusion with heart and mind. Vortex of divine energy gives spiritual determination to persist through continual tests. Re-establishes us in our own power.	Defiant, reactive, resists the trials of life.	Belief that the world offers greater pleasure than Spirit.
12	The Angel of Reversal	Baba Yaga	Invites us to let go of the ego-driven personality and identification with "I." Mastery of non-attachment. Giving up the mortal for the immortal sense of existence. The final step before regeneration.	Hoards material possessions, lives without inspiration.	Fear of loss and deprivation, in the cellar of the self.
13	The Angel of Ultimate Release	Kali	The energy of metamorphosis. Help with letting go. The freedom of surrender. Heralds a new cycle of learning. Release of the earthly plane. New vitality springing forth from the soul. The ability to be still.	Cannot recognize when a phase of life is complete.	Fear of death of the ego, identification of the body as self.

#	Angel		Description		
14	The Angel of Temperance	Uma	Provides a surge of raw cosmic energy that allows us to charge ourselves. Energy gives way to intuitive perception and true optimism. The light body is activated and exits in its multi-colored splendor.	Lack of vitality, isolated, impatient, wastes energy.	Fear of the future, lack of trust in the divine plan.
15	The Angel of the Illumined Shadow	Hecate	Helps us know all things and recognize that we know nothing. Assists us in staying grounded through frequency shifts. Maintains equilibrium in relationships. Enjoys modern conveniences without attachment.	Projects shadow, invasive, opinionated, narrow-minded.	Fear of not having enough, dominated by desires.
16	The Angel of Strength + Nurturing	Demeter	The Gatekeeper to the Realm of Cosmic Consciousness. Offers the steadfastness to live infused with Spirit no matter what is going on around us. Prompts us to follows the highest vision.	Resentment, easily irritated, feels trapped, controlling.	Given Self up to serve others, over-active sense of duty.
17	The Angel of the Galactic Beam	Nuit	Welcomes us to the Realm of Cosmic Consciousness. Creates a new context assisting us in our evolution. Motivates us to be in service to humanity which is a requisite to receiving energy from the Master Self.	Focuses on religion instead of spirituality, blocks Spirit.	Doesn't realize that God/Goddess is within each of us
18	The Angel of the Lunation Cycle	Artemis	Emanates the opalescent, tranquil, refined, silvery vibration of the Moon. Transduces energies from galactic beams into encodements. Waxing and waning, it pulsates alternating currents of electromagnetic energies.	Out of touch with the cycles of life, unreliable.	Over-socialized, overly influenced by the media
19	The Angel of Multidimensionality	Hathor	Teaches us to tune into the subtle vibrations that are transmitted through our glandular system. Opening of the psychic regulatory system. Rebirth as a galactic star-child. Opens portals to other dimensions.	Frequently ill, shut down, not open to evolution, haughty.	Chakras shut down, electrostatically over-charged
20	The Angel of Cosmic Consciousness	Maat	Has full access to all realms in the Universe and the 12 dimensions of consciousness. Takes us beyond space and time. Ushers us through dimensional portals where we access galactic levels of consciousness.	Vulnerability to legal problems, manipulative.	Gives power away to others, doesn't want to be first to evolve
21	The Angel of the One Heart	Gaia	Dominion on the Earth plane. Mastery of the language of the heart. Assists us in connecting with the power of Universal Love. Generates harmonic energy. Reradiation from the inner chamber of the heart.	Uses resources carelessly, uninspired.	Feels dominated, in the game for what can gain for self

Chapter Notes

Introduction

1. Harvey, 1984, page 45.
2. Jung, 1960, page 25.

Chapter 1 – Archetypes

1. Bjorkman, 1985, page 45.
2. Engelsman, 1979, page 14.
3. Jung, 1960, page 20.
4. Whitmont, 1982, page 123.
5. Carey, 1988, page 205.
6. von Franz, 1992, page 37.
7. Boulter, 1989, page 3, unpublished manuscript *Visualization and Creative Thinking*.
8. Ornstein, 1977, page 37.
9. Carey, 1988, page 207.
10. Alter, 1993, page 41.
11. Ibid, pages 41-42.
12. Ibid, page 42.
13. Whitmont, 1982, page 189.
14. Ibid, pages 189-190.
15. Jung, 1960, page 23.
16. Whitmont, 1982, pages 201-202.
17. Ibid, page 187.
18. Goodrich,1989, page 205.
19. Whitmont,1982, page 188.

Chapter 11 – The Angels

1. Unity School of Christianity, 1939, Metaphysical Bible Dictionary— "Judgment," page 377.
2. Price, 1993, page 237.
3. Ibid, page 98.
4. Carey, 1988, page 36.

5. Dr. David Ash, March 1994, in proxy Conclave of Michael, Banff, Canada.
6. Unity School of Christianity, 1939, Metaphysical Bible Dictionary— "Ark," page 64.
7. Woer, 1989, page 75.
8. Carey ,1988, page 59.
9. Yankelovich Partners Inc., December 1993, see "Angels Among Us", *Time Magazine,* page 46, survey of 500 Americans.
10. Snow, 1978, page 85.
11. Leary, 1989, page112.
12. Carey, 1988, page 205.
13. Ibid, page 216.
14. Leary, 1989, page 8.
15. Unity School of Christianity, 1939, Metaphysical Bible Dictionary— "Ark," page 64.
16. Ibid, "Christ," page 150.
17. Ibid, "ascension," page I, Addenda.
18. Ibid, "supper, great," page 635.

Chapter 111 – The Evolutionary Map

1. Veggi and Davidson, 1995, page 63.
2. Hoaglan, Richard, 1994,*The Face on Mars* video.
3. Melchizadek, Drunvalo, *1995, Flower of Life* video series.
4. Price , 1995,page 10.
5. Ibid
6. Lamy, 1981, page 18

Chapter IV – The Dreamer

1. Nichols, 1980, page 41.
2. Ibid, page 24.
3. Ibid, page 31.
4. Ibid, pages 30-31.
5. Walker, 1984, page 60.
6. Michel, 1966, page 116.
7. Noble,1983,page 129.
8. Nichols, 1980,page 68.
9. Noble, 1983, page 132.

Chapter V – Persephone

1. Nichols, 1980, pages 48–49.
2. Gadon, 1989, page 159.
3. Ibid— page 159.
4. Rudyar, 1972, page 94.
5. Nichols, 1980, page 51.

Chapter VI – Isis

1. Hall, 1901, pages XLVI, XLVIII.
2. Nichols, 1980, page 80.
3. Kinstler, 1985, page 21.49.
4. Bleeker, 1983, page 33.
5. Nichols, 1980, page 73.
6. Graves, 1979, page 18.
7. PBS video, The Lost Years of Jesus
8. Woer, 1989, page 41.
9. Clow, 1995, page 225.
10. Kinstler, 1985, pages 21–22.
11. Clow, 1995, page 48.
12. Mascetti, 1990, page 161.
13. Ibid, page159–160.
14. Douglas, 1972, page 121.

Chapter VII – Hera

1. Unity School of Christianity, 1939, Metaphysical Bible Dictionary— "Magdalene," page 415.
2. Wanless,1986, page 27.
3. page 88, Nichols
4. Ibid.
5. Nichols, 1980, page 95.
6. Walker, 1984, page 68.
7. Bolen, 1992, page 139.
8. Walker, 1984, page 68.

9. Unity School of Christianity, 1939, Metaphysical Bible Dictionary— "vessels," page 673.
10. Ibid—"Marriage," page 424.
11. Ibid—"wedding garment," page 676.
12. Walker, 1983, pages 585-595.
13. Cavander, 1974, page 105.
14. Statistics from Statistics Canada.
15. Ibid.
16. George, 1992, page 211.
17. Marciniak, 1995, pages 97-98.
18. Unity School of Christianity, 1939, Metaphysical Bible Dictionary— "prosperity," page 536.

Chapter VIII – Pele

1. Unity School of Christianity, 1939, Metaphysical Bible Dictionary— "Flaming Sword," page 217.
2. Nichols, 1980, page 108.
3. Ibid, page 106.
4. Pelletier, 1978, page 16.
5. Nichols , 1980, page 108.

Chapter IX – Inanna

1. Wanless, 1986, page 37.
2. Unity School of Christianity, 1939, Metaphysical Bible Dictionary— "Ur," page 668.
3. Nichols, 1980, page 123.
4. Ferguson, 1996, page 17.
5. Gadon, 1989, page 120.
6. Ibid, page 116.
7. Sitchin, 1990, page 15.
8. Ibid, page 19.
9. Ferguson, 1996, page xiv.
10. Ibid, page 24.
11. Ibid, page 20.
12. Gadon, 1989, page 121.
13. Ibid, page 122.
14. Gadon, 1989, page 125.
15. Whitmont,1982, page 136.
16. Ibid.
17. Ibid, page 134.
    Gadon, 1989, page 127.
    Wolkstein and Kramer, 1983, page 38.

20. Whitmont, 1982, page 136.
21. Ibid, page 134.
22. Ibid.
23. Ochshorn, 1983, page 22
24. Gadon, page 128.
25. Ibid, page 128.
26. Ibid.
27. Starck and Stern, 1993, page 34.
28. Whitmont, 1982, page 136.
29. Whitmont, page 134.
30. Kinstler, 1985, page 183.
31. Perrera, 1989, page .
32. Kinstler, 1985, page 170.
33. Ibid, page 171.
34. Price, 1993, page 81.
35. Ibid.

Chapter X - Aphrodite

1. Bolen, 1992, page 224.
2. Walker, 1984, page 82.
3. Ibid.
4. Walker, page 81.
5. Ibid.
6. Walker, 1983, page 130.
7. Ibid, page 44.
8. Ibid.
9. Ibid.
10. Bolen, 1971, page. 224.
11. Ibid, page 233.
12. Walker, 1984, page 81.
13. Nichols, 1980, page 135.
14. Unity School of Christianity, 1939, Metaphysical Bible Dictionary—"Asheroth," page 70.
15. Bolen, 1977, page 225.
16. Nichols, 1980, page 136.
17. There are many references to this myth, one being Goodrich, 1989, page 226.
18. Whitmont, 1982, page 136.

Chapter XI - Medusa

1. George, 1992, page 155.
2. Goodrich, 1989, page 68.
3. Whitmont, 1982, page 135.
4. Noble, 1983, page 67.
5. Unity School of Christianity, 1939, Metaphysical Bible Dictionary—"Sabbath," page 563.
6. Noble, 1983, page 68.
7. Wanless, 1986, page 46-47.
8. Whitmont, 1982, page 141.
9. Ibid.
10 Price, 1993, page 108.
11. Ibid, page 112.

Chapter XII - Kuan Yin

1. George, 1992, page 155.
2. Goodrich, 1989, page 68.
3. Whitmont, 1982, page 135.
4. Noble , 1983, page 67.
5. Unity School of Christianity, 1939, Metaphysical Bible Dictionary—"Sabbath," page 563.
6. Noble, 1983, page 68.
7. Wanless, page 46-47.
8. Whitmont, 1982, page 141.
9. Ibid.
10. Price, 1993, page 108.
11. Ibid, page 112.

Chapter XIII - Hestia

1. Cheiro, 1988, page 65.
2. Nichols, 1980, page 175.
3. Kinstler, 1985, page 244.
4. Nichols, 1980, page 166.
5 Price, 1993, refers to the Angel of Discernment
6. Ibid, page 170.

Chapter XIV - Athena

1. Nichols, 1980, page 188.
2. Downing, 1981, page 110.
3. Ibid, page 118.
4. Ibid, page 113.
5. Ibid.
6. Ibid, page 141.
7. Ibid.
8. Book out of print.
9. Ibid, page 149.

Chapter XV - Lillith

1. Walker, 1983, page 541.
2 Konraad, 1983, page 22.

3. Noble, 1983, page 89.
4. Nichols, 1980, page 208.
5. Walker, 1983, page 541.
6. Ibid, page 543.
7. Internet reference humm@ccat.sas.upenn.edu
8. Whitmont, 1982, page 157.
9. Unity School of Christianity, 1939, Metaphysical Bible Dictionary— "Red Sea," page 543.
10. Ibid.
11. Whitmont, 1982, page 184.
12. Unity School of Christianity, 1939, Metaphysical Bible Dictionary— "Eden" page 181.
13. Ibid.
14. Whitmont, 1982, page 289.
15. Ibid, page 291.
16. See Estes, 1992, Women Who Run With the Wolves, for a full description of the Wild Woman archetype.
17. Price, 1993, page 159.
18. Ibid, page 165.

Chapter XVI – Baba Yaga

1. Nichols, 1980, page 221.
2. Ibid, page 179.
3. Internet PbYaga@http:// cent1.lancs.ac.uk/~gec95020
4. Estes, 1992, page 77.
5. Ibid, page 92.
6. Vilenskaya, 1995, page 2.
7. Estes, page 97.
8. Nichols, 1980, page 224.
9. Price, 1993, page 170.
10. Ibid.
11. Ibid, page 172-173.
12. Ibid, page 173.
13. Unity School of Christianity, 1939, Metaphysical Bible Dictionary— "Sacrifices," page 565.
14. Ibid.

Chapter XVII – Kali

1. Mookerjee , 1988, page 61.
2. Brown, 1983, page 110.
3. Mookerjee, 1988, page 62.
4. Unity School of Christianity, 1939, Metaphysical Bible Dictionary— "Akrabbim," page 39.
5. Mookerjee, 1988, page 62.
6. Ibid.
7. Brown, 1983, page 112.
8. Ibid, page 113.
9. Ibid, page 114.
10. Mookerjee, 1988, page 62.
11. Ibid, page 116.
12. Whitmont, 1982, page 57.
13. Mookerjee, 1988, page 61.
14. Price, 1993, pages 185-186.

Chapter XVIII – Uma

1. Murphy, 1983, page 192.
2. Noble, 1983, page 108.
3. Unity School of Christianity, 1939, Metaphysical Bible Dictionary— "poise," page 533.
4. Murphy, page 196.
5. Unity School of Christianity, 1939, Metaphysical Bible Dictionary— "poise," page 533.
6. Murphy,1983, page 199.
7. Ibid.
8. Noble, 1983, page 107.
9. Price, 1993, pages 193-194.
10. Ibid, page 196.
11. Ibid, page 197.
12. Ibid, page 198.
13. Ibid.

Chapter XIX – Hecate

1. Walker, 1983, page 366.
2. Noble, 1980, page 115.
3. Unity School of Christianity, 1939, Metaphysical Bible Dictionary— "Phoenix," page 529.
4. Ibid.
5. Unity School of Christianity, 1939, Metaphysical Bible Dictionary— "Phoenicia," page 529.
6. Neumann, 1994, page 64-118.
7. Ibid , page 106.
8. Noble, 1983, page 113.
9. Ibid, page 213.
10. Ibid.

Chapter XX – Demeter

1. Walker, 1984, page 116.
2. Gadon, 1989, page 160.
3. Ibid, page 143.
4. Ibid, page 144.
5. Stone,1979, page 371.
6. Gadon, 1989, page 146.
7. Ibid, page 144.
8. Ibid.
9. Ibid, page 157.
10. Ibid, page 154.
11. Woer, 1989, page 309.
12. Gadon,1989, page 155.
13. Vilenskaya, 1995, page 3.
14. Gadon, 1989, page 155
15. Woer, 1989, page 3.
16. Gadon, 1989,page 160.
17. Ibid.
18. Ibid, page 156.
19. Harvey, 1984, page 47.

Chapter XXI – Nuit

1. Crowley,1969, page 113.
2. Jung, 1979, page 380.
3. Nichols, 1980, page 296.
4. Unity School of Christianity, 1939, Metaphysical Bible Dictionary— "Pleiades," page 533.
5. Ibid, "Stars," page 629.
6. Noble, 1980, page 125.
7. page 298 Nichols
8. Whitmont, 1982, page 157.
9. Veggi and Davidson, 1995, page 45.
10. Price, 1993, page 234-235.
11. Ibid, pages 238-239.

Chapter XXII – Artemis

1. Whitmont, 1982, page 32.
2. Unity School of Christianity, 1939, Metaphysical Bible Dictionary— "Artemas," page 66.
3. Ibid, "Pleiades," page 533.
4. Ibid.
5. Estes, 1992.

6. Ibid, page 29.
7. Downing, 1981, page 167.
8. Ibid.
9. Whitmont, 1982, pages 199-200.
10. Ibid, page 182.
11. Clow, 1995, page 138.
12. Neumann, 1994, page 112.

Chapter XXIII – Hathor

1. Konraad, 1983, page 20.
2. Hall, 1901, pages 258-259.
3. Nichols, 1982, page 333.
4. Lamy,1981, page 68.
5. Drunvalo Melchizedek, *The Flower of Life*, Video 3.
6. Clow , 1995, page 224.
7. Bleeker, 1983, page 31.
8. Ibid.
9. Clow, 1995, page 94.
10. Schul and Petit, 1975, page 41.
11. Wilks, 1979, page 100.
12. Michel, 1973, page 99.
13. Ibid, page 105.
14. Ibid, page 115.
15. Ibid.
16. Veggi and Davidson, 1995, page 101.
17. Woer, 1989, page 91.
18. Bleeker, 1983, page 40.
19. Ibid, page 44.
20. Ibid, page 47.
21. Woer, 1989, page 64.
22. Unity School of Christianity, 1939, Metaphysical Bible Dictionary— "Hor," page 284.
23. Bleeker, 1983, page 43.
24. Unity School of Christianity, 1939, Metaphysical Bible Dictionary— "Asheroth," page 70.
25. Bleeker, 1983, page 41.
26. Ibid, page 44.
27. Ibid.
28. Ibid, page 48.
29. Clow, 1995, page 145.

Chapter XXIV – Maat

1. Lamy, 1981, page 17.
2. Stone, 1979, page 9.
3. Walker, 1984, page 130.
4. Lamy, 1981, page 51.
5. Unity School of Christianity, 1939, Metaphysical Bible Dictionary— "Judgment," page 376.
6. Ibid, "Kingdom," page 388.
7. Ibid, "Logos," page 405.
8. Ibid.
9. Ibid.
10. Ibid, "thought," page 654.
11. Stone, Joshua, 1995, page 141.
12. Ibid, page 146.

Chapter XXV – Gaia

1. Downing, 1981, page 135.
2. Ibid, page 50.
3. Ibid, page 51.
4. Ibid, page 50
5. Goodrich, 1989, page 194.
6. Ibid, page 197.
7. Ibid, pages 197-198.
8. Downing, 1981, page 51.
9. Ibid, pages 50, 51, 54.
10. Noble, 1983, page 142.
11. Gadon, 1989, page 341.
12. Downing, 1981, page 155.
13. Ibid, page 51.
14. Ibid, page 135.
15. Wolke, 1995, page 1.
16. Ibid.

Photo Credits

Preface

Page x: Photograph of the Great Pyramid as seen across the gardens of Mena House Oberoi Hotel which overlooks the Giza plateau in Cairo, Egypt. Mena House was formerly the palace of King Mena. Photo by Carmen Boulter.

Introduction

Page xvi: The Gate of Power, also known as the Gate of the Sun, Tihuanaco, Bolivia. Photo by Josef Szujker.

Archetypes

Page xxi: Two magnificent pillars guarding the entrance to the Holy of Holies, the sacred sanctuary at the temple of Karnak, Egypt. One pillar has a papyrus flower and the other has a blue lotus flower. Photo by Suze Baumann.

Angels

Page 10: Original art for *Angels and Archetypes* drawn by Robert H. Foster.

The Evolutionary Map

Page 15: Top is the Evolutionary Map. Bottom is the Angels and Archetypes Astrological Template. Both are original art created for *Angels and Archetypes* by Michael Freeman.

The Dreamer

Page 25: Angel and Archetype Rune for The Dreamer. All 22 original glyphs by Carmen Boulter. All 22 photographs of Angels and Archetypes Runes by Brian McCutcheon.

Page 26: Original water color art by Dwayne Edward Rourke entitled *The Dreamer* created for *Angels and Archetypes*. The Dreamer gazes through an archway at the galaxy.

Page 30: The Angel of Karmic Destiny is about to enter through the doorway to the third dimension. Photographed at The Recoletta in Buenos Aires, Argentina, by Carmen Boulter.

Persephone

Page 36: Persephone from impressive life size relief located in the museum at The temple to Demeter, Eleusis, Greece, fourteen miles outside of Athens. Photo by Boyd Holloway.

Page 41: The Angel of Surrender anchored to the mundane world seeking spiritual release. Photographed at the Recoletta in Buenos Aires, Argentina, by Carmen Boulter.

Isis

Page 46: Relief of Isis off temple wall at Edfu, Egypt. Photo by Suze Baumann.

Page 51: The Angel of Cosmic Intelligence sits patiently. Photographed at the Recoletta in Buenos Aires, Argentina, by Carmen Boulter.

Hera

Page 56: Hera's House display at the National Archaeological Museum in Athens, Greece. Photograph by Boyd Holloway.

Page 62: The Angel of Prosperity with her large vessel symbolizing her ability to contain and to prosper. Photographed at the Recoletta in Buenos Aires, Argentina, by Carmen Boulter.

Pele

Page 66: Original water color art by Dwayne Edward Rourke entitled *Pele* created for *Angels and Archetypes.* The goddess Pele blasts forth from an erupting volcano in all her fiery majesty.

Page 69: The Angel of Empowerment walks with confidence fully facing all that crosses her path. Photographed at the Recoletta in Buenos Aires, Argentina, by Carmen Boulter.

Inanna

Page 74: Inanna makes her descent into the Underworld and then ascends on the *stairway to heaven*. Original water color art by Dwayne Edward Rourke created for *Angels and Archetypes*.

Page 81: The Angel of Descent flies freely between the Upperworld and the Underworld. Photographed at the Recoletta in Buenos Aires, Argentina, by Carmen Boulter.

Aphrodite

Page 86: Aphrodite sitting peacefully in a sea shell representing her birth in the sea. Photographed by Boyd Holloway at the National Archeological Museum in Athens, Greece.

Page 91: The Angel of Love gazes adoringly at a goddess seated on her throne. Photographed at the Recoletta in Buenos Aires, Argentina, by Carmen Boulter.

Medusa

Page 96: Head of Medusa photographed at Didyma, Turkey by Geordie Facey. Similar representations of Medusa are found scattered all over the Greek Islands and Turkish coast showing how widespread the Amazon warrior women's territory was.

Page 98: The Angel of Focus concentrates as she plays her instrument. Photographed at the Recoletta in Buenos Aires, Argentina, by Carmen Boulter.

Kuan Yin

Page 102: Fifteenth century carved wooden statue of Kuan Yin from China. Photo courtesy of the Darion Collection.

Page 104: The Angel of Peace is suspended in tranquillity. Photographed at the Recoletta in Buenos Aires, Argentina, by Carmen Boulter.

Hestia

Page 108: Hestia's energy filling an entire house. Original water color art by Dwayne Edward Rourke created for *Angels and Archetypes*.

Page 110: The Angel of Discernment makes evaluations from her heart. Photographed at the Recoletta in Buenos Aires, Argentina, by Carmen Boulter.

Athena

Page 116: Life size statue of Athena carrying a shield with a Gorgon mask embossed on it (mask not visible at this angle). Photograph by Boyd Holloway, national Archaeological Museum, Athens, Greece.

Page 120: The Angel of Magnetic Resonance seen reaching toward heaven with her heart open and her thymus chakra pointed up. Photographed at the Recoletta in Buenos Aires, Argentina, by Carmen Boulter.

Lillith

Page 126: Lillith appearing with wings and with bird feet holding ancient Egyptian geometric symbols. Photograph courtesy of Alan Humm.

Page 130: The Angel of Courage and Conviction making a pledge. Photographed at the Recoletta in Buenos Aires, Argentina, by Carmen Boulter.

Baba Yaga

Page 134: Interpretive image of Baba Yaga sitting at the base of a tree in a mossy forest. Original water color art by Dwayne Edward Rourke created for Angels and Archetypes.

Page 137: The Angel of Reversal seen pouting and contemplative. Photographed at the Recoletta in Buenos Aires, Argentina, by Carmen Boulter.

Kali

Page 144: Kali with her four arms shown standing on the body of her husband. Photograph courtesy of the Glenbow Museum, Calgary, Alberta.

Page 147: The Angel of Ultimate Release carries a maiden as he stands on the body of the devil seen holding a pitchfork. Photographed at the Recoletta in Buenos Aires, Argentina, by Carmen Boulter.

Uma

Page 152: Original water color art of Uma writhing and dancing by Dwayne Edward Rourke created for *Angels and Archetypes*.

Page 154: The Angel of Temperance balances energy solemnly holding her crossed hands over her heart. Photographed at the Recoletta in Buenos Aires, Argentina, by Carmen Boulter.

Hecate

Page 160: Life size statue of Hecate as the triple goddess. Each of three faces of the statue represent the virgin, the mother, and the crone. Photographed in the National Archaeological Museum in Athens, Greece by Boyd Holloway.

Page 163: The Angel of the Illumined Shadow walks proudly forward. Photographed in the National Archaeological Museum in Athens, Greece by Boyd Holloway.

Demeter

Page 168: Huge bust of Demeter, shoulder width of 30 inches on display in the museum at Eleusis, Greece. Note Gorgon medallion on her heart. Photo by Boyd Holloway.

Page 174: The Angel of Strength and Nurturing is carrying a child and stands within the *tower* of her own strength. Photographed at the Recoletta in Buenos Aires, Argentina, by Carmen Boulter.

Nuit

Page 178: Original fresco of Nuit classically displayed with her fingers and feet touching the Earth. Eight by ten foot fresco photographed in four sections at the temple of Hathor at Dendera, Egypt by Ron Rathburn. Reconstructed and color enhanced in photoshop by Carmen Boulter.

Page 180: The Angel of the Galactic Beam contains the Galaxy within her outspread arms. Angel photographed at the Recoletta in Buenos Aires, Argentina, by Carmen Boulter. Galaxy from NASA collection http://images.jsc.nasa.gov/html/home.htm, May 1996.

Artemis

Page 186: Enlargement of a tiny metal artifact of Artemis from an elaborate collection of excavated remains. Photographed at the National Archaeological Museum in Athens by Boyd Holloway.

Page 190: The Angel of the Lunation Cycle proudly transmits energy from the moon. Angel photographed at the Recoletta in Buenos Aires, Argentina, by Carmen Boulter. Moon from Michael Myers http://www.netaxs.com/~mhmyers/moon.tn.html, April, 1996.

Hathor

Page196: Face of Hathor recently excavated near Memphis, Egypt. Photograph by Ron Rathburn.

Page 202: The Angel of Multidimensionality flows freely between dimensional portals. Photographed at the Recoletta in Buenos Aires, Argentina, by Carmen Boulter.

Maat

Page 208: Maat holding her feather of Truth from carved fresco at Abydos, Egypt. Photograph by Ron Rathburn.

Page 211: The Angel of Cosmic Consciousness holding a cross representing Christ consciousness. Photographed at the Recoletta in Buenos Aires, Argentina, by Carmen Boulter.

Gaia

Page 216: Photograph of the Earth from space from http://images.jsc.nasa.gov/images/pao/sts49/10065092.jpg, April 1996.

Page 219: The Angel of the One Heart gives and receives energy from the Earth. Angel photographed at the Recoletta in Buenos Aires, Argentina, by Carmen Boulter. Photo of Earth as above, page 216.

Applications

Page 220: Photograph of Gwendolyn A. Jansma and Frances Murphy taken at a ritual near San Diego.

Bibliography

ADLER, Margot, *Drawing Down the Moon: Witches, Druids, Goddess-Worshippers, and Other Pagans in America Today*, Beacon Press, Boston, 1979

ALDRED, Cyril, *Akhenaten: King of Egypt*, Thames and Hudson, London, 1988

ALESANDRINI, Kathryn Lutz, "Imagery-eliciting strategies and meaningful learning", *Journal of Mental Imagery,* Volume 6, 1982, pages 120-140

ALLEN, Paula Gunn, *Grandmothers of the Light: A Medicine Woman's Sourcebook,* Beacon Press, Boston, 1991

ALTER, Wendlyn, "The yang heart of yin: on women's spiritual nature", *The Quest,* Winter 1993, pages 40-45

ANKA, Darryl, *Bashar: Blueprint for Change, A Message From Our Future*, New Solutions Publishing, Simi Valley, 1990

ARCHER, John, "Biological explanation of psychological sex differences", *Exploring Sex Differences*, Barbara Lloyd and John Archer [Eds.], Academic Press, New York, 1976

ARROYO, Stephen, *Astrology, Psychology, and the Four Elements: An Energy Approach to Astrology and Its Use in the Counseling Arts,* CRCS Publications, Reno, 1975

BANDURA, Albert; WALTERS, Richard; *Social Learning and Personality Development*, Holt Rinehart and Winston, New York, 1963

BARDWICK, Judith M., *Readings on the Psychology of Women,* Harper and Row, New York, 1972

BARTLEY, Sandra Lee, *Feminism and Domination: Studies in the Phenomenology of Oppression,* Routelidge, New York, 1990

BASSERMANN, Lujo, *The Oldest Profession: A History of Prostitution*, translated by James Cleugh, Stein and Day, New York, 1968

BERNBAUM, Edwin, *Sacred Mountains of the World*, Sierra Club Books, San Francisco, 1990

BIANCHI, Suzanne M.; SPAIN, Daphne, *American Women: Three Decades of Change*, Special Demographic Analyses, U.S. Department of Commerce Bureau of Census, June 1984

BIRKHAUESER-OERI, Sibylle, *The Mother: Archetypal Image in Fairy Tales,* Inner City Books, Toronto, 1988

BJORKMAN, Rut, *Saints and the Enlightened: Light From Another Dimension,* Aurum Verlag, Freiburg, 1985

BLEEKER, C.J., "Isis and Hathor: two Ancient Egyptian goddesses", *The Book of the Goddess Past and Present*, Carl Olson Ed., Crossroads Press, New York, 1983, pages 29-48.

BLY, Robert, *Iron John - A Book About Men,* Random House, New York, 1990

BOLEN, Jean Shinoda, *The Ring of Power: The Abandoned Child, The Authoritarian Father, and the Disempowered Feminine,* Harper and Row, San Francisco, 1992

————, *Goddesses in Everywoman: A New Psychology of Women,* Harper, New York, 1971

————, *Gods in Everyman: A New Psychology of Men's Lives and Loves*, Harper, New York, 1989

BOWLBY, John, "The nature of the child's attachment to his mother", *International Journal of Psycho-Analysis*, Volume 58, 1958, pages 350-373

BRAASCH, Gary, STRAFFORD, Kim R., *Entering the Grove,* Peregrine Smith Books, Salt Lake City, 1990

BROOKS-GUNN, Jeanne; MATHEWS, Wendy S., *He and She: How Children Develop Their Sex-Role Identity,* Prentice Hall, Englewood Cliffs, 1974

BROWN, C. Mackenzie, "Kali, the mad mother", *The Book of the Goddess Past and Present,* Carl Olson Ed., Crossroads Press, New York, 1983, pages 110-123.

BUDAPEST, Zsuzsanna E., *Feminist Book of Lights and Shadows,* Luna Publications, Los Angeles, 1976

————, *The Grandmother of Time*, Harper and Row, San Francisco, 1989

BUDGE, E.A. Wallis, *The Egyptian Book of the Dead*, Dover, New York, 1983

BUNKER, Barbara Benedict, "Power; collusion; intimacy-sexuality; support: breaking the sex role stereotypes in social and organizational settings", *Beyond Sex Role Stereotypes,* Alice G. Sargent (Ed), West Publishing Company, St. Paul, 1975

BURNHAM, Sophy, *Angel Letters*, Ballentine Books, New York, 1991

BURT, Kathleen, *Archetypes of the Zodiac,* Llewellyn Publications, St. Paul, 1988

BURTON, Judith M., "Developing minds: the first symbols", *School Arts Magazine,* Volume 80:2, 1980, pages 60-65

CAMERON, Anne, *Daughters of Copper Woman,* Press Gang Publishers, Vancouver, 1981

CAMERON, Avail; KUHRT, Amelia (Eds), *Images of Women in Antiquity,* Crumb Helm, New York, 1983

CAMPBELL, Joseph, ROBERTS, Richard, *Tarot Revelations*, Vernal Equinox Press, San Anselmo, 1979

CAMPBELL, Joseph, *The Power of Myth,* Doubleday, New York, 1988

——, *Primitive Mythology: The Masks of God,* Penguin, New York, 1959

——, *Creative Mythology: The Masks of God,* Penguin Books, New York, 1968

CAPONIGRO, Paul, *Megaliths,* Little, Brown, and Company, Boston, 1972

CAREY, Ken, *The Starseed Transmissions*, Harper, San Francisco, 1982

——, *The Return of the Bird Tribes*, Harper, San Francisco, 1988

CAVANDER, Kenneth, "Love and death in Ancient Greece", Horizon, Volume 16, April 1974, pages 102-106

CHEIRO, *Cheiro Book of Numbers: The Complete Science of Numerology, How Numbers Affect Your Health, Fortune, Life, and Marriage,* Prentice Hall, New York, 1988

CHERNIN, Kim, *Reinventing Eve: Modern Woman in Search of Herself,* Harper and Row, New York, 1987

——, *The Obsession: Reflections on the Tyranny of Slenderness,* Harper and Row, New York, 1987

——, *The Hungry Self: Women Eating and Identity,* Harper and Row, Toronto, 1985

CHESLER, Phyllis, "Mother-hatred and mother-blaming: what Electra did to Clytemnestra", *Women and Therapy,* Volume 10:1-2, 1990, pages 71-81

CHICAGO, Judy, *The Dinner Party Needlework: Embroidering Our Heritage*, Anchor Press, New York, 1980

——, *The Dinner Party: A Symbol of Our Heritage*, Anchor Press, New York, 1979

CHOPRA, Deepak, *Ageless Body Timeless Mind: The Quantum Alternative to Growing Old,* Harmony Books, New York, 1993

CHRIST, Carol P., "Symbols of the Goddess and God in feminist theology", *The Book of the Goddess Past and Present,* Carl Olson Ed., Crossroads Press, New York, 1983, pages 231-251.

————, *Diving Deep and Surfacing: Women Writers on the Spiritual Quest*, Beacon Press, Boston, 1980

CLOW, Barbara Hand, *Eye of the Centaur: A Visionary Guide to Past Lives,* Bear and Company, Sante Fe, 1989

————, *Heart of Christos: Starseeding from the Pleides*, Bear and Company, Sante Fe, 1989

————, *Signet of Atlantis: War in Heaven Bypass*, Bear and Company, Sante Fe, 1992

————, *The Pleiadian Agenda: A New Cosmology for the Age of Light*, Bear and Co. Sante Fe, 1995

COHEN, Daniel, *Ancient Greece,* Doubleday, New York, 1990

COHEN, Yolande, "Thoughts on women and power", Feminism in Canada: From Pressure to Politics, G. Finn, A. Miles (Eds.), Black Rose Books, Montreal, 1981

COTTERELL, Arthur, *The Minoan World*, Charles Schibner's Sons, New York, 1979

CROWLEY, Aleister, *777,* Level Press, San Francisco, 1965

————, *The Book of Thoth: Egyptian Tarot*, Samuel Wiser Inc., York Beach, 1969

CUNNINGHAM, Elizabeth, *The Return of the Goddess: A Divine Comedy,* Station Hill Press, New York, 1992

DANIEL, Alma, WYLLIE, Timothy, RAMER, Andrew, *Ask Your Angels*: Ballentine, New York, 1992

DAVISON, Ronald C., *Astrology: The Classic Guide to Understanding Your Horoscope*, CRSC Publications, Sebastopol, 1987

DeBEAUVOIR, Simone, *The Second Sex*, Bantam Books, New York, 1970

————, *When Things of the Spirit Come First*, Pantheon Books, New York, 1982

DeCASTILLEJO, Irene Claremont, *Knowing Woman: A Feminine Psychology*, Harper and Row, New York, 1973

DeGRECE, Michel, *Greece*, Fernand-Nathan Beau Livres, Paris, 1983

DeLASZLO, Violet S., *Psyche and Symbol: A Selection from the Writings of C.G. Jung*, Doubelday, New York, 1958

DINER, Helen, *Mothers and Amazons: The First Feminine History of Culture,* translated by John Philip Lundin, Julian Press, New York, 1965

DINNERSTEIN, Dorothy, *The Mermaid and the Minotar: Sexual Arrangements and Human Malaise*, Harper and Row, San Francisco, 1976

DOWLING, Colette, *The Cinderella Complex: Women's Hidden Fear of Independence*, Pocket Books, New York, 1981

DOWNING, Christine, *The Goddess: Mythological Images of the Feminine*, Crossroad Press, New York, 1981

———, "The Mother Goddess among the Greeks", *The Book of the Goddess Past and Present*, Carl Olson Ed., Crossroads Press, New York, 1983, pages 49-59

DURUY, Victor, *The Greeks*, Crescent Books, New York, 1980

DYRENFORTH, Sue R.; WOOLEY, Orland W.; WOOLEY, Susan C.; "A woman's body in a man's world", *A Woman's Conflict - The Special Relationship Between Women and Food*, Jane Rachel Kaplan [Ed.], Prentice Hall, Englewood Cliffs, 1980, pages 30-57

EDINGER, Edward F., *Ego and Archetype: A Fascinating Synthesis of C.G. Jung's Fundamental Psychological Concepts*, Penguin Books, New York, 1972

EDWARDS, Carolyn McVicker, *The Storyteller's Goddess: Tales of the Goddess and Her Wisdom*, Harper, San Francisco, 1991

EISLER, Riane, *The Chalice and the Blade,* Harper, San Francisco, 1988

ENGELSMAN, Joan Chamberlain, *The Feminine Dimension of the Divine,* The Westminster Press, Philadelphia, 1979

ERBE, Peter O., "A cosmic birth", *Connecting Link*, Issue 24, 1994, pages 20-31

ERIM, Kenan T., *Aphrodisias: City of Venus Aphrodite*, Facts on File Publications, New York, 1986

ESSENE, Virginia, Ed., *New Cells, New Bodies, New Life,* S.E.E. Publishing Company, Santa Clara, 1991

ESTES, Clarissa Pinkola, *Women Who Run With the Wolves: Myths and Stories of the Wild Woman Archetype,* Ballentine, New York, 1992

———, *The Gift of Story: A Wise Tale About What is Enough*, Ballentine Books, New York, 1993

EVSLIN, Bernard, *Medusa,* Chelsea House Publications, New York, 1987

FALUDI, Susan *Backlash: The Undeclared War Against American Women*, Doubleday, New York, 1991

FEDER, Bernard and Elaine, *The Expressive Arts Therapies: Art, Music, and Dance as Psychotherapy*, Prentice-Hall, New Jersey, 1981

FELDMAN, Judith F.;BRODY, Nathan; MILLER, Stephen A.; "Sex differences in non-elicited neonatal behaviors", *Merill Palmer Quarterly,* Volume 26:1, 1980, pages 63-73

FERGUSON, Ann, "On conceiving motherhood and sexuality: a feminist materialist approach", *Sexual Democracy*, Westview Press, Boulder, 1991, pages 154-182

FERGUSON, Marilyn, *The Aquarian Conspiracy: Personal and Social Transformation in the 1980's*, J.P. Tarcher, Los Angeles, 1976

FIELD, D.M., *Greek and Roman Mythology*, Hamlyn, London, 1977

FINE ARTS MUSEUMS OF SAN FRANCISCO, *The Rainbow Book*, Shambhala Publications, Berkley, 1975

FISH, Jefferson M., "Direct versus indirect approaches to imagery and psychotherapy: the status of the transference explanation", *Journal of Mental Imagery*, Volume 4:1, 1980, pages 161-163

FOLEY, Helene, *Reflections of Women in Antiquity*, Gordon and Breach, New York, 1981

FORWARD, Dr. Susan, *Men Who Hate Women and The Women and the Women Who Love Them: When Loving Hurts and You Don't Know Why,* Bantam, New York, 1986

FOWLES, John; BRUKOFF, Barry, *The Enigma of Stonehenge,* Collins Publishing, Toronto, 1980

FRAZIER, Kendrick, *Solar System: Planet Earth*, Time-Life Books, Alexandria, 1985

FREEMAN, Rita J., "Reflections of beauty as it relates to health in adolescent females", *Women and Health,* Volume 9:2-3, 1984, pages 29-45

FULLER, Buckminster, "Goddesses of the twenty-first century", *Saturday Review*, March 2, 1968, pages 12-46

———, "Why women will rule the world", *McCalls*, Volume 95, March 1968, pages 10-11

GADON, Elinor W., *The Once and Future Goddess: A Sweeping Visual Chronicle of the Sacred Female and Her Reemergence in the Cultural Mythology of Our Time*, Harper and Row, Sam Francisco, 1989

GEORGE, Demetra, *Mysteries of the Dark Moon: The Healing Power of the Dark Goddess*, Harper, San Francisco, 1992

GIBBS, Nancy, "Angels among us", *Time*, December 27, 1993, pages 46-53

GIBRAN, Kahil, *The Broken Wings*, The Citadel Press, New York, 1957

GIMBUTAS, Marija, *The Civilization of the Goddess: The World of Old Europe*, Harper, San Francisco, 1991

———, *The Language of the Goddess*, Harper and Row, New York, 1989

————, *The Goddesses and Gods of Old Europe: 6500-3500 BC Myths and Cult Images*, University of California Press, Berkley, 1974

GIOSEFFI, Daniela, Earth Dancing: Mother Nature's Oldest Rite, Stackpole Books, Harrisburg, 1980

GIOVANNI, Garbini, *The Ancient World*, McGraw-Hill Book Company, New York, 1966

GOLDENBERG, Naomi R., *Changing of the Gods: Feminism and the End of Traditional Religions*, Beacon Press, Boston, 1979

GOLDSMITH, Martin, *Moon Phases: A Symbolic Key*, Whitford Press, Westchester, 1988

GOODRICH, Norma Lorne, *Priestesses*, Harper Perennial, New York, 1989

GOODWATER, Leanna, *Women in Antiquity: An Annotated Bibliography*, The Scarecrow Press, Metuchen, 1975

GOODWIN, Malcolm, A*ngels, An Endangered Species, Simon & Schuster*, New York, 1990

GLUBOK, Shirley Ed., *Discovering Tut-ankh-Amen's Tomb*, McMillan Publishing Company, New York, 1963

GRALTON, M.A.; HAYES, Y.A.; RICHARDSON, J.T.E.; "Introversion- extroversion and mental imagery", *Journal of Mental Imagery*, Volume 3:1-2, 1979, pages 1-10

GRAVES, Robert, *New Larousse Encyclopedia of Mythology*, Prometheus Press, London, 1979

GRAY, Eden, *A Complete Guide to the Tarot*, Bantam, New York, 1970

GREEN, Jeff, *Pluto: Evolutionary Journey of the Soul*, Llewellyn Publications, St. Paul, 1989

GREEN, Landis Knight, The Astrologer's Manual: Modern Insights Into An Ancient Art, Arco Publishing Company Inc., New York, 1975

GRIGSON, Geoffrey, *The Goddess of Love: The Birth, Triumph, Death, and Return of Aphrodite*, Constable and Company, London, 1976

GRISCOM, Cris, *Ecstacy is a New Frequency*, Fireside, New York, 1987

GROSVENOR, Melville Bell, "Journey into golden Greece and Rome", *National Geographic*, October, 1968, pages 550-567

HALEY, Jay, *Uncommon Therapy*, General Publications, Toronto, 1973

HALL, Nor, *The Moon and the Virgin: Reflections on the Archetypal Feminine*, Harper and Row, New York, 1980

HALLETT, Judith P., "Sappho and her social context: sense and sensuality", *Signs: Journal of Women in Culture and Society*, Volume 4:3, pages 447-464

HAND, Robert, *Horoscope Symbols*, Whiteford Press, West Chester, 1981

HANNA, Barbara, *Encounters With the Soul: Active Imagination as Developed by C.G. Jung*, Sigo Press, Los Angeles, 1981

HARRIS, James Renel, *Egyptian Art*, Spring Books, London, 1966

HARVEY, David, "Women in Ancient Greece", *History Today*, Volume 34, August 1984, pages 45-47

HAWASS, Zahi; LEHNER, Mark; "The Sphinx: who built it and why?", *Archaeology*, September/October 1994, pages 30-47

HAWKINS, Gerald S., *Beyond Stonehenge*, Harper and Row, New York, 1973

HAWTHORNE, Nan, *Loving The Goddess Within: Sex Magick For Women*, Delphi Press, Oak Park, 1991

H'DOUBLER, Margaret N., *Dance: A Creative Art Experience*, The University of Wisconsin Press, Madison, 1940

HEINSOHN, Gunnar; STEIGER, Otto, "The elimination of medieval birth control and the witch trials of modern times", *International Journal of Women's Studies*, Volume 4:2, 1981, pages 193-214

HIROVEN, Kaarle, "Matriarchal survivals and certain trends in Homer's female characters", *Annales Academie Scientiarum Fennicae*, Ser. B., Volume 152, Helsinki: Svomalainen Tiedeakatemian, 1968

HOBSON, Alan, *Share the Flame: The Official Retrospective Book of the Olympic Torch Relay*, Whitecap Books, Vancouver, 1988

HODGSON, Joan, *Reincarnation Through the Zodiac*, CRCS Publications, Reno, 1973

HORNUNG, Erik, *The Valley of the Kings: Horizon of Eternity*, Timken Publishers, New York, 1982

HOUSTON, Jean, *The Hero and the Goddess: The Odyssey as Mystery and Initiation*, Ballentine, New York, 1992

———, *The Possible Human: A Course in Enhancing Your Physical, Mental, and Creative Abilities*, J.P. Tarcher, Los Angeles, 1982

HUTCHINSON, Marcia G., "Current feminist issues in psychotherapy", *Women and Therapy*, Volume 1:3, 1982, pages 59-67

HUTT, Corinne, "Sex differences in human development", *Social Issues on Developmental Psychology*, Helen Bee [Ed.], Harper and Row, New York, 1972

KOLBENSCHLAG, Madonna, *Kiss Sleeping Beauty Goodbye: A Book that Breaks the Spell of Feminine Myths*, Bantam, New York, 1977

KOLLER, John M., *The Indian Way: Asian Perspectives*, Macmillan Publishing, New York, 1982

KONRAAD, Sandor, Numerology: Key to the Tarot, Para Research, Rockport, 1983

KRAMER, Samuel Noah, *Cradle of Civilization,* Time Inc., New York, 1967

LAMY, Lucie, *Egyptian Mysteries: New Light on Ancient Spiritual Knowledge,* Crossroad, New York, 1981

LANGLEY, Erica, SCHNIREL, Shirley, *Goddess Channeling Cards* E.E. Printing Inc., Salt Lake City, 1987

LEARY, Timothy, *Info-Psychology: A Navigational Guide for Piloting the Evolution of the Human Individual,* Falcon Press, Las Vegas, 1989

LEE, Carol, "Matriarchal study group papers", *Feminist Review*, Volume 2, 1979, pages 74-81

LEMESURIER, Peter, *The Great Pyramid Decoded*, Element, Rockport, 1977

LeMIEUX, David, *The Ancient Tarot and Its Symbolism,* Cornwall Books, New York, 1985

LEONARD, Linda Schierse, *Meeting the Madwoman: An Inner Challenge for Feminine Spirit*, Bantam, NewYork, 1993

———, *On the Way to the Wedding: Transforming the Love Relationship,* Shambhala, Boston, 1987

———, Witness to the Fire: Creativity and the Veil of Addiction, Shambhala, Boston, 1989

———, *The Wounded Woman: Healing the Father-Daughter Relationship*, Shambhala, London, 1983

LEVI, Peter, *Atlas of the Greek World,* Andromeda Oxford Ltd., NewYork, 1991

LINCOLN, Bruce, *Emerging From the Crystals: Rituals of Women's Initiation,* Oxford University Press, New York, 1991

LING, Roger, *The Greek World: The Making of the Past,* Peter Bedrick Books, New York, 1976

LONG, Kim, *The Moon Book,* Johnson Books, Boulder, 1988

LUKE, Helen M., *Woman, Earth, and Spirit: The Feminine in Symbol and Myth,* Crossroad Press, New York, 1981

LUXTON, Leonora, *Astrology, Key to Self Understanding: A Guide to Karma, Reincarnation, and Spiritual Astrology*, Llewellyn Publications, St. Paul, 1978

MALIDOMA, Patrice Some, *Ritual: Power Healing and Community,* Swan Raven and Company, Portland, 1993

MALIN, David, MURDIN, Paul, *Colors of the Stars,* Cambridge University Press, Cambridge, 1984

MALYUTIN, B.I., "Shaping theoretical thinking on the basis of images", *Voprosky Psikhologii,* Volume 1, 1981, pages 90-99

MANLEY, John, *Atlas of Prehistoric Britain,* Oxford University Press, New York, 1989

MANN, Edward W., *Orgone, Reich, and Eros,* Simon and Schuster, New York, 1973

MARCH, Marion D., McEVERS, *The Only Way to Learn Astrology: Volume 1, Basic Principles,* A.C.S. Publications Inc., San Diego, 1976

MARCIANO, Theresa D., "Why are men unhappy in patriarchy?", *Marriage and Family Review,* Volume 9:3-4, 1985-1986, pages 17-30

MARCINIAK, Barbara, *Bringers of the Dawn: Teachings from the Pleiadians,* Bear and Company, Sante Fe, 1992

————, *The Pleiadians: Harmonics of Frequency Modulation and the Human DNA,* John Hornecker Life Sciences Center, Pacific Grove, 1990

————, *Earth: Pleiadian Keys to the Living Library,* Bear and Company, Sante Fe, 1995

MARONEY, Heather Jon, "Embracing motherhood: new feminist theory", *Feminism and Political Economy,* Toronto, 1987, pages 22-44

MASCETTI, Manuel Dunn, *The Song of Eve: An Illustrated Journey into the Myths, Symbols, and Rituals of the Goddess,* Simon and Schuster, New York, 1990

MASLOW, Abraham H., *Toward a Psychology of Being,* Van Nostrand Reinhold, New York, 1968

MATHEWS, Caitlin, *The Elements of the Goddess,* Element, Rockport, 1989

McBRIDE-SMITH, Barbara, "Medusa", *Stories Told at the National Storytelling Festival,* Jonesborough, Tennesse, 1992, pages 104-109

McGUINNESS, Diane; McLAUGHLIN, Lorraine; "An investigation of sex differences in visual recognition and recall", *Journal of Mental Imagery,* Volume 6, 1982, pages 203-212

MILANOVICH, Dr. Norma J., *Sacred Journey to Atlantis,* Athena Publishing, New York, 1992

MILLER, John; UHLINGER, Dean, *Desert Light: Myths and Visions of the Great Southwest,* Chronicle Books, San Francisco, 1993

MILLMAN, Dan, *The Way of the Peaceful Warrior: A Book That Changes Lives,* H.J. Kramer, Berkley, 1980

MICHELL, John, *The View Over Atlantis,* Abacus, London, 1973

MISCHEL, Walter, "A social learning view of sex differences in behavior", *The Development of Sex Differences*, Eleanor Macoby [Ed.], Stanford University Press, Stanford, 1966, pages 56-81

MONAGHAN, Patricia, *The Book of Goddesses and Heroines,* Llewellyn Publications, St. Paul, 1981

MONTE, Christopher F., *Beneath the Mask: An Introduction to the Theories of Personality*, Holt Reinhart and Winston, New York, 1980

MONTGOMERY, Ruth, *Strangers Among Us: Enlightened Beings From a World to Come*, Coward, McCann & Geoghegan, New York, 1979

MOOKERJEE, Ajit, *Kali: The Feminine Force*, Destiny Books, New York, 1988

MOORE, Thomas, *The Care of the Soul: A Guide for Cultivating Depth and Sacredness in Everyday Life,* Harper Collins Publishers, New York, 1992

MORGAN, Elaine, *The Descent of Woman*, Bantam Books, New York, 1972

MORGAN, Fiona, *Daughters of the Moon Tarot,* Daughters of the Moon Press, Willis, 1984

MORRISON, James K.; COMETA, Michael S.; "A cognitive reconstructive approach to psychotherapeutic use of imagery", *Journal of Mental Imagery*, Volume 4:1, 1980, pages 35-42

MOSS, Howard A., "Sex, Age, States as Determinants of Mother- Infant Interaction", Merill Palmer Quarterly, Volume 39, 1968, pages 401-408

MURDOCK, Maureen, *The Heroine's Journey: A Woman's Quest for Wholeness*, Shambhala, Boston, 1990

MURPHY, Joseph M., "Oshun the dancer", *The Book of the Goddess Past and Present*, Carl Olson Ed., Crossroads Press, New York, 1983, pages 190-201.

NASH, June, "The Aztecs and the ideology of male dominance", *Signs: Journal of Women in Culture and Society*, 4:2, pages 349-362

NATIONAL GEOGRAPHIC SOCIETY, *Ancient Egypt: Discovering Its Splendor,* Washington, 1978

NEIMARK, Philip John, *The Way of the Orisa: Empowering Yourself Through the Ancient African Religion of Ifa,* Harper Collins Publishers, San Francisco, 1993

NEUMANN, Erich, *The Great Mother: An Analysis of the Archetype,* Princeton University Press, New Jersey, 1955

———, "The moon and consciousness", *The Fear of the Feminine: and Other Essays on Feminine Psychology*, Bollingen Series #4, Princeton University Press, Princeton, 1994, pages 64-118

NEWTON, Esther; WEBSTER, Paula, "Matriarchy: As women see it", *Cultural Variations,* Volume 4:25, 1973, pages 72-87

NICHOLLS, Arthur, *The Seven Wonders of the World*, Studio Vista, London, 1976

NICHOLS, Sallie, *Jung and Tarot: An Archetypal Journey*, Samuel Wiser Inc., New York, 1980

NICHOLSON, Shirley, *Goddess Re-Awakening: The Feminine Principle Today,* Quest Books, Wheaton, 1989

NOBLE, Vicki, *Motherpeace: A Way to the Goddess through Myth, Art, and Tarot,* Harper, San Francisco, 1983

NOLES, Steven W.; CASH, Thomas F.; WINSTEAD, Barbara; "Body image, physical attractiveness, and depression", *Journal of Consulting and Clinical Psychology*, Volume 53:1, 1985, pages 88-94

OCHSHORN, Judith, "Ishtar and Her Cult", *The Book of the Goddess Past and Present,* Carl Olson Ed., Crossroads Press, New York, 1983, pages 16-28.

OKEN, Alan, *Soul Centered Astrology: A Key to Your Expanding Self,* Bantam, New York, 1990

ORBACH, Susie *Between Women: Love, Envy, and Competition in Women's Friendships,* Penguin, New York, 1987

ORDWAY, Fredrick I., *Pictorial Guide to Planet Earth*, Thomas Y. Crowell Company, New York, 1975

ORNSTEIN, Robert, *The Psychology of Consciousness,* Harcourt, Brace, Jovanovich, New York, 1977

PAGE, Michael, INGPEN, Robert, *Encyclopedia of Things That Never Were: Creatures, Places and Things*, Viking Penguin Inc., New York, 1987

PAGELS, Elaine H., "What became of God the Mother? Conflicting images of God in early Christianity", *Signs: Journal of Women in Culture and Society*, Volume2:2, 1976, pages 293-303

PALMER, Helen, *The Enneagram: The Definitive Guide to the Ancient System for Understanding Yourself and Others in Your Life*, Harper and Row, San Francisco, 1988

PANTEL, Pauline Schmitt (Ed), *A History of Women: From Ancient Goddesses to Christian Saints*, Harvard University Press, Cambridge, 1992

PARK, H.W.; WORMELL, D.E.W., *The Delphic Oracle,* Volumes,1 and 2 Oxford Basil, Blackwell, 1956

PATRICK, Richard, *All Colour Book of Egyptian Mythology,* Octopus Books, London, 1972

————, *All Colour Book of Greek Mythology*, Octopus Books, London, 1972

PAUL, Diana, "Kuan-Yin: Savior and Savioress in Chinese Pure Land Buddhism, *The Book of the Goddess Past and Present,* Carl Olson Ed., Crossroads Press, N.Y., 1983, pages 161-175.

PELLTIER, Robert, *Planets in Houses: Experiencing Your Environment*, Whitford Press, West Chester, 1978

PEMBROOK, Simone, "Women in Charge: the function of alternatives in early Greek tradition and the ancient idea of Matriarchy", *Journal of the Warburg and Courtauld Institute,* XXX, 1967, pages 1-35

PERADOTTO, J.J.; SULLIVAN, J.P. (Eds), *Women in the Ancient World: the Arethusa Papers,* State University of New York Press, New York, 1984

PERRERA, Sylvia Brinton, *The Scapegoat Complex: Toward a Mythology of Shadow and Guilt*, Inner City, New York, 1986

————, *Descent to the Goddess: A Way of Initiation for Women*, Inner City, New York, 1989

PETERSEN-LOWARY, Sheila, *The 5th Dimension: Channels to a New Reality,* Fireside, New York, 1988

PHILLIPS, Sheridan; KING, Suzanne; DuBOIS, Louise; "Spontaneous activities of females versus male newborns", *Child Development*, Volume 49, 1978, pages 590-597

POIGNANT, Roslyn, *Oceanic Mythology,* Paul Hamlyn, London, 1967

POLLACK, Rachel, *Tarot Readings and Meditations,* The Aquarian Press, Wellingborough, 1986

POMEROY, Sarah B., *Goddesses, Whores, Wives, and Slaves: Women in Classical Antiquity*, Schocken Books, New York, 1975

PONDER, Catherine, *The Healing Secret of the Ages*, Parker Publishing Inc., New York, 1967

PORTER, Elliot, *Monuments of Egypt*, University of Mexico Press, Albuquerque, 1990

————, *The Greek World,* E.P. Dutton, New York, 1962

POWELL, Anton, *The Greek World,* Equinox (Oxford) Ltd., New York, 1989

PRICE, John Randolph, *The Angels Within Us; A Spiritual Guide to Twenty-two Angels that Govern our Lives*, Fawcett Columbine, New York, 1993

PRIDEAUX, Tom, "Ancient Egypt Part I: the marvels of Egypt's past", *Life*, Volume 64:14, 1968, pages 42-59

———, "Ancient Egypt part II: kings and gods", *Life,* Volume 64:15, 1968, pages 58-74

———, "Ancient Egypt part III: the miracle of strength and grace", *Life,* Volume 64:16, pages 62-79

RAGGHIANTI, Carlo Ludovico, *Treasures of the Egyptian Museum,* Newsweek Books, New York, 1969

RAMPA, T. Lobsang, *The Third Eye,* Ballentine, New York, 1956

RAPHAELL, Katrina, *The Crystalline Transmission: A Synthesis of Light,* Aurora Press, Sante Fe, 1990

READER'S DIGEST, *The World's Last Mysteries: In Search of Fabled Lands,* The Reader's Digest Association, Pleasantville, New York, 1976

REDFIELD, James, *The Celestine Prophecy: An Adventure,* Satori Publishing, Hoover, 1993

ROBERTS, Jane, *Seth Speaks,* Bantam, New York, 1972

ROBERTS, Richard, *Tarot Revelations,* Vernal Equinox Press, San Anselmo, 1982

ROGERS, Carl, *On Becoming a Person,* Houghton Mifflin, Boston, 1961

ROMAN, Sanayu; PACKER, Duane, *Opening to Channel: How to Connect With Your Guide,* H.J. Kramer, Tiburon, 1984

ROSENBLUM, Karen E., "The conflict between the genders: an appraisal of contemporary American femininity and masculinity", *Conflict Between and Within Genders,* pages 94- 103

ROTH, Gabrielle, *Maps to Ecstasy: Teachings of an Urban Shaman,* New World Library, San Rafael, 1989

ROTHERY, Guy Cadogan, *The Amazons in Antiquity and Modern Times,* Francis Griffiths, London, 1910

RUDHYAR, Dane, *The Astrological Houses: The Spectrum of Individual Experience,* CRCS Publications, Reno, 1972

———, *An Astrological Mandala: The Cycle of Transformation and Its 360 Symbolic Phases,* Vintage Books, New York, 1973

———, *Person Centered Astrology,* Aurora Press, New York, 1976

RUETHER, Rosemary Radford, *Womanguides: Readings Toward a Feminist Theology,* Beacon Press, Boston, 1985

SAMS, Jamie, *The Thirteen Original Clan Mothers: Your Sacred Path to Discovering the Gifts, Talents, and Abilities of the Feminine Through the Ancient Teachings of the Sisterhood,* Harper, San Francisco, 1993

SCHAEFF, Anne Wilson, *Women's Realities: An Emerging System in a White Male Society*, Harper, San Francisco, 1981

SCHUL, Bill; PETTIT, Ed, *The Secret Power of Pyramids*, Fawcett Publications, Greenwich, 1975

SCOTT, Clifford, "Some embryological, neurological, psychiatric, and psycholanalytic implications of the body scheme", *International Journal of Psychoanalysis,* Volume XXIX:3, 1948, pages 141-155

SHKLOVSKII, I.S.; SAGAN, Carl, *Intelligent Life in the Universe,* Delta, New York, 1966

SHONTZ, Franklin C., "Body image and its disturbances", *International Journal of Medicine,* Volume 5:4, 1974, pages 461-472

SHORTER, Edward, *A History of Women's Bodies,* Basic Books, New York, 1982

SHOSTROM, E.L., *Personality Orientation Inventory,* Educational and Industrial Testing Service, 1963

SHUTTLE, Penelope; REDGROVE, Peter, *The Wise Wound: Myths, Realities, and Meanings of Menstruation,* Bantam Books, New York, 1978

SINGER, June, *Boundaries of the Soul: The Practice of Jung's Psychology,* Anchor Books, New York, 1953

SITCHIN, Zecharia, *The Twelfth Planet,* Avon Books, New York, 1978

————, *The Stairway to Heaven,* St. Martin's, New York, 1980

————, *The War of Gods and Men,* Avon Books, New York, 1985

————, *The Lost Realms,* Bear and Company, Sante Fe, 1988

————, *Genesis Revisited: Is Modern Science Catching Up With Ancient Knowledge?,* Avon Books, New York, 1990

SJOO, Monica; MOR, Barbara, *The Great Cosmic Mother: Rediscovering the Religion of the Earth ,* Harper and Row, San Francisco, 1987

SNOW, Chet B.; WAMBACH, Helen; *Mass Dreams of the Future,* Deep Forest Press, Crest Park, 1989

SNOW, Loudell F.; JOHNSON, Shirley M., "Myths about menstruation: victims of our own folklore", *International Journal of Women's Studies,* Volume 1:1, 1978, pages 64-72

SOLARA, *11:11: Through the Gateway,* Star Borne Unlimited, Charlottesville, 1992

SPRETNEK, Charlene [Ed.], *The Politics of Women's Spirituality: Essays of the Rise of Spiritual Power Within the Feminist Movement,* Anchor Books, New York, 1982

————, *States of Grace: The Recovery of Meaning in the Post Modern Age,* Harper, San Francisco, 1991

STARCK, Marcia, STERN, Gynne, *The Dark Goddess: Dancing With the Shadow*, Crossing Press, Freedom, 1993

STARHAWK, *The Fifth Sacred Thing: A Magnificent Novel That Will Transform Our Vision of the Future*, Bantam, New York, 1993

———, *The Spiral Dance: A Rebirth of the Ancient Religion of the Great Goddess*, Harper and Row, New York, 1979

STEIN, Diane, T*he Goddess Book of Days*, the Crossing Press, Freedom, 1992

STEINEM, Gloria, *Revolution From Within*, Little, Boston, 1992

———, *Moving Beyond Words,* Simon and Schuster, New York, 1994

STEINER, Rudolph, *Atlantis and Lemuria*, Tri State Press, Clayton, 1989

STEPANICH, Kisma K., *The Gaia Tradition: Celebrating the Earth in Her Seasons*, Llewellyn Publications, St. Paul, 1991

STEVENS, Dr. Anthony, *Archetypes: A Natural History of the Self*, Quill, New York, 1983

STONE, Merlin, *When God Was a Woman*, Harcourt, Brace, Javanovich, New York, 1976

———, *Ancient Mirrors of Womanhood: A Treasury of Goddess and Heroine Lore from Around the World,* Beacon Press, Boston, 1979

———, "The Great Goddess: who was she?", *The Politics of Women's Spirituality,* C. Spretnek [Ed.], Anchor Books, New York, 1982

SWAN, James A., *Sacred Places: How the Living Earth Seeks Our Friendship,* Bear & Company, Sante Fe, 1990

THIERENS, A.E., *Astrology and The Tarot,* Newcastle Publishing, Philadelphia, 1975

THORNDIKE, Joseph J. Jr., *Discovery of Lost Worlds*, American Heritage Publishing, New York, 1979

THORSTEN, Geraldine, *The Goddess in Your Stars: The Original Meaning of the Sun Signs,* Fireside, New York, 1980

———, *God Herself: The Feminine Roots of Astrology*, Doubleday and Company Inc., New York, 1980

TIEROU, Alphonse, *Doolpe: The Eternal Laws of African Dance*, Harwood Academic Publishers, Philadelphia, 1992

TOMPKINS, Peter, *Secrets of the Great Pyramids,* Harper and Row, New York, 1971

TYLDESLEY, Joyce, *Daughters of Isis: Women of Ancient Egypt,* Penguin Books, New York, 1994

UHLINGER, Lee, MILLER, John, *Desert Light: Myths and Visions of the Great Southwest*, Chronicle Books, San Francisco, 1993

UNITY School of Christianity, *Metaphysical Bible Dictionary*, Unity Village, 1939

VEGGI, Athon; DAVIDSON, Alison, *The Book of Doors Divination Deck: An Alchemical Oracle from Ancient Egypt*, Destiny Books, Rochester, 1995

VINCENT, L.M., *Competing With the Sylph - Dancers in the Pursuit of the Ideal Body Form*, Andrews and McMeel, New York, 1979

Von FRANZ, Marie-Louise, *Creation Myths,* Spring Publications Inc., Dallas, 1972

————, *Time: Rhythm and Response*, Thames and Hudson, New York, 1992

WALKER, Barbara G., *The Crone: Woman of Power, Age, and Wisdom,* Harper, San Francisco, 1985

————, *The Woman's Dictionary of Symbols and Sacred Objects*, Harper, San Francisco, 1988

————, *The Woman's Encyclopedia of Myths and Secrets,* Harper and Row, San Francisco, 1983

————, *The Secrets of the Tarot: Origins, History, and Symbolism,* Harper and Row, San Francisco, 1984

————, *Amazon*, Harper Collins, San Francisco, 1992

WAMSLEY, James S., "Art: echoes of Egypt", *Architectural Digest*, September 1984, pages 106-111

WANLESS, James, *New Age Tarot: Guide to the Thoth Deck*, Merill West Publishing, Carmel, 1986

WARNER, Rex; HURLIMANN, Martin; *Eternal Greece*, Thames and Hudson, London, 1971

WENDORF, Fred; SAID, Rushdi; SCHILD, Romuald; "Egyptian prehistory: some new concepts", *Science,* Volume 169:3951, September 18, 1970, pages 1161-1169

WESLEY, Frank; WESLEY, Claire; *Sex Role Psychology,* Human Sciences Press, New York, 1977

WHITMONT, Edward C., *Return of the Goddess*, Crossroads Press, New York, 1982

WILKS, William, *Science of a Witches Brew*, Access Publications Limited, Salt Spring Island, 1979

WILLIAMS, Hector, "Secret rites of Lesbos", *Archeology,* July- August 1994, pages 24-40

WILLIAMS, Jerry, *Contemporary Astrology*, Para Research. Rockport, 1977

WILLIS, Ellen, *No More Nice Girls: Countercultural Essays,* Wesleyan University Press, Hanover, 1992

WOER, Samuel Aun, *The Perfect Matrimony,* Universal Christian Gnostic Movement of the USA (New Order), Washington, 1989

WOLF, Naomi, *Fire With Fire: The New Female Power and How It Will Change the Twenty-first Century*, Random House, Toronto, 1993

———, *The Beauty Myth*, Vintage Books, Toronto, 1990

WOLKE, Gerry, *"The heart of the matter", Tachyon Healing and the Physics of Love,* http://www.community.net~tachyon/THATPOL.html

WOLKSTEIN, Diane, KRAMER, Samuel Noah, Inanna, Queen of Heaven and Earth, Harper and Row, New York, 1983

WOMBWELL, Felicity, *The Goddess Changes: A Personal Guide to Working With the Goddess*, Mandala, London, 1991

WOODMAN, Marion, *The Owl Was a Baker's Daughter: Obesity, Anorexia Nervosa, and the Repressed Feminine,* Inner City Books, New York, 1980

———, *Addiction to Perfection: The Still Unravished Bride*, Inner City Books, 1982

———, *The Pregnant Virgin: A Process of Psychological Transformation*, Inner City, New York, 1985

———, *The Ravaged Bridegroom: Masculinity in Women,* Inner City Books, Toronto, 1990

———, *Leaving My Father's House: A Journey to Conscious Femininity*, Shambhala, Boston, 1992

———, *Conscious Femininity: Interviews With Marion Woodman*, Inner City Books, Toronto, 1993

WOUDHUYSEN, Jan, *Tarot Therapy: A New Approach to Self Exploration*, Jeremy P. Tarcher Inc., Los Angeles, 1979

WRIGHT, F.A., *Feminism in Greek Literature From Homer to Aristotle*, Routledge, London, 1923

YOLEN, Jane, *Sister Light Sister Dark*, Tom Doherty Associates, New York, 1988

———, *White Jenna*, Tom Doherty Associates, New York, 1989

YOUNG-EISENDRATH, Polly, *Hags and Heros: A Feminist Approach to Jungian Psychotherapy with Couples*, Inner City, New York, 1984

YOUNGBLUT, John R., *Shaping a Personal Myth to Live By*, Element, Rockport, 1992

YWAHOO, Dhuyani, *Voices of Our Ancestor: Cherokee Teachings from the Wisdom Fire,* Shambhala, Boston, 1987

ZAKIN, David F.; BLYTHE, Dale A.; SIMMONS, Roberta G.; "Physical attractiveness as a mediator of the impact of early pubertal changes for girls", *Journal of Youth and Adolescence*, Volume 13:5, 1984, pages 439-450

ZIMMER-BRADLEY, Marion, *The Mists of Avalon,* Ballentine Books, New York, 1982

———, *The Fall of Atlantis*, Beacon Publishing, Riverdale, 1983

———, *The Firebrand,* Pocket Books, New York, 1987

———, *The Forest House,* Viking Penguin, New York, 1994

Index

A

abandoned
29, 36, 41, 57, 78,
80, 81
abduction
36, 37, 40
Acropolis 118
active imagination
28
Adam
126, 127, 128
Africa
49, 74, 95, 152,
154
African dance 154
African Queen 95
Age of Aquarius 49
Age of Leo 197
Age of Light
13, 16, 49,
69, 197
agriculture 172
alcoholism 40
Alexandria 48, 199
All Hallow's Eve
217
All Souls' Day 217
Amazon priestess
96, 116
Amazon tribes 95
Amazon Woman 95
Amazons 6, 95, 96
Amenti 178, 197
American Indians
196
Anakim 74
ancient Egyptian
female royals 200
ancient Egyptian
goddess cults 95

ancient Greece
56, 109, 159,
167, 216
ancient Hindu
goddess 143
ancient mystery
schools 156, 163,
209
ancient oracles 201
ancient records 47
ancient temple
dances 201
anima
2, 20, 26, 79, 87, 89,
97, 102, 117, 127,
129, 134, 138, 187,
188, 189, 190, 199,
200, 216, 218
animus
2, 26, 87, 96,
115, 117
animus possessed
117
animus-driven
Woman 115
Anubis 208
Anunnaki
74, 75, 76,
78, 79
anzu bird 75
Apollo 108, 216
Aquarian Age 13
archetypal complex
2, 9
archetypal vocabu-
lary 38
archetypal Zodiac
66
Artemas 186

artificial insemina-
tion 75
Aryan tribes
96, 160
ascend
11, 14, 21, 49,
73, 79, 80, 101,
145, 147, 153, 154,
172, 211, 212
ascended master
101, 154
ascended state 14
ascending spiral of
evolution 145
ascension
14, 18, 101,
139, 198, 202, 215
astral projection
212
astrological sky
chart 199
astrological transits
49
astronauts 217
Australian aborigi-
nes 195
authentic self 135
authoritarianism 7
automatic writing
51, 154,
Aztecs 196

B

bad hair days 136
band of illumination
120
bardo 179, 198,
208

belle dame sans
merci 97
belly dancing
154, 201
betrayal
8, 61, 80, 116
Bible 7, 127, 160
bija 102
biological rhythms
185
birth of horticulture
172
blackness 146
bodhisattva 101
Buddhism
101, 102
bulimia 39
bulimic personality
39

C

calendars 6
candlelight 121
Candlemas 187
canonical Bible 127
celestial
bodhisattvas 101
celestial realms 11
celibacy 57
celibate men 57
Ceremony of the
Weighing of the
Heart 208, 209
chakras
95, 133, 155, 202,
203, 210, 217
chambers in the
pyramids 21
chaos
16, 107, 137, 199
chastity belt 58
children of the
goddess 57

Christ
7, 14, 48, 57,
58, 73, 86, 127,
130, 145, 151, 152,
153, 155, 196, 209,
212
Christ Conscious-
ness 14, 73, 130,
151, 152, 153, 196
Christ-current 152
Christing 155
co-dependency
61, 68, 89
cobra 95
collective initiation
29, 35
collective shadow
69, 88, 159
collective uncon-
scious
1, 7, 9, 58, 66, 120,
137, 172, 211
communication gap
2
compulsive eating
40
conscious feminine
3, 35, 79, 80, 160
conspiracy of silence
8, 35, 68, 189
consumerism 61
Contact with Angels
12
containment
8, 50, 56
control of the mind
209
cosmic conscious-
ness
15, 17, 19, 20, 21,
90, 174, 180, 203,
207, 208, 210
cosmic currents 153
cosmic dancer 144
cosmic duty 16

Cosmic Gate 17,
66, 177
Cosmic Intelligence
18, 50, 51, 52,
202
cosmic intervals
198
cosmic orgasms
212
Cosmos
2, 16, 30, 45,
51, 65, 115, 129,
143, 145, 151, 152,
154, 177, 178, 203,
211
Council of Trent 57
Cows 200
Coyote 26
creative thinking 3
Crete 36, 95, 160
crone
19, 35, 37, 46,
50, 85, 96, 128,
133, 159, 160, 162,
168, 171, 187
Cronos 86, 108
crown chakra
202, 203, 211, 212
crucifixion 148
crystal core of the
Earth 65, 66
crystals 109, 201
cultural context
2, 3, 120
culture of the God-
dess 57, 160
cyclic nature of the
Universe 145
Cyprus 86

D

Dancing on the body
of a man 144

dark sister 78, 81
Death 143
death and dying 7, 8,
    13, 19, 35, 38, 42,
    45, 78, 79, 80, 108,
    134, 135, 137, 145,
    148, 168, 169, 170,
    189, 199, 208, 217
December 21, 2011
    212
decoded DNA 60
Delphic Oracle 8,
    216
demon lovers 28
Dendera 199
denial
    5, 8, 28, 35, 3
    9, 40, 47, 60, 61,
    68, 80, 116, 139,
    146, 147, 159
Descending passage
    21
Devi Mahatyma 144
devil
    85, 130, 159, 161
Dione 86
Dionysian 89
Dionysus 108
divine child 173
divine human
    prototype 17, 178
divine magic of
    sexuality 199
divining rods 52
Djwhal Khul 137
DNA
    60, 120, 133, 203,
    210, 212
Dog Star 208
dolphins 201
door of compensa-
    tion 40
double Maat 208
dragon lines 170

dream language
    27, 28
dreamtime
    88, 90, 212
dualistic thinking 7
duality 8, 11, 12,
    14, 16, 19, 20,
    73, 81, 121, 125,
    145, 152, 210,
    211
Dumuzi
    76, 77, 79, 80
Durga 144
dysfunctional family
    39

E

Ea 79
earth currents 170
earthly queenship
    78
earthquakes
    61, 67, 218
earth's grid 50
Easter Island 201
ecological con-
    sciousness 14
Ecstatic Dancer 151
Eden 126, 127
Edfu 199
Egyptian Book of
    the Dead 198
Egyptian Queen of
    Heaven 195
Egyptian Sky
    Mother 177
Eighth dimension
    210, 212
electromagnetic
    13, 16, 27, 95, 120,
    151, 152, 197, 202
electromagnetic
    energy
    16, 95, 202

electromagnetic field
    13, 16
electromagnetic
    frequency adjust-
    ment 120
electrostatic energy
    95, 202
Eleusinian Mysteries
    38, 107, 168, 169,
    170, 171
Eleusis
    37, 38, 168, 170
eleventh dimension
    212
emotional bodies
    16, 120, 191
emotional lessons 8
encodements 50,
    190, 191, 197,
    203
Enki 76, 77, 79
Enlil 77, 79
envy 58, 89, 96
Ephesus 186
Ereskigal 78
Eros 87
eternal flame
    108, 109,
    111
etheric field
    14, 187
etheric wings 202
Eve 2, 7, 28, 58,
    62, 76, 81, 103,
    118, 127, 128, 130,
    134, 152, 155, 160,
    173, 181, 185, 189,
    215, 217
evolution of con-
    sciousness
    130, 208
evolutionary pro-
    gramming 14
evolutionary step
    14, 172

exalted goddess 77
excessive television 40
excommunicated 57
extraterrestrials 201
eyes of Truth 209

F

fate 13, 115, 169
father-daughter relationship 120
fear of death 169
feather of Truth 208
female Pharaoh 200
female-oriented, cyclic cosmology 207
feminine deity 75
feminine power 57, 76, 126
feminine principleS 55, 76, 108, 144
femme fatale 97
Fifth dimension 16, 21, 155, 211, 212
Fifth Kingdom of God 155
fire-walk 201
First dimension 210, 212
first menstruation 59
flamenco 154, 201
flower-yoni 126
Fourth dimension 11, 16, 196, 211
free will zone 31, 16
Freud 28
Fritz Perls 29
funerary practice 47
future incarnations 49

G

galactic beams 13, 181, 191
galactic clarion call 16
galactic star-child 203
galactic synchroni-zation 50
Galaxy 46, 95, 177, 212
gambling 40
Garden of Eden 126, 127
Gate of Power 65, 66, 68
gateways 78, 80
gender gap 2
genetic code 14, 199
genetic transmuta-tions 74
geological plates 67
Geshtinanna 79
Gestalt therapy 29
Giglamesh 75
Giza plateau 197, 198
global family 218
global psychic renewal 6
Gnostic doctrines 27
God of Wisdom 76, 77
Goddess cultures 76
goddess of procrea-tion 116
goddess wisdom 135
golden wings 95
Gorgons 96
gorilla 119

Gospel of Saint John 198
grace 5, 8, 9, 12, 51, 65, 68, 78, 79, 80, 89, 95, 98, 102, 103, 109, 130, 147, 152, 178, 186
Great Cosmic Mother 172, 188, 212
Great Mother 6, 19, 57, 60, 108, 126, 167, 172, 212
Great Pyramid 21, 50, 197, 198, 202
Great Round 20, 115, 145, 207, 215
group meditations 102
group mind 181
guemilère 153
guilt 8, 30, 68, 138, 163, 179
gypsy 50

H

Hades 36, 37, 117, 136, 171
Hall of Judgment 198, 208
Hall of Records 48, 197
Hanged Man 133, 135
harlot of hell 128
Harmonic Conver-gence 50, 155
Hathor cult 199
Hatshepsut 200
healing secrets 48
hearth 18, 107, 108

heartspace 50, 219
Hebraic tradition
  126
hell 7, 56, 60,
  78, 86, 128, 135,
  173, 209
Hermes 51, 108
Hermeticism 51
heroine
  56, 95, 134, 135
hierarchical culture
  2
hieros gamos 187
High Priestess
  45, 49, 78, 96
Higher Self
  9, 52, 87, 107,
  137, 138, 153,
  154, 202, 208,
  210, 219
Himalayas 162
Hindu philosophy
  145
Holy Fire of Spirit
  65
Holy Spirit 45, 73,
  107, 178
holy woman 159
Homer
  86, 108, 173
Homeric hymns
  108
honoring of the
  Goddess 85, 108
Hopi legends 202
Horus 48
huluppu tree
  80, 125
humanitarian
  97, 179, 207, 215,
  218
Hungarian 133
hunter-gatherer
  cultures 172
huntress

186, 187, 188
Hymn to Hathor
  200

I

idealized feminine
  27, 89
identification with
  the aggressor 117
illusion
  7, 18, 27, 29,
  39, 40, 41, 52,
  143, 145, 148
Immaculate Concep-
  tion 56
immortality
  14, 47, 115,
  159, 170, 178, 200,
  208, 212
incarnations
  14, 17, 30, 48,
  49, 148, 190, 198,
  208, 210
incest 35, 39, 117
incestuous 117
Indian mythology
  145
individuation
  35, 107, 110, 120
initiate animals 20
initiate priestess
  20, 77
initiate scribes 48
initiation
  8, 12, 18, 21, 29, 35,
  36, 42, 48, 51, 81,
  85, 87, 107, 134,
  135, 137, 139, 152,
  153, 168, 170, 179,
  180, 212
inner chamber of the
  heart 219
inner sanctuary
  110, 111
Inquisition 7

instability in male-
  female relation-
  ships 2
integrate the mascu-
  line aspect 90
Iron Maiden 119

J

Jester 25, 26
Jesus 7, 48, 77,
  91, 148, 198
Joker 25
journal writing 29
Jung
  1, 2, 26, 27, 28,
  29, 65, 87, 117

K

Ka 16, 17,18, 19,
  30, 31, 49, 91,
  97, 129, 137,
  143, 144, 145,
  146, 147, 185,
  187, 198, 201,
  211, 217
Kali woman
  146, 147
karma 16, 30, 49,
  91,129, 145, 185,
  211, 217
karmic burdens 137
karmic responsibili-
  ties 49
Keeper of the
  Records 48, 51
King Minos 161
Kingdom of God
  155, 198
Knossos 160, 161
Kundalini energy
  217

L

La Loba 187

language of the heart 208
law of abundance 18
left brain 5
level of initiation 179
levitate 21
ley lines 216
light body 13, 14, 133, 144, 155, 202, 203, 210
light workers 16, 17, 18
linear thinking 6
linear time 49
Lord Archangel Michael 207
lotus 126
Lucifer 159, 163
Lulus 75
Luna 4, 17, 180, 185, 190, 191
lunar rapture 191
lunation cycle 6, 17, 143, 151, 180, 185, 187, 190, 191
lust 125
luxurious baths 121
lygus plant 59

M

Machu Picchu 74, 201, 202
Madwomen 28
Magic 4, 6, 20, 35, 42, 46, 47, 48, 97, 108, 127, 134, 135, 151, 170, 171, 185, 195, 199
Magic rites 48
magic spells 97

magnetic crystalline mantle of the Earth 203
magnetism 3, 26, 89, 197
magnetism of a lover 89
marriage 55, 56, 57, 58, 60, 61, 75, 76, 77, 80, 85, 87, 129, 180, 187, 197
Mary Magdalene 48, 57, 77
masculinized 96, 116
Master Self 130, 156
materiality 11, 14, 61, 137, 161, 163
maternal attachment 36
matriarchal spirit 7, 168
Matriarchate 6
matrilineal accession 200
Mayan calendar 49, 155, 212
Meat-eaters 188
megalithic structures 1
Melchizedek 196
Memphis 199
menstrual blood 60, 126
menstruation cycles 6
merry month of May 57
Mesopotamia 77, 127, 179
metamorphosis 147
Metis 96, 116, 117

Milky Way 177
Minoan Snake Goddess 95
mistress of love 199
Mistress of the World 126
molestation 35, 39, 41
monogamy 56, 57, 58, 60
moon 6, 8, 15, 20, 25, 35, 37, 45, 47, 51, 55, 59, 60, 65, 66, 77, 95, 101, 126, 127, 134, 136, 151, 60, 161, 167, 172, 177, 185, 186, 187, 188, 190, 191, 200, 210, 211, 215, 217
moon blood 60, 126, 127
Moon consciousness 161
moon cycles 59, 136
Moon in Aries 66
Moon in Aquarius 177
Moon in Cancer 167
Moon in Capricorn 160
Moon in Gemini 35
Moon in Leo 186
Moon in Libra 101
Moon in Pisces 25
Moon in Sagittarius 151
Moon in Scorpio 134
Moon in Taurus 215

Moon in Virgo 45
moon time 59, 136
moon-spirit 161
moontime rituals 59
mother archetype
17
Mother God 14,
17, 56, 108,
173, 200
Mother of Tender-
ness 48
mother-daughter
relationship 168,
169, 171
mudra 102, 144
multidimensional
learning 35
multidimensional
Universe 17
mutation 74, 107,
108, 190, 202,
203, 208
mystery of procrea-
tion 6

N

Nanna 77
navel of the Earth
216
navel stone 216
Nefertiti 200
Nefilim 74
Nephthys 46
Netters 199
New Testament 7
next Universe 212
Nibiru 74
Nile 46, 47, 48,
50, 51, 199
ninth dimension
212
North American
Native traditions
185

not to save the
drowning man 88

O

objective witness
102
off-planet colonies
201
Olympian Greece 36
Olympian Pantheon
58, 108
Oracles 50, 90,
109, 201
Orion nebula 210
orisha 152
Osiris
46, 47, 51, 169
Our Lady of Infinite
Space 177
out-of-body experi-
ence 147
over-exercise 40

P

pagan 50, 57
pagan times 50
pajama party 90
palmistry 50
papyrus 48, 199,
208
parlor sittings 201
past-life memories
210
paternity 57, 58
patriarchal con-
sciousness 7, 161
patriarchal daughter
39, 58, 118, 120
patriarchal values 6
peak experience
212
pendulum 52
perfectionistic
38, 118

phoenix rising 160
photon band
197, 212
photonic light 211
pile of seeds 87
pineal gland 202
Piscean Age 49
pituitary gland 202
planetary align-
ments 49
planetary shifts 136
Plato 87
Pleiadians 74, 197
PMS 136
polarity 5, 9, 41,
45
Pollyanna 162
portal 19, 20,
21, 27, 65, 66,
74, 147,177,179,
197, 212
Poseidon 108
pre-dynastic Egypt
50
pre-menstrual
syndrome 68,
136
primal conscious-
ness 145
primordial
1, 80, 145, 168, 169
procession
37, 49, 168, 170
processional cycle
49
procreation envy
58, 96
projection
26, 39, 40, 41,
87, 90, 111,
116, 162, 209,
211, 212
projection holder
116

psyche
1, 2, 5, 8, 25,
27, 29, 30, 31,
37, 38, 39, 40,
41, 73, 87, 88,
90, 91, 110, 120,
133, 134, 135,
136, 163, 170,
173, 177
psychic center 95
psychic regulatory
center 202
psychometry 50
psychosocial field 1
psychosomatic
illness 68
purified water 121
pythoi jar 56

Q

Queen of Heaven
and Earth
18, 73, 76
Queen of the Sea 86

R

Ra 4, 5, 46, 60,
129, 154, 201
radiation 74, 103
Realm of Cosmic
Consciousness
15, 17, 19, 20,
21, 90, 174, 180
Realm of Renuncia-
tion 15, 17, 19,
90, 121, 129, 139,
174
Realm of Roles
15, 17, 18, 19, 90,
174
receptive feminine
26
Red Sea 126, 128
reincarnation
48, 127, 145

relationship
2, 3, 5, 8, 27,
28, 47, 52, 55,
58, 61, 80, 87,
88, 89, 90, 91,
97, 103, 110, 117,
118, 119, 120, 129,
137, 138, 146, 147,
163, 167, 168, 169,
171,187,189, 208
released from the
mundane world
153
repression of the
feminine 2, 8,
116
resurrection
137, 148, 160,
209
retrieve golden
fleece 88
rewrote history 96
Rhea 56, 108
Riddle Mother 27
right-brain domi-
nant 3
rites 8, 29, 35,
48, 57, 77, 168,
173, 188, 199
rites of passage
35, 188
rule of thumb 59
Russian 133

S

sacrament of sex 77
sacred chamber 21
sacred flame
12, 18, 107, 109
sacred geometry
201
sacred marriage bed
75, 76, 80

sacred priestesses
77
sacred rites 8
sacred sites 201
Samadhi 212
Sanskrit 126
scapegoat
39, 40, 119, 127
Second dimension
210, 211
sensationalism of
culture 14
serpent energy
199, 200
serpents 75
Set 7, 11, 18,
19, 21, 35, 40,
46, 47, 56, 58,
76, 77, 87, 88,
101, 108, 126,
144, 146, 188,
208, 212
seven wonders of
the ancient world
186
Seventh dimension
211, 212
sex-roles stere-
otypes 2
sexual abuse
8, 35, 103
sexual addiction 40
sexual charm 85
sexual magic 171
shadow
2, 5, 6, 8, 17,
18, 20, 26, 28,
38, 40, 41, 47,
50, 65, 67, 69,
73, 78, 79,80,
81, 87, 88, 117,
118, 126, 135,
144, 146, 148,
153, 159, 161, 162,
163, 171, 173

Shakti 145
shaman 76
shamanic call 27
shamanic experiences 35
shamanism 137
sheitels 127
Shiva 145
Sinai 199
single parent 51
Sirian energy 196
Sirius 16, 46, 48, 195, 197, 208
sixth dimension 211
666 85
Slavic 133
snakes 95, 97
solar consciousness 6
sort 30, 87, 110, 135
sorted the seeds 135
soul doves 200
soul group 49
soul's destiny 21
Source 5, 14, 36, 61, 74, 107, 118, 153, 173, 180, 198, 202, 211, 215, 216, 218
spaceship commander 210
Sphinx 20, 48, 197, 202
spiritual debts 25
spiritual gurus 201
spiritual illumination 179
spiritual mystery schools 31
spiritual warriors 95, 162

Spring Equinox 187
Standing Persons 185
starry beings 48
Stone Persons 185
Stonehenge 201
strands of DNA 60, 133, 203, 210, 212
subconscious 8, 13, 29, 30, 41, 66, 190
Sumerian culture 74, 76, 77, 125
Sumerian cuneiform tablets 74
Sumerian texts 125
Sun in Aquarius 177
Sun in Aries 66
Sun in Cancer 196
Sun in Capricorn 115
Sun in Gemini 85
Sun in Leo 125
Sun in Libra 207
Sun in Pisces 55
Sun in Sagittarius 96
Sun in Scorpio 143
Sun in Taurus 73
Sun in Virgo 108
sympathy for the devil 161
synchronicity 4, 27, 203, 210

T

taming a lion 125
tango 154
Tantric tradition 145

Tarot 25, 35, 45, 55, 65, 67, 73, 85, 95, 101, 107, 115, 125, 130, 133, 143, 151, 159, 167, 177, 179, 185, 195, 207, 215
Tarot Chariot 95
Tarot Death 143
Tarot Devil 159
Tarot Emperor 65
Tarot Empress 55, 67
Tarot Fool 25
Tarot Hanged Man 133
Tarot Hermit 107
Tarot Hierophant 73
Tarot High Priestess 45
Tarot Judgment 207
Tarot Justice 101
Tarot Lovers 85
Tarot Magician 35
Tarot Moon 185
Tarot Star 177
Tarot Strength 125
Tarot Sun 195
Tarot Temperance 151
Tarot Tower 167
Tarot Wheel of Fortune 115
Tarot World 215
teleport 21
Temple 48, 170
temple 12, 14, 18, 19, 20, 37, 45, 48, 49, 50, 56, 76, 77, 86, 108, 118, 159, 160, 161, 168, 170, 171, 186, 198, 199, 200, 201, 209, 216

temple priestess
76, 77, 160, 209
Temples of Isis 48
tenth dimension
212
terrestrial portal
65, 177
The Book of Coming
Forth into Day
198
The Fool 25, 26
The Golden One
199, 200
The Kuan Yin
woman 103
The Lost Years of
Jesus 48
the pit 21, 202
the secure feminine
188
Thebes 199
third dimension
11, 13, 16, 196, 211
Thoth
51, 125, 199,
208
thought is creative
17, 209
thymus 95, 202
Tihuanaco 74
trance dancing
153, 154
transcend
1, 14, 27, 31,
35, 95, 102, 145,
152, 207, 209,
218
Tree of Knowledge
75, 179
Trickster 25, 26
trinities 55
triple goddess
46, 85
turned men to stone
97
twelfth dimension
210, 211, 212
twelve chakras
133, 203, 210

twelve strands of
DNA
133, 203, 210, 212

U

ultimate creatrix
143
ultimate release
17, 147, 148
unconditional love
30
universal civilization
1
Universal law 11
Universal Mind 51
universal permis-
siveness 26
uraeus 95
Uranus 86
Uroboros 25

V

vagina dentata 134
veneration of the
goddess 199
Venus 16, 196
vessel for holiness
45
vestal virgin
107, 108, 110
vibrational
densification 17
vibrational fre-
quency
3, 16, 62, 155,
202, 210
violet hour 20, 177
virgin goddess
35, 116
Virgin Mary 56, 86
virgin-mother-crone
triplicity 96
visualization
50, 102, 191, 209
volcanoes 67
vortex 61, 73, 95,
129, 211

W

way shower 107
whales 201
whore-saint 153
Wild Woman
128, 185, 187
wing point 202
winged lioness 197
winter solstice 187
wise woman
50, 96, 159, 162, 171
witch 97
withdrawal of
projections 90
woman who be-
longed to herself
89
womb of Mother
Earth 21
women-centered
Goddess culture
18, 168
worldwide medita-
tion 50
worship of the
goddesses 77

Y

yantra 102
yin and yang 3
yogis 162
Yoni 126
Yoruba tradition
152

Z

Zeus
36, 37, 56, 58,
86, 96, 116, 117,
118, 167, 170
zodiac 55, 66,
133, 178, 199

If you would like Carmen Boulter to give a lecture or teach a workshop on *Angles and Archetypes* in your area, you can contact her in writing:

Angels and Archetypes
#410 1201 SW 12th Ave.
Portland, Oregon 97205
USA

Profile of the Author

Carmen in the Amazon Basin, Peru 1995

Carmen Boulter, also known by her spiritual name *Carmella*, is an educator, a therapist, and an adventurer. She has pursued her interest in the feminine, the secrets of the ancients, and in higher levels of consciousness throughout her career. Carmen has maintained a private practice for 17 years counseling women, couples, and families. Since 1979, she has traveled extensively in North America teaching workshops and public speaking. Trained in Educational Psychology as a counselor, Carmen founded the *Women's Therapy and Research Center* in Calgary, Canada, where she facilitated 17 programs focusing on eating disorders, compulsive behaviors, body image, visualization, self-esteem, assertiveness, and family therapy. As Director of the Center, she supervised graduate students in Social Work and in Psychology. She also supervised Research Assistants at the College level. During that time, she published a quarterly magazine called *The Transformer*, focusing on issues of personal transformation for women.

Writing *Angels and Archetypes* has been a labor of love for Carmen. Research for the project began in 1985. Over ten years, she sifted through hundreds of books and articles and traveled to sacred sites all over the world in search of clues pertaining to goddess-centered cultures, the Amazon tribes of women warriors, sacred rituals, and ancient Mystery Schools. This journey took Carmen to archaeological sites in Europe, Egypt, Turkey, Iran, Afghanistan, Pakistan, India, and Nepal. Since, Carmen has returned to Egypt and Greece, traveled to Easter Island, Argentina, Chile, Peru, and Bolivia.

Currently, Carmen teaches two programs: *Angels and Archetypes* which enlivens the material in this book through ritual theater and drama therapy; she also teaches *Women with Wings*, a dance therapy program using techniques which can ultimately raise vibrational frequency. Carmen is available for private sessions and works with past-lives to promote contact with higher levels of consciousness. She is now creating a set of 44 *Angels and Archetypes Cards* and writing her next book.

If you would like Carmen Boulter to give a lecture or teach a workshop on Angles and Archetypes in your area, contact her in writing:

Angels and Archetypes
#410 1201 SW 12th Ave.
Portland, Oregon 97205
USA